WARNING AND RESPONSE TO THE MOUNT ST. HELENS ERUPTION

SUNY Series in Environmental Public Policy
Lester W. Milbrath, Editor

Thomas F. Saarinen & James L. Sell

WARNING AND RESPONSE TO THE MOUNT ST. HELENS ERUPTION _____

State University of New York Press _____ Albany

Published by
State University of New York Press, Albany
©1985 State University of New York

For information, address State University of New York
Press, State University Plaza, Albany, N.Y., 12246

Library of Congress Cataloging in Publication Data

Saarinen, Thomas F. (Thomas Frederick)
    Warning and response to the Mount St. Helens eruption.
    (SUNY series in environmental public policy)
    Includes bibliographical references and index.
    1. Volcanic activity prediction. 2. Saint Helens, Mount (Wash.)—
Eruption, 1980. I. Sell, James L., 1947-   . II. Title. III. Series.
QE527.5.S23   1984   363.3'495   84–46
ISBN 0-87395-915-9
ISBN 0-87395-916-7 (pbk.)

10 9 8 7 6 5 4 3 2 1

CONTENTS

LIST OF FIGURES _____

LIST OF MAPS _____

LIST OF TABLES ─────────────────

PREFACE _____

As we conducted our survey of officials involved in the Mount St. Helen's eruptions, we found that a "volcanic community" existed, of people who were brought together by the shared experiences of responding to the emergency. It was easy to identify key actors, people who had earned the respect of their co-workers. There was a kind of catharsis, as well, many people shared hours of time with us, telling all they could about the good and bad. To those people, whose names must remain confidential, we owe a great debt, and we hope this study may in some small part repay their trust. We also owe thanks to the community of researchers who shared information with us and to the people who helped us in the essential tasks of typing, editing, and drafting—the list is too long to present fully. We are additionally in debt to the people who reviewed our manuscript— John Allen, Jeremy Anderson, Bob Christiansen, Rocky Crandell, Phil Cogan, Dick Buck, Dick Bullock, Robert Geipel, Tom Kilijanek, Dan Miller, Don Mullineaux, Don Nichols, Eric Schuster, John Sorensen, Barry Voight, and Forrest Willcox—who added immeasurably to the accuracy of this volume. A special thanks goes to Gilbert White and Bob Alexander of the Hazard Research Center at Boulder, Colorado, for their help in developing this project. We also have to thank our families, who have lived with the volcano for so long—Penny, Caryl, Amber, and Sascha.

This material is based upon work supported by the National Science Foundation under Grant No. PFR–8002581. Any opinions, findings, and conclusions or recommendations expressed in this publication are those of the authors and do not necessarily reflect the views of the National Science Foundation.

INTRODUCTION _____

The amount of foreknowledge and warning for the Mount St. Helens volcanic eruption was probably greater than for any previous geologic hazard in United States history. The public, and/or responsible officials, had a series of warnings as information on this volcano passed through successive stages from a routine research publication, to the issuing of a potential hazard notification, and, still later, to the initiation of a hazard watch. These warnings, and the regulations developed as a result of them, reduced the death toll of the May 18 eruption. However, many people remained unwarned, or unconvinced of the danger in spite of the great amount of information disseminated to the public through government channels and intensive media coverage.

In the introductory chapter we outline the main warning activities provided by the United States Geological Survey (henceforth USGS), other public agencies, and the media, prior to and as a response to the heightened volcanic activity; describe in some detail the physical event, its social and economic impacts; and conclude with a short statement of the major benefits and the major oversight of the warning activity.

In subsequent chapters we trace in more detail the warnings and responses to the Mount St. Helens volcanic eruption based on our questionnaire survey of 130 main participants. To provide a sense of the sequence of events we follow the warning process agency by agency in a roughly chronological order (see also figure 1). Chapter 2 on the USGS, chapter 3 on the United States Forest Service (henceforth USFS), and chapter 4 of the state of Washington Department of Emergency Services (henceforth DES) analyze the warning activities.

Figure 1.   Chronology of Major Events in the Mount St. Helens Warning and Response.

1978

December 20   USGS notifies Washington DES of potential volcanic hazard from Mount Baker and Mount St. Helens

1980

March 20   First earthquakes near Mount St. Helens

March 25   First closure of land around the volcano

March 26   USFS calls first planning meeting

March 27   First eruption

USGS initiates hazard watch

Sixty people evacuated in Skamania County

April 1   FAA establishes restricted airspace zone

April 3   Governor proclaims state of emergency, establishes Mount St. Helens Watch Committee

USGS notice of harmonic tremor

April 5   National Guard begins manning roadblocks

April 30   State closure area proclaimed

USGS notice of bulge on the north flank

May 14   Equipment airlifted from camps near Spirit Lake

May 17   State patrol escorts homeowners to Spirit Lake

May 18   8:32 A.M., Catastrophic eruption begins, USGS-FS receive reports

8:35 USFS begins emergency response and notification of other agencies

8:48 Washington DES notified

9:00 Weather Service issues flash flood watch around volcano

9:30 Weather Service issues first ash warning

9:45 Ash reaches Yakima

10:15 DES issues statewide warning

11:00 First Toutle mudflow reaches Interstate 5

11:45 Ash reaches Spokane

1:20 P.M. National Guard begins helicopter search and rescue (SAR) missions

1:38 DES issues second warning

2:00 Interstate 90 closed at Ritzville

3:00 Ash reaches Missoula, Montana

5:00 Eruption begins to subside

May 21   Presidential disaster declaration, FEMA begins coordinating and public information activities

May 25   Second major eruption

Ash hits west side of Cascades

May 30	Most east side roads cleared of ash
	Termination of SAR body recovery activities
June 12	Third major eruption
June 22	Fourth major eruption
August 8	Fifth major eruption

The responses to the major volcanic eruption of May 18 are analyzed in chapter 5, dealing with the local activities west of the Cascades, chapter 6, on local events east of the Cascades, and chapter 7 on the United States Federal Emergency Management Agency (henceforth FEMA). The final section consists of chapter 8, an analysis of some aggregate statistics, and chapter 9, conclusions.

The roughly chronological arrangement of chapters also serves to gradually expand the area of concern from the volcano itself to the forests surrounding the mountain, to the statewide warning system, and, after the major eruption, to federal involvement in a national disaster.

WARNING ACTIVITIES

Warnings Prior to 1980 Volcanic Activity
The abstract in the slim, informative "Blue Book" of Dwight Crandell and Donal Mullineaux published in 1978 opens with the statement: "Mount St. Helens has been more active and more explosive during the last 4,500 years than any other volcano in the conterminous United States." In the publication, the past behavior and future probabilities of volcanic eruptions are succinctly outlined and the areas likely to be affected by lava, pyroclastic flows, mudflows, floods, and ash are clearly marked on maps (Crandell and Mullineaux 1978). In addition, the bulletin includes step by step instructions for identifying the warning signs of an eruption, monitoring the premonitory events, and informing both governmental agencies and private companies. This publication was a product of a research program focused on hazard appraisals for the volcanoes in the Cascade Range. A report discussing the Mount St. Helens hazard appraisal appeared in *Science* as early as 1975, and geologists and some USFS personnel were aware of the work one or two years earlier (Crandell, Mullineaux, and Rubin 1975).

In recent years, as reports on various volcanoes reached publication stage, they were forwarded to the USGS hazards information coordinator, and, after evaluation, notices of potential hazards were issued. This notification is in keeping with the USGS responsibility to provide timely and effective warnings with respect to geological hazards (U.S. Department of the Interior 1977). It has been doing so since 1977 (Saarinen and McPherson 1981).

Mount St. Helens was the eighth notice of the new USGS hazard warning system. On December 20, 1978, a letter was sent to the Washington State governor's representative from the USGS notifying federal, state, and local officials of the potential hazard. The governor's representative misinterpreted the notification, thinking an eruption was imminent, and a special meeting involving representatives of many state of Washington government departments and USGS officials was called in January, 1979, to clarify the situation. Although at the time this action was regarded an overreaction, the meeting might, in retrospect, have been useful in alerting state officials to the potential problem.

Warnings After Volcanic Activity Began
On March 20, 1980, the first of a series of moderate earthquakes, measuring about local magnitude 4, was detected on seismographs operated by the University of Washington in cooperation with the USGS's earthquake studies program. The subsequent seismic activity beneath and within Mount St. Helens and the initial steam eruption on March 27 led to further monitoring and to the decision to initiate a hazard watch for the volcano the next day. Since then, the volcanic activity has stimulated great interest as may be seen in the extensive and continuous coverage in local, national, and international news. Mount St. Helens clearly qualifies as a major media event.

Within the state of Washington and the immediate vicinity of the volcano, major efforts were made to once again inform responsible officials of the potential hazard after the hazard watch was initiated. The USGS shipped two hundred copies of the Crandell and Mullineaux report to Vancouver, Washington, for distribution to appropriate persons. By then the interest level was so high that thousands of copies of the report could have been given away had they been available. Many of the USGS geologists were then stationed in the USFS offices for the Gifford Pinchot National Forest which contains the volcano. Thus Vancouver, Washington, became the main information center for the developing events.

As the monitoring activity for the volcano watch continued, frequent news conferences were provided under the leadership of the USFS. In the immediate aftermath of the initial eruption, these news conferences were held three times a day and were scenes of great intensity as the radio, television, and press personnel, who had converged on Vancouver, grilled the spokespersons for the USGS, the USFS, the state DES, and the sheriffs of the local counties demanding clarifications of statements, explanations of discrepancies, and, occasionally, answers to unanswerable or embarrassing questions. Clearly, there was a high demand for information.

The leadership of the USFS in organizing the daily press conferences is to be commended. These press conferences saved harassed officials, responding to the disaster, from the necessity of confronting each reporter separately, and they provided the media with a single, centralized source so they could gain an overall perspective on the most recent developments. They also helped keep rumors to a minimum. USGS officials were kept busy both before and after the May 18 eruption, not only in explaining probable risks but in discounting imaginary ones; some examples include fears that watermelon—sized bombs would destroy Morton, that a new bulge was developing on the south side of the mountain, that the dam of debris at Spirit Lake might break, that a lava flow might reach the Kelso—Longview area, or that Mount Margaret (north of Spirit Lake) is a volcano.

The USFS also took the initiative in gathering many of the local officials (figure 2) to develop the Mount St. Helens Contingency Plan, which laid out the steps to be taken by each agency in the event of an eruption (Osmond 1980). Some of the flavor of the earliest organizational meetings is provided by Sorensen (1981). Several other agencies developed contingency plans before the major eruption of May 18. These included the Washington State Department of Emergency Services, the 9th Army Division, the Federal Aviation Administration, and the Washington National Guard.

In addition, as significant changes were noted from the monitoring, letters were sent by the USGS to the director of the Department of Emergency Services. These letters were sent when harmonic earthquake tremors occurred, and when the bulge on the north flank of the mountain developed.

THE PHYSICAL EVENT

From the foregoing, it is clear there was a great deal of warning and discussion about the activity of Mount St. Helens prior to the major eruption which began at 8:32 A.M. on Sunday, May 18, 1980. This catastrophic eruption had several major aspects including landslides, mudflows, ashfalls, pyroclastic flows, and a lateral blast, all of which merit discussion.

Geography and Geology

Mount St. Helens (see map 1) is near the middle of the Cascade Range of the Pacific Northwest, about 45 miles northeast of Vancouver, Washington. The Cascades, part of the "Ring of Fire" around the Pacific Ocean, is a range of volcanic mountains. At least five of these volcanoes have been active in historic time, and geologic records indicate that for the last 12,000 years there has been an average of at least one eruption in the Cascade Range per century (Crandell and Mullineaux 1975, 23).

Before the eruption of May 18, 1980, Mount St. Helens (figure 3) reached an elevation of 9,677 feet, with a symmetrical glacier—covered

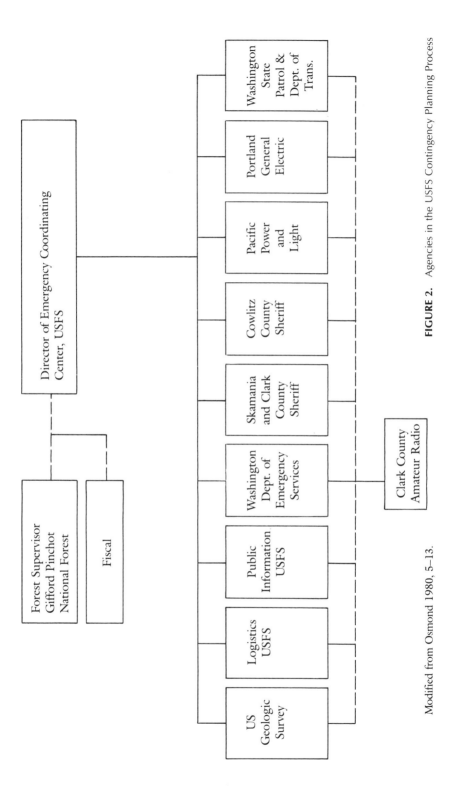

FIGURE 2. Agencies in the USFS Contingency Planning Process

Modified from Osmond 1980, 5–13.

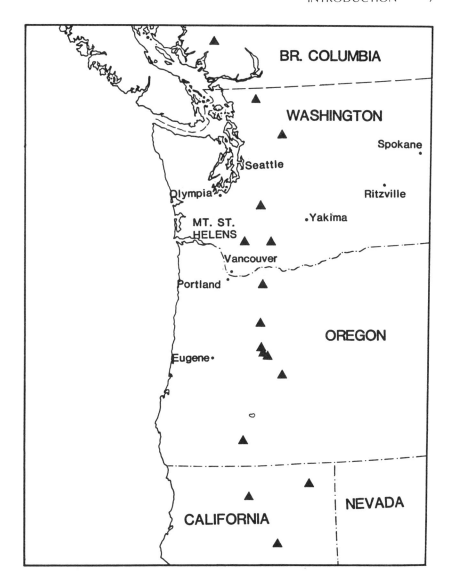

MAP 1. The Cascade Volcanoes and Their Relation to the Tectonic Plates of the "Ring of Fire." From Decker and Decker 1981, 5.

cone that led to its sometimes sobriquet of the "Fujiyama of America" (Harris 1980, 166). Most of the existing cone was formed in the last thousand years, overlying an older volcanic center whose history goes back 36,000 years. During the last 1,500 years, Mount St. Helens has repeatedly erupted domes, tephra, and pyroclastic flows of dacite and, additionally,

FIGURE 3. The "Fujiyama of America."

lava flows and tephra of andesite (Hoblitt, Crandell and Mullineaux 1980, 555). Some basalt lava flows also occurred, the most recent having erupted on the south side about 100–200 a.d. Basalt, andesite, and dacite differ especially in the amount of silica they contain, basalt with the least and dacite with the highest percentage. This chemical composition affects the viscosity and, hence, the explosiveness of the lava. Basalt lava is generally fluid and tends to erupt quietly because gas escapes relatively easily and does not build up to an explosive force. Dacite magma is more viscous and tends to build domes; it is more explosive than basalt because gases do not easily escape. Andesite is intermediate between the two; at Mount St. Helens some andesite eruptions have been explosive and some have only formed lava flows (Crandell and Mullineaux 1978, C5–C7).

The volcano is drained by tributaries of three river systems (see map 2): the two forks of the Toutle River on the north and northwest, the Kalama on the west, and the Lewis to the south and east. All of these are tributaries of the Columbia, although the Toutle flows into the Cowlitz River before it enters the Columbia near Longview, Washington. The Lewis River has been dammed to form three reservoirs created for hydroelectric power generation, with the uppermost, Swift Reservoir, directly south of the volcano. To the north is Spirit Lake, created by a mudflow dam from earlier eruptions across the North Fork of the Toutle (Crandell and Mullineaux 1978, C2).

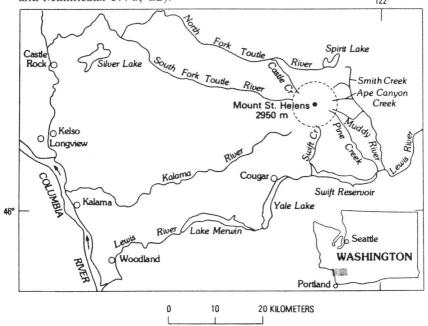

MAP 2. Major Streams in the Mount St. Helens Area. From Crandell and Mullineaux 1978, C2).

Precursors to Catastrophe

Recent activity was first noticed on the afternoon of March 20, 1980, with an earthquake of local magnitude 4 centered just north of the volcano's summit. Seismic activity increased rapidly to peak on March 25, when seismographs near the mountain were saturated to the point that individual earthquakes could not be distinguished (8–10 earthquakes per hour of more than 3.2 magnitude). After a few days of seismic shocks of this sort, it became increasingly apparent the earthquakes were of volcanic origin. Interestingly, earthquake frequency decreased (see figure 4) from the March 25 peak to the cataclysmic eruption of May 18 (Geophysics Program 1980, 529–30), although the earthquakes tended to become increasingly larger. In that period there were over 10,000 earthquakes (Endo et al. 1981).

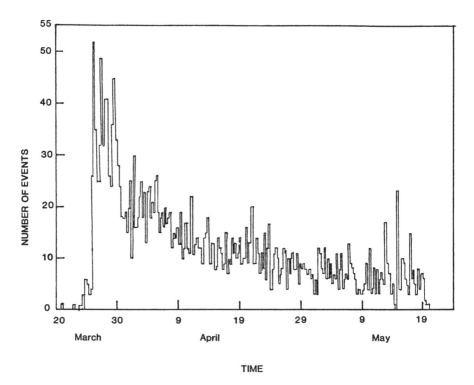

FIGURE 4.   Earthquake Activity in the Mount St. Helens Area: March 20–May 18, 1980. From Geophysics Program 1980, 530.

The first eruption occurred on March 27, blowing out steam and ash, and forming a small crater on the summit (figure 5). These phreatic (steam) eruptions continued intermittently until April 25, leaving the volcano quiescent for the next ten days before resuming on May 7. On April 1, the first harmonic tremor appeared. A harmonic tremor is a continuous, low level signal lasting an extended period of time, usually ten to thirty minutes, and is associated with the underground movement of magma or eruptions in progress (Geophysics Program 1980, 530; Christiansen 1980, 532; Endo et al. 1981). After the initial eruption a graben (a depression formed by faulting) appeared, trending east—west across the summit and "nearly bisecting the old snow—and—ice filled summit crater" (Christiansen 1980, 532). An area on the north flank of the mountain was found to be bulging at the rate of about 5 feet per day. The maximum deformation of this area in the two months before May 18 reached nearly 500 feet (150 meters, according to Moore and Albee 1981, 123). USGS scientists monitoring the mountian viewed this bulge as the prelude to a landslide, and possibly an eruption, but were not quite sure when this event would happen:

> Although it was hoped that changes in seismicity and in the rate of deformation on the north flank, as well as other precursors, might give warning of a major slope failure, the possibility that such a failure might occur resulted in the closing of the area north of the volcano by civil authorities. That such a slope failure might trigger an eruption was also considered a distinct possibility. The event finally occurred, however, essentially without warning at 0832 on the morning of May 18 (Christiansen 1980, 532).

Catastrophe: The May 18 Eruption

The May 18 eruption of Mount St. Helens released some 1.7×10^{18} joules of thermal and mechanical energy (Decker and Decker 1981, 68). Although this amount of energy is equivalent to that released by 400 megatons of nuclear explosive, the comparison is somewhat misleading, especially in terms of the rate of explosion. Instead of releasing that amount of energy in a flash, as in a thermonuclear explosion, the volcano's energy was released over a longer period, thus:

> The volcano's sustained power output might therefore be compared to the serial detonation of some 27,000 Hiroshima—size bombs: nearly one a second for nine hours. For another comparison, the power generated by Mount St. Helens on May 18 was on the order of 100 times the generating capacity of all US electric—power stations (Decker and Decker 1981, 68).

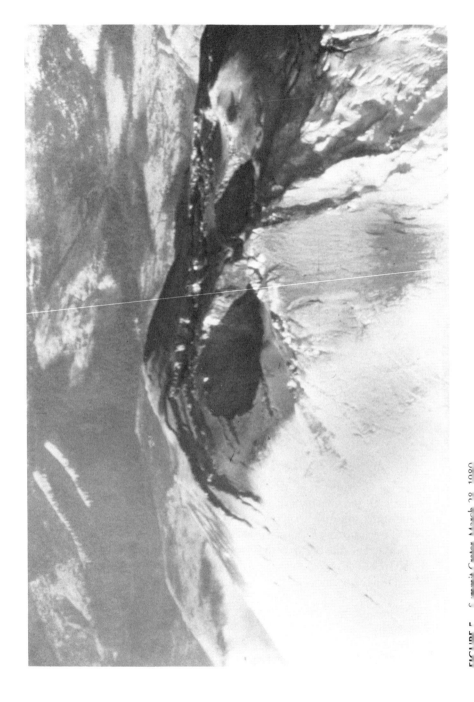

FIGURE 5. Summit Crater, March 29, 1980.

The Mount St. Helens explosion was the greatest volcanic eruption in the conterminous United States (forty eight states) in historic times. This huge release of volcanic energy removed the top of the mountain (figure 6), reducing its elevation 1,313 feet, to 8,364 feet (Findley 1981b, 714; Moore and Albee 1981, 134). Approximately one cubic mile (2.7km³) of material was displaced from the mountain, about 15 percent of which was new magma (Lipman et al. 1981, 632). The crater formed was about 2500 feet deep, broken on the north side to form a great "amphitheater" one by two miles across (Christiansen 1980, 532; Hammond 1980–81, 2–7). From the blast alone, some 230 square miles were devastated (Christiansen and Peterson 1981, 22) in a fan—shaped area reaching to the Green River about 15 miles north (see map 3).

There were five major aspects of the eruption of May 18; a rockslide—avalanche, a lateral blast, pyroclastic flows, mudflows, and an extensive ashfall. The following sections will discuss each of these events in turn.

The Rockslide-Avalanche
With the bulge growing at a rate of 5 feet per day since early April, the north flank became progressively less stable and approached a state at which an avalanche could occur. On the morning of May 28, this slide was triggered by an earthquake of 5.1 magnitude at 8:32 A.M.; in turn, the slide triggered the eruption (figure 7). Two geologists (one from the Washington State Division of Geology and Earth Resources) were flying directly over the mountain at the time, at an altitude of 11,000 feet. According to one of these observers,

> As we were looking directly down on the summit crater, everything north of a line drawn east-west across the northern side of the summit crater began to move as one gigantic mass. The nature of the movement was eerie, like nothing we had ever seen before. The entire mass began to ripple and churn up, without moving laterally. Then the entire north side of the summit began sliding to the north along a deep-seated slide plane. I was amazed and excited with the realization that we were watching this landslide of unbelievable proportions slide down the north side of the mountain toward Spirit Lake. We took pictures of this slide sequence occurring but before we could snap off more than a few pictures, a huge explosion blasted out of the detachment plane (Stoffel 1980, 10–11).

This avalanche was the largest on earth in historic times (Voight, personal communication, 1982). Over two-thirds of a cubic mile of rock and glacial ice moved downslope, accelerating to 150 miles per hour (70 meters per second) as it was lubricated by exploding steam. The avalanche divided into several lobes. One lobe topped Coldwater Ridge and reached

FIGURE 6. The Eruption of Mount St. Helens, May 18, 1980.

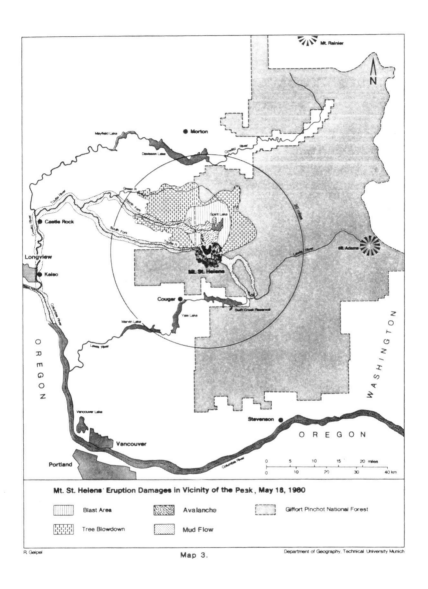

MAP 3.   Mount St. Helen's Eruption Damages in Vicinity of the Peak, May 18, 1980.

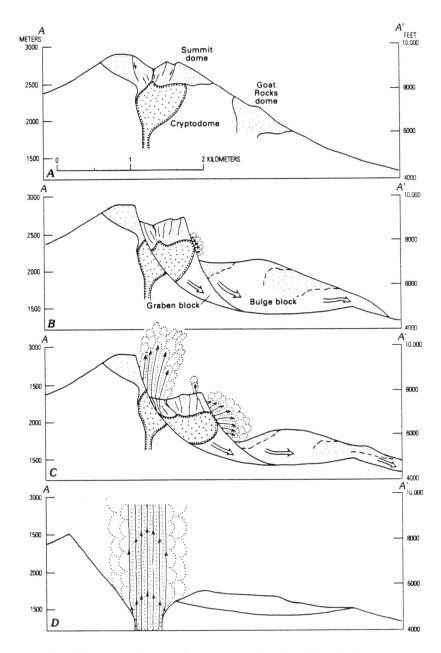

FIGURE 7. Mount St. Helens: Profile Changes, Avalanche and May 18 Eruption. From Moore and Albee 1981.

Coldwater Creek, about 4.5 miles from the base of the volcano. Another portion moved north into Spirit Lake, raising a wave over 850 feet (260 meters) over the original lake surface which scoured the shoreline and washed back into the lake bed (raised about 200 feet by avalanche material), carrying with it a mass of logs and other debris. The main lobe traveled down the valley of the North Fork Toutle River (figure 8). In ten minutes, a 14 mile (22 kilometer) stretch of the valley was filled with a hummocky deposit one mile wide and 150 feet thick on average (Voight, personal communication, 1982; Voight et al. 1981, 351).

The Lateral Blast
The slide opened the north side of the mountain like a great gate, exposing the magma chamber inside (see figure 7). With the pressure of this "lid" suddenly removed, the pent up power of high pressure gases was released in a lateral explosion which surged northward at speeds reaching over 700 miles per hour (325 meters per second—Keiffer 1981, 391). According to one expert, the explosion "was a classic *nuée Peléanne d'explosion* or directed explosion cloud, similar to the event at Mount Pelée, May 8, 1902" (Korosec 1980, 13). The lateral blast devastated 230 square miles in a fanlike area to the north, reaching about 18 miles down the North Fork of the Toutle, 15 miles north to the Green River, and 12 to 13 miles northeast. Temperatures were estimated at about 400 degrees–620 degrees Fahrenheit (207 degrees–327degrees Centigrade), enough to melt the plastic on a camper 13 miles north (Decker and Decker 1981, 74; Keiffer 1981, 393; Korosec 1980, 13–14). The devastation caused by the blast can be roughly divided into three zones. In an inner zone of about 6 miles was an area of nearly complete destruction, as the power of the initial explosion obliterated the formerly dense forest, leaving a scorched, barren plain between the volcano and Spirit Lake (figure 9). Beyond this area was a zone 6 to 10 miles across where almost all the trees were blown down, charred, and stripped of their bark (figure 10). In this blowndown area, the power of the initial blast was weakened, but the force of gravity "energized the dense, fluidized mass" so that it rolled onward in a cloud of "turbulent eddies and curving streamlines." As the turbulence settled the hot cloud flowed into a thin fringe zone, leaving the trees standing but singed to death (figure 11). The blast deposit totalled about .04 cubic miles of material (Decker and Decker 1981, 6; Christiansen 1980, 532).

The Mudflows and Floods
The May 18 eruption removed an estimated 70 percent of the glacial ice on the mountain, much of which was melted (Brugman and Meier 1981, 743). This meltwater, as well as water from the volcano's hydrothermal system and the Toutle River, combined with ash and avalanche debris to

FIGURE 8. Avalanche Deposits in the Toutle Valley.

FIGURE 9. Blast Zone: Looking South from Spirit Lake to the Crater.

FIGURE 10.   Blowdown Area.

FIGURE 11.   Singed Trees.

form a number of huge mudflows. The greatest mudflows moved down the North and South Forks of the Toutle, depositing mud into the Cowlitz and Columbia Rivers to a distance of 75 miles downstream (Janda et al. 1981, 461). Other large mudflows moved down Pine and Smith Creeks into Swift Reservoir south of the mountain, raising its level 2 feet (Janda et al. 1981; Korosec 1980, 15).

Several mudflows occurred in the Toutle-Cowlitz-Columbia River system, causing extensive flash flooding downstream. The first major flow moved down the South Fork of the Toutle, cresting at Silverlake, near the confluence of the North and South Forks, at 10:50 A.M.. This flow produced a peak flow of 47,000 cubic feet per second at the Silverlake gauging station, greatly exceeding the previous maximum discharge of 37,600 measured in 1910. The largest flow (down the North Fork) crested at about 7:00 P.M. on May 18, destroying the Silverlake stream gauge. High water marks at the site, together with information extrapolated from the Castle Rock gauging station, indicated the flood reached a stage of more than 53 feet, 30 feet higher than the previous flow. The estimated discharge of this flow was approximately 150,000 cubic feet per second, comparable to a 10,000 year flood on the river (Decker and Decker 1981, 79; Janda et al. 1981, 470; Corps of Engineers, 1980, 1–1; "Toutle River Receives Extensive Damage" 1980, 17). This deluge caused a great deal of damage, especially considering that the mudflows had a consistency of wet cement, much heavier than clean water, giving them the power to damage even strongly built structures.

After May 18, about two and one-half billion cubic yards of avalanche and mudflow material clogged the channels of the Toutle, Cowlitz, and Columbia rivers (map 3). Some 14 to 16 million cubic yards choked a ten-mile stretch of the Columbia around the mouth of the Cowlitz at Longview. The massive shoaling on this stretch became evident when an ocean-going ship ran aground in 16 feet of water. The navigation channel to Portland, normally 40 feet deep and 600 feet wide, was filled. The shoaling in the navigation channel stranded thirty-one ships in the Portland, Vancouver, and Kalama harbor areas, and another fifty ships enroute to the area were forced to stand off at the mouth of the Columbia or reroute to other ports. Intensive dredging enabled ships to pass through the channel after five days.

Another 33 to 40 million cubic yards of mud filled the channel of the Cowlitz an average depth of 15 feet from Castle Rock to the Columbia (see figure 12). The bankful channel capacity of the river at Castle Rock was reduced about 80 percent from 70,000 cubic feet per second to less than 13,000 (the week before the eruption the flow was 6000—8000 cfs). This clogging of the channel increased the flood danger—flood stage after the eruption was reduced from 34 to 25 feet (Corps of Engineers 1980,

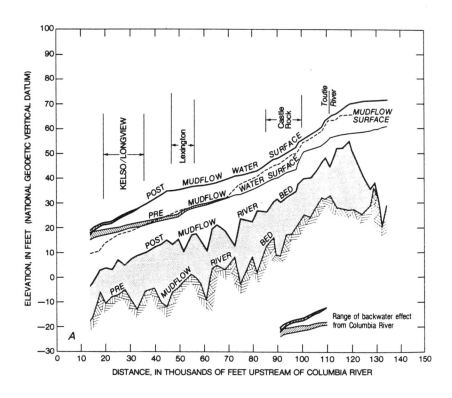

FIGURE 12. Profile of the Cowlitz River. From Corps of Engineers 1980, 1–10.

1–1 to 1–11; "Toutle River Receives Extensive Damage" 1980, 17). The old channel on the North Fork of the Toutle was replaced by two smaller channels flowing on either side of the debris fill. This debris fill (both avalanche and mudflow) is loose and potentially unstable, causing problems for the entire system:

> Erosion potential is very high, and even normal fall and winter flows will cause the transport of much sediment downstream into the Cowlitz. The Cowlitz cannot carry the amount of sediment expected to be transported; as a consequence, material will settle out into the river bottom, thereby reducing its water carrying capacity and expanding its flood plains (Corps of Engineers 1980, 1–12).

Pyroclastic Flows
Also associated with the Mount St. Helens eruption on May 18 were a number of pyroclastic flows. Proclastic flows are hot masses of gas, ash, and rock fragments. The mixture of hot air and other gases gives the flow great fluidity, while the ash and rock fragments have a density that enables great acceleration under the force of gravity (Crandell and Mullineaux 1978, C11–C12). Their total volume was about .05 cubic miles, covering the blast-scoured slope between the crater and Spirit Lake (including the south shore of the lake itself). Temperatures in the flows were estimated at about 600 degrees–1350 degrees F (Banks and Hoblitt 1981, 295).

Ashfall
Although most of the force of the inital lateral blast was directed to the north, an ensuing vertical eruption lasted over nine hours. This vertical eruption generated a plume of ash that reached up to 63,000 feet and dispersed about .16 cubic miles of material into the atmosphere (Korosec 1980, 16; Sarna-Wojcicki et al. 1981). The prevailing winds over the volcano on May 18 were toward the east northeast (National Weather Service 1980) and the ash fell mainly on eastern Washington, northern Idaho, and western Montana. The plume was tracked by satellite, radar, and ground observations. An isochron map (map 4) provides information about the time areas were first affected. For the first thirteen miles, the impetus of the blast moved the plume at about 100–150 miles per hour. For the next 600 miles, the winds carried the ash at an average speed of 60 miles per hour (Sarna Wojcicki et al. 1981, 581).

The thickness of ashfall from the plume is shown in map 5. As can be seen from the map, the thickness of ashfall generally decreases with distance from the mountain, with the exception of a "hump" near Ritzville. This depositional pattern generally reflects the fineness of the particles. As would be expected, the size of the grains decreased with distance, the

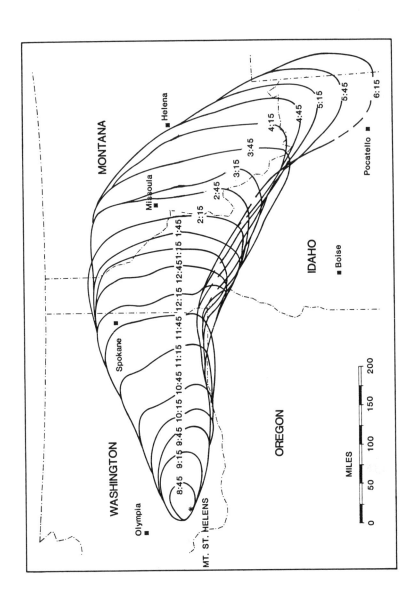

MAP 4. Isochron Map of Time Areas Were Reached by the Ash Plume, May 18, 1980. From Sarna-Wojcicki et al. 1981.

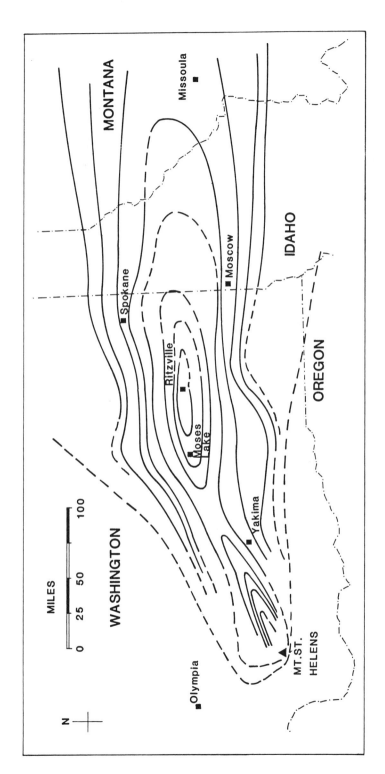

MAP 5. Isopach Map of Thickness of Ash, May 18, 1980. From Sarna-Wojcicki et al 1981.

smaller ones being carried further. As a result of this pattern Yakima (about 90 miles from the volcano) was covered by sand-sized particles, while the ashfall received by Ritzville (about 200 miles away) had the texture of talcum power (Decker and Decker 1981, 76; Sarna-Wojcicki et al. 1981, 581–582; McLucas 1980a, 11–12). When looking at the isopach map (map 5), one obvious anomaly is the peak of heavy ashfall surrounding Ritzville. This fall reached about 2.75 inches of very fine talc-like material (Sarna-Wojcicki et al. 1981, 584).

The ashfall caused many problems in eastern Washington. The day of May 18 became pitch black as the cloud came over head (figure 14). Machinery was affected by the abrasive and electrical nature of the ash, communities were isolated, people feared for their health and the condition of the crops in the predominantly agricultural area, and, in general, those few inches of ash brought a highly technological system to its knees. Ritzville, which probably received the worst of it, was isolated for almost a week, and the 1800 residents had to put up with the extra burden of 2000 travelers stranded when the highways closed. The different types of ash varied in the ease with which they could be handled. The sandlike material around Yakima was not very dusty and could be picked up easily. The talc-like material near Ritzville was very light and easily disturbed. It had to be dampened to be picked up, and even the slightest wind (or turbulence from passing vehicles) would blow it back into the cleared spaces. This ash will affect eastern Washington for many years even with no further ashfalls (McLucas 1980b, 6).

Social and Economic Impacts
The most dramatic social impact was the loss of some sixty lives, the first fatalities in historic time in the continental United States due to a volcanic eruption. Many missing and presumed dead were probably killed instantly by the blast in locations immediately north of the mountain, while other further away were asphyxiated by the effects of hot volcanic ash (Ota, Snell, and Zaitz 1980). Floods and mudflows led to the evacuation of hundreds of riverside residents.

East of the Cascades, the ashfall brought normal activities to a halt in most of eastern Washington and on into Idaho and Montana. Even a small amount of ash was sufficient to disrupt community systems and cause a major inconvenience, while larger amounts constituted a disaster (Warrick et al. 1981). Recovery time was a direct function of ash depth. Despite the initially paralyzing effect of the ashfall, communities proved surprisingly resilient and were soon back to normal. So highly stimulating was the event that it could be regarded as a "peak experience" for many individuals, and much community solidarity was evident in the clean-up operations (see also Anderson 1983).

Preliminary estimates of $2.7 billion damages (Rainier National Bank 1980; May 1982) were later succeeded by estimates of short term losses to the economy of Washington State on the order of $860–$970 million (Hunt and MacCready 1980; May 1982). Over half the loss was forest damage (approximately $450 million) in the blast zone where some 230 square miles were either laid bare, left with fallen timber marking the direction of the blast, or singed. Next in amount of losses were clean up costs ($270 million), agricultural losses ($40 million), and damaged or destroyed property ($85 million)—mainly roads, bridges, and other property in the blasted and flooded areas.

Two-thirds of the clean-up costs were concentrated in the immediate area of the volcano and downstream to the Columbia. A major portion was due to the need for dredging the Toutle, Cowlitz, and even the Columbia River where ocean-going traffic was stopped for about a week. Twenty-seven bridges and 170 miles of road were destroyed. Housing losses included sixty-one totally destroyed, fifty five heavily damaged, and sixty four cut off by mud with a temporary displacement of hundreds of residents along the Toutle. In addition, flooding at Castle Rock covered the Cowlitz County Fairgrounds and two nearby subdivisions (Schuster 1981, 705; Corps of Engineers 1980, 1–1; "Toutle River Receives Extensive Damage" 1980, 18).

East of the Cascades, the clean up problem was ash removal. Appreciable amount of ash fell on four states, with the greatest concentration in certain eastern Washington counties where expenses involved in the ash removal exceeded the local ability to pay. Most of the agricultural damages were concentrated in these same areas as well (Cook et al. 1981). The major losses were to the hay crop. Wheat, apple, and potato crops were normal or above normal. The record wheat crop may have been partly due to the ash "mulch" on the surface, but the ash's abrasive qualities caused damage to the mechanical equipment used in harvesting. Note the large amount of dust being raised by the harvesting operations in figure 16.

MAJOR BENEFITS AND OVERSIGHTS OF THE WARNINGS

In assessing the preparation for and reaction to these damaging events, only the most beneficial and worst aspects of the warning system will be discussed here. The major benefits were derived from the establishment of a restricted zone which reduced the fatalities from the eruption. In contrast, the major oversight in the warning system was the failure to effectively warn people in the ashfall areas.

Major Benefits of the Warnings
As a result of the many earthquakes, the observed deformations, and other

physical indications that Mount St. Helens was building toward an eruption, restricted zones were set up around the mountain. As early as March
25, the USFS set up a Red Zone, closing off the whole mountain above
timberline (map 6,). From the moment the roadblocks were set up to
prevent entrance to the area, the officials experienced great difficulty enforcing the restriction (Sorensen 1981). On April 3, Washington State
Governor Dixy Lee Ray declared a state of emergency which allowed
National Guard units to aid local law officials in keeping out the public.
Evading the roadblocks became a game. It was easy to find alternative
routes, especially when enterprising local people began selling maps of the
many logging roads in the areas. This same public discounting of the
hazard was documented by Green, Perry, and Lindell (1980) who interviewed residents of Toutle/Silverlake and Woodland, small communities
close to the volcano.

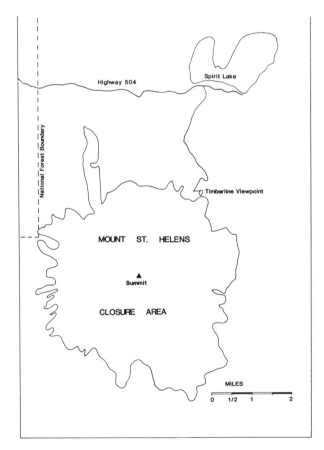

MAP 6. First USFS Closure Area, March 25, 1980. From Osmund, 1980.

Not only the public discounted the hazards. The major lumber companies discounted them as well and were capable of exerting strong political pressure. When the state Red and Blue Zones were finally made official on April 30, portions of the Red Zone boundaries bore a closer resemblance to divisions between federal lands and state-controlled and lumber company property than to defined geologic hazard zones (see maps 7 and 8). All activities were to be banned from the Red Zone. Certain activites were allowed in the Blue Zone during daylight hours and access was possible with permission. Consequently, logging could continue very close to the western side of the volcano.

In spite of all these problems, the establishment of restricted zones did prevent greater loss of life from the blast. Even so, a bit of luck was involved, for the death toll would surely have been higher if the major eruption had occurred on a weekday, when logging was in full swing, rather than on a Sunday or later in the day on that Sunday. Estimates of how many lives were saved as a result of the warnings and restrictions vary from a few hundred, the number who might normally be there on a weekend in May, to as high as 100,000. The size of these estimates depends on the assumptions of the estimator as to how many people would have converged on the area to see the volcanic activity if free access had been allowed.

The interest level was high and remains so, as may be seen in the growth of a thriving souvenir industry at main roadside sites from which the mountain is visible. T-shirts, ash, volcanic rock, postcards, picture-books, refreshments, and a variety of items made from volcanic rock were all available. On the first anniversary of the destructive eruption, celebrations in Toutle, Castle Rock, Silverlake, and other nearby small towns commemorated the event with parades, prayers for the dead, and the sale of souvenirs ("Towns Have a Blast a Year After the Big One", 1981).

Major Oversight of the Warning
The major oversight of the warning system was the failure to adequately inform the people in the ashfall areas about the problems they could face. The USGS clearly described these problems in the Blue Book (see map 9 and figure 13), but did not ensure the public east of the Cascades was aware that:

> Tephra eruptions can also result in psychological stress by blocking roads and causing people to be isolated, by causing darkness during daylight hours, by increasing acidity and turbidity in exposed water supplies, and by interrupting telephone, radio, and electrical services. Exposure to one or more of these stresses may lead to panic even though an individual's health or life is not directly endangered. Damage to property results largely from the weight of

Map 7.

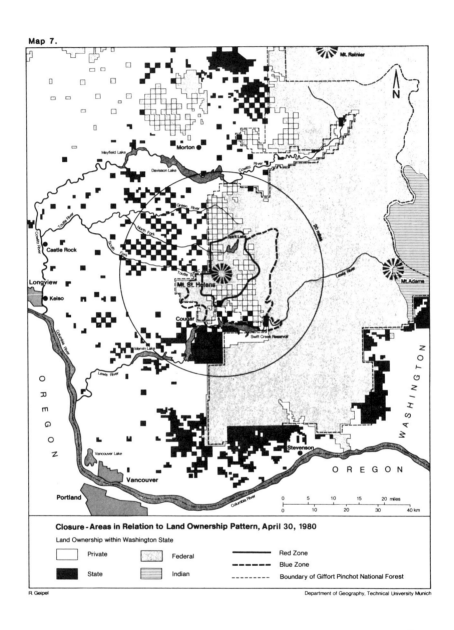

Closure - Areas in Relation to Land Ownership Pattern, April 30, 1980

Land Ownership within Washington State

Private	Federal	——— Red Zone
State	Indian	- - - - - Blue Zone
		- - - - - Boundary of Giffort Pinchot National Forest

R. Geipel

Department of Geography, Technical University Munich

MAP 7. Closure Areas in Relation to Land Ownership Pattern, April 30, 1980.

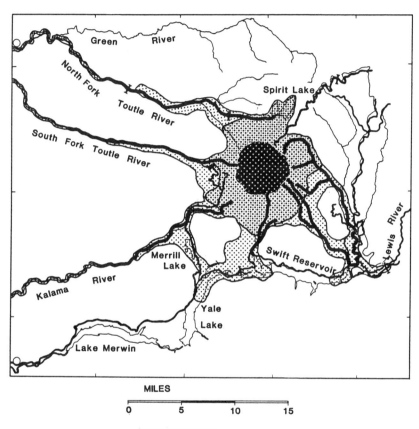

MILES

| 0 | 5 | 10 | 15 |

TYPE OF EVENT

MAGNITUDE	pyroclastic flow	mud-flow	Max. Ash Thickness (in.) at 20 mi.	at 50 mi.
Large			39	12
Medium			4	3
Small			1	0-1

I   Roadblock May 18,1980

MAP 8.   Mount St. Helens: Geologic Hazard Zones Near the Volcano. From Miller, et al, 1981.

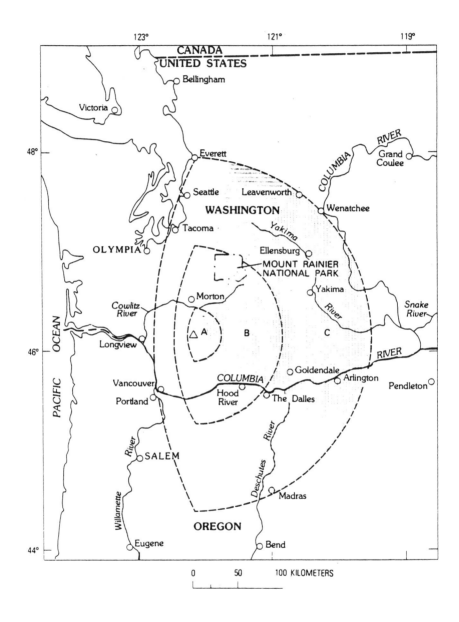

MAP 9. Mount St. Helens: Ashfall Hazard Zones in Washington. From Crandell and Mullineaux 1978.

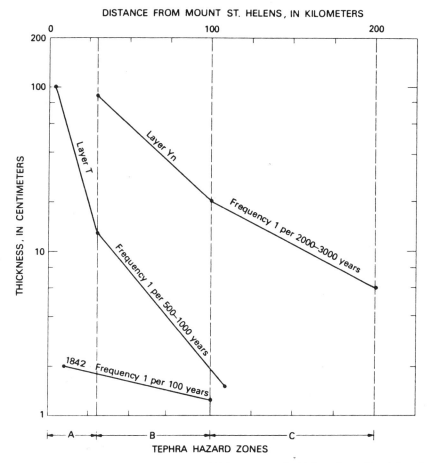

FIGURE 13.   Relative Frequencies of Ashfall from Mount St. Helens. From Crandell and Mullineaux 1978.

tephra, especially if it becomes water soaked, from its smothering effect, from abrasion, and from corrosion. Machinery is especially susceptible to the last two effects (Crandell and Mullineaux 1978), C 11).

The USGS scientists, with little experience in direct communication with the public, saw themselves as technical advisors. They perhaps assumed their report would be read and that, somehow, the people who needed to know would get the necessary information. The report was sent to some key public officials, but there was little follow-up to see that it had reached all those with responsibilities to act in hazard situations. One might argue that people who received the information might not have used it anyway, but our survey results plainly indicate that those who received the Blue Book were more likely to make some adjustment to the volcanic hazard then those who did not.

The USGS scientists were not at all reluctant to relinquish the public information role to the USFS officials, who became heavily involved because the Mount St. Helens area was under their jurisdiction. After the hazard watch was declared, the USGS representatives were kept too busy responding to local demands for information as well as assessing the geologic nature of the hazard, to follow up on warning the public. The intensity of the demands on them during their period of high excitement forced them to work up to twenty hours a day for several weeks. Even with such long hours they were unable to attend to all the legitimate requests for their time with which they were inundated.

Many members of the USFS were aware of the hazard and they very quickly responded to the increased seismic activity by closing off the area, setting up a public information office at their headquarters in Vancouver, Washington, and developing a contingency plan for an eruption. Their main responsibility was for the forest areas. These, and the areas immediately adjacent, corresponded closely to the most serious geologic hazard zones identified by the USGS. Thus, the USFS concentrated their main efforts on what were perceived to be the areas of most serious danger to life and property, essentially the areas immediately adjacent to the mountain and in the valleys down which mudflows and floods were likely to descend. Only two of the some sixty-six key contacts among public officials and private industry representatives in their contingency plan were from the areas east of the Cascades, which later were covered with ash. Both of these representatives were from Yakima County which borders the USFS land on the east.

The state of Washington Department of Emergency Services was the agency responsible for warning the public. Unfortunately, this agency was neglected, underfunded, and directed by an inexperienced political appointee rather than by a hazards professional. It had been rated as having one of the worst disaster response programs in the country (Ota, Snell, and Zaitz 1980). As a result, the DES did not have the personnel to conduct independent geological assessments, nor did it take advantage of the geological expertise in Washington universities or the state government. Rather than take the initiative, the DES followed the lead of the Vancouver headquarters. Although the agency sent out information on the volcano's activities to all county offices, it did not specify how this information was relevant to eastern Washington. When the major eruption took place on May 18, the state of Washington Department of Emergency Services was still in such a state of disarray that its warning to the local communities was delayed almost two hours.

Before May 18, the local officials in eastern Washington receiving the

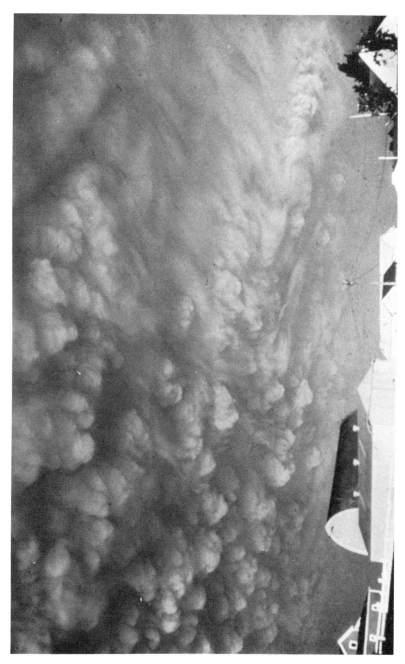

FIGURE 14. Ash Cloud Over Ritzville, May 18, 1980.

reports on the increasing activity of Mount St. Helens tended to regard them as irrelevant to their activities. After all, Mount St. Helens was a distant Cascade peak. Consequently, the information was not acted upon. On May 18, as the ash cloud approached (figure 14), many people thought it was a thundercloud or dust storm and were completely unprepared for any heavy ashfall. Thus, roads were soon closed, motorists stranded, and normal activity came to a standstill. Each community tended to improvise in handling the emergency situation and, in at least one case, all emergency vehicles were soon out of commission when ash clogged the engines. Later, as the cleanup began, problems arose related to how to handle the ash. The ash clean-up was complicated by variations in the physical properties of the ash from place to place, so it could not be handled in a uniform manner.

Questions and fears developed about medical effects. Children might enjoy the ease with which they could stir up a dust cloud, but parents worried about the potential health effects (figure 15). Similar concerns arose related to the effects of the ash on vehicles or mechanical equipment or on crops (figure 16). The Federal Emergency Management Agency, which became involved when a federal disaster declaration was made official, soon developed a series of technical bulletins to answer some of these questions, but such information would have been even more useful a few weeks or months earlier.

Since the May 18 eruption, people's perceptions of volcanoes have changed considerably. The warning system has also become more effective

FIGURE 15. Child Kicking Up Dust.

FIGURE 16. Harvesting in the Ash—Eastern Washington.

than before. From the predictions based on physical measurements to the dissemination of data to the public, the system is much improved. Logging is once more taking place though restricted zones are still in force. Crews have emergency evacuation plans and are in direct contact with the headquarters from which warnings are issued. For most of the eruptions after May, 1980, predictions were made at least several hours in advance and people were warned and evacuated efficiently.

This, then, is our view of the general outline of events. The succeeding chapters provide more detail and flavor, and substantiate the outline by reference to the results of our questionnaire survey. Much of the discussion is necessarily qualitative because of the relatively small number of individuals interviewed within any one agency or geographical area (map 10 and appendix B). Since our sample of 130 consisted of almost all the individuals most directly involved in hazard warning and response activities by virtue of their positions, no advantage would be gained by an increase in numbers for it would only be adding people from more peripheral positions. Wherever possible we have supplemented our questionnaire results with information from other published sources. Direct quotations are freely used throughout the book because we feel they communicate certain attitudes and shades of meaning vividly and parsimoniously. We assume the reader realizes we do not always agree entirely with the sentiments expressed. On the other hand, we do consider them important because, whether right or wrong, they illustrate interpretations which may form the basis for many decisions.

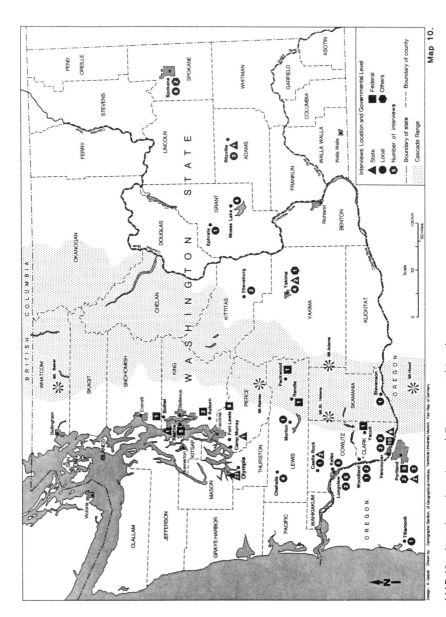

MAP 10.   Interviews: Location and Governmental Level.

THE GEOLOGISTS _____

A major theme of the previous chapter was the large amount of fore-knowledge and warning about the likelihood of a volcanic eruption at Mount St. Helens. Years before the major eruption, the USGS had developed an excellent report providing the public with information and maps showing where lava, pyroclastic flows, mudflows, floods, and ash would most probably occur. With the notable exception of the magnitude of the avalanche and initial blast, which were unprecedented in the 4500-year history upon which the report was based, the volcanic events at Mount St. Helens followed approximately the pattern sketched out previously in the "Blue Book" of Crandell and Mullineaux (1978; see Decker 1981; Miller, Mullineaux, and Crandell 1981).

    Interesting social science questions stem from these circumstances. How does one get such excellent scientific information, available well in advance of the natural event, to those who should use it, in a form that leads them to adopt appropriate mitigation measures? How well did the USGS, who developed this information, succeed in this dissemination? We have already indicated that there was a great deal of warning activity, from the first publication of scientific investigations to a series of official warnings. There was also sufficient national publicity, as Mount St. Helens became active, to easily qualify as a major media event. In the remainder of the book, we propose to assess the effectiveness of this warning activity by analyzing the results of a questionnaire survey of those most directly involved in the warning and response to the volcanic eruptions of Mount St. Helens. As we examine these data we will attempt to show which things worked, which didn't, and why. We begin by tracing the main warning activities of the major agencies involved, and then by assessing the responses by geographic area and by agency. In this chapter we start with the reawakening of the volcano, and the role of USGS and other scientists responsible for the earliest response to the precursors of the Mount St. Helens eruptions.

DETECTION AND REACTION TO PRECURSORS BY UNIVERSITY OF WASHINGTON GEOPHYSICISTS

On Thursday, March 20, 1980, an earthquake was recorded by a seismometer a little more than two miles from the summit of Mount St. Helens. It was of local magnitude 4.2, a moderate earthquake, but the strongest recorded in the southern Washington Cascades since the instruments had been installed some seven years earlier as part of a USGS volcano monitoring program (Geophysics Program 1980). The information was logged at the Geophysics Department of the University of Washington, where messages from seismic stations throughout the state of Washington are received.

The first reaction to this event was to install four seismic stations in the region to supplement the existing stations. Fortunately, several portable seismographs that store their data on tapes, scheduled for use on another joint USGS-University of Washington project, were available. The USGS in Menlo Park was informed about the earthquake. When the aftershocks persisted the following day, the stations were installed, three in the valleys adjacent to the mountain, the fourth, a telemetered station, twenty-two miles away. These stations were installed with the help of the USFS because of snowy conditions. Much driving was done that weekend by Steve Malone, Craig Weaver, and several graduate students as they analyzed the tapes from the mountains. On March 25, a television station helicopter was volunteered to help establish another telemetered station high on the mountain. To place it, they had to dig down through four feet of snow.

Over the weekend of March 22 and 23, the earthquakes persisted. The seismologists, who had received the Blue Book of Crandell and Mullineaux when first published, knew there was the possibility of an eruption. On Saturday, March 22, they contacted the USFS to warn about potential snow avalanches. The seismologists first mentioned the possibility of an eruption to the USFS on Sunday, March 23. Although the type of earthquake sequence they were observing had been known to precede volcanic eruptions elsewhere in the world, there was no precedent from the United States or the Cascades. There was also the possibility of such an earthquake swarm occurring without an eruption. Furthermore, the scientists were cautious because of publicity over Mount Baker a few years previously, where the initial extensive press coverage was not followed by a major event.

The seismologists decided Monday morning to call Crandell and Mullineaux at the USGS office in Denver. Mullineaux left for Vancouver the next day. He had previously been contacted by Chuck Tonn of the USFS who knew of the felt earthquake on March 20. The seismologists also came out with a press statement on Monday, March 24, saying that an intense sequence of earthquakes was going on and that this sequence was similar to those preceding eruptions. By this time, the small professional staff at the geophysics lab were convinced that a volcanic mechanism was necessary to explain the concentrated high level of seismicity. They arranged to watch the seismographic records around the clock, a practice which continues as part of the ongoing hazard warning system. Among the seismologists, the constant surveillance became known as the "Captain System." The person on night shift was referred to as "Captain Midnight," those on day and evening shift as "Captain Daylight" and "Captain Twilight."

On Tuesday, March 25, the seismic activity reached a peak. The seismologists were in constant touch with the USGS, calling every half hour because of the intensity. They were, as one said, "going bananas." In the early stages they only had the USGS public phone number, but somehow always managed to get through despite the busy lines. Later, a hot line was installed so they could make immediate connections. Even the installation of a hot line did not end communication problems, for it came into a room that was not always manned. This problem was not solved until the second or third week of April. In addition to the USGS and USFS, the seismologists had contacts with the state of Washington Department of Emergency Services (DES). The latter group did not have a trained geologist on their staff so they were dependent on the interpretations of the seismologists. Eventually, the DES got most of their data from the USFS Vancouver headquarters.

The seismic data were also available to other people. Almost anyone who called and seemed to have a good reason was allowed access through the phone. This could have led to potential problems, for the data were raw and arriving so fast that mistakes were possible. In the early phases, these records were updated three to four times per day.

The devotion to duty and esprit de corps displayed by the seismologists from the time of the first earthquake was typical of most of the professional personnel with definite responsibilities in dealing with the hazard of Mount St. Helens. Among the seismologists, these qualities were seen in the installation and monitoring of the seismic stations in the field throughout the weekend following the first earthquake, in the twenty-four hour surveillance of the seismic activity afterwards, and in their determined efforts to make sure that those most concerned were kept well informed of the developments. These tasks became more difficult as excitement about the earthquakes grew and they were forced to spend more time with the media. This time drain was seen as their greatest problem, for it detracted from their ability to do their scientific work. Eventually, they were given important help by university public relations people who fielded the questions from the public and media.

The warning for Mount St. Helens, which began with the USGS hazard appraisal program for volcanoes in the Cascade Range, had proceeded very well to this point. The scientific and agency personnel called on to play roles were generally very well informed about the potential hazards and about who should be told. They had seen the Blue Book of Crandell and Mullineaux and many knew them personally. The USGS scientists were thus contacted directly, not only by the seismologists, but even earlier by the USFS personnel in the field. The foresters, already alerted by the University of Washington group, had observed the avalanches triggered by some of the initial earthquakes, and knew the potential significance of these events. The pertinent USGS personnel were contacted very early both at Denver and Menlo Park. While the seismologists continued to monitor and send in data they were "relieved when Don Mullineaux and the experts arrived to make the determinations." They were quite content to step back and become seismologists once more.

THE USGS: INITIAL RESPONSE TO VOLCANIC PRECURSORS

Soon after the first earthquakes, the volcano experts at the USGS were alerted and became actively involved in assessing the significance of the seismic activity. They were concerned, but had to admit two possibilities, an earthquake swarm of tectonic orgins, or a volcanic precursor. On Monday, March 24, those at the Denver office consulted each other and telephoned many individuals, ranging from Forest Service employees on the mountain and at the Vancouver, Washington, headquarters to the seismologists at the University of Washington, as well as some of their own colleagues at Reston, Virginia, Golden, Colorado, and Menlo Park, California (Miller, Mullineaux, and Crandell 1981). By Tuesday it was decided that Don Mullineaux would go to Vancouver, Washington. His co-author, Dwight, "Rocky," Crandell, stayed at the Denver headquarters where he wrote a statement, based on their research, of what might happen should an eruption occur. He also began fielding questions from the news media in Denver.

Meanwhile, at Menlo Park, the West Coast headquarters of the USGS, other volcano experts were equally active. They also could see the possibility of a volcanic eruption as reports of earthquakes on Mount St. Helens were received. One USGS scientist, in Seattle for other reasons, was asked to remain there to augment the seismic monitoring group at the University of Washington. The intense seismic activity of March 25 convinced many that an eruption was imminent and the chief geologist decided a group should get together and make plans. Bob Christiansen was placed in charge of monitoring activities on March 26, and on the morning of March 27 a group was gathered to make preparations. Before that group could do anything, the first steam eruption occurred on March 27. That same day, the USGS officially initiated a hazard watch and sent formal notices from Reston to inform officials of this change in status from a potential hazard to a hazard watch.

Two main activities were seen as most important by those in charge of the hazard watch—monitoring and hazard assessment. Once the steam eruptions began, geologists from Denver and Menlo Park were sent to Vancouver, Washington. They were provided with space in the USFS headquarters there. Within a few days, fifteen to twenty people had arrived and were being organized for monitoring and assessing hazards.

> The script called for Mullineaux to be in overall charge and be the USGS spokesman; Christiansen to be responsible for monitoring activities and Crandell for hazard assessments. As time went on and it was necessary to maintain the sanity of people at Vancouver by rotating them out from time to time, the three would double up. At times Chris was "spokesman" when Mullineaux and Crandell were out and Dan Miller was "assessor" and at other times when Chris was gone [Robert] Decker or [Donald] Peterson came in to replace him. Similarly at times Crandell doubled up as both spokesman and "assessor" (Nichols, personal communication, 1982).

THE MAJOR PROBLEM FOR USGS OFFICIALS: THE LACK OF MANPOWER

The first USGS official on the scene at Vancouver was Donal Mullineaux. He arrived the night of March 25, was picked up the next morning by Ed Osmond of the USFS, and they "went full blast." The next morning he met with the contingency planning group at the USFS and provided information from the Blue Book as well as other details and updates. He presented the same information again, and again, and again, to federal, state, and local agencies, businesses, industrial groups, community groups, and individuals at public committee meetings and press conferences. As other USGS representatives arrived they were drawn into the same activity. The major limiting factor they were to face in the following weeks was time and personnel. It was a total immersion experience, with people working twenty hours a day for weeks at a time, kept alert and active by the varied stimuli of a "once in a lifetime event."

The major problem noted by all USGS personnel later interviewed was a lack of trained and experienced manpower. All spoke of the extreme pressure placed all day long on those present. In spite of sixteen to twenty hour days, many legitimate requests remained unfilled at the end of each day. This pressure is reflected in comments such as,

> We were running 20 hours a day for 3½ weeks. I had never been involved in that before. I took a day off after two weeks.

> Personally I totally underestimated the demands required, [we were] working under extreme pressure all day long.

> Pictures taken of me show what it did to my health.

At this early stage there simply were not enough support personnel to free the geologists to do the most essential tasks: "Priorities were set on the basis of who had the ear. Requests could not be dealt with systematically. There was just too much pressure." In one way or another all the USGS personnel, even those brought in to do monitoring work, became involved in providing public information. There was also a spillover effect into the nearest university, Portland State, where all the geologists became "instant vulcanologists" because of the demand for information by the public and media.

A major task Rocky Crandell had to accomplish after his arrival on March 29 was to enlarge the volcanic hazards map in the Blue Book to a more useful scale. This map was to be used for planning, to help other agencies decide on boundaries such as for restricted zones. He stated that, "The first map I did between the hours of one and five one morning simply because it was not possible to do it in the daytime. Six telephones were ringing incessantly."

The importance of the hazard assessment study of Mount St. Helens is underlined by this quotation, for it clearly indicates that the emergency period is definitely not the best time for planning. One of the very fortunate aspects of the Mount St. Helens eruption was that this volcano was one of the very few for which a detailed hazard assessment was available. This preparation was not entirely accidental, since the Cascade volcano hazards appraisal program was designed to identify the peaks most likely to erupt. The good judgment of the USGS scientists in selecting Mount St. Helens for detailed study paid off. Had there been no such study, there would have been a much weaker basis for warning activities and no time available to remedy the deficiency during the emergency period, since it takes several years to gather the necessary information (Miller, Mullineaux, and Crandell 1981).

There were many reasons advanced to explain the lack of trained manpower, seen as the greatest problem by the USGS officials interviewed.

The unprecedented nature of the event was basic. As one official said, "We never had an eruption like this before so we never had an organization equipped to deal with it." This position was eloquently expressed as follows: "The problem was simply in establishing communication and working out our role under the pressure of a changing event, public demand for information, and people demanding access." One respondent bluntly stated that the USGS officials "operated on a shoestring until May 18 since their 'trouble money' was used up."

Others indicated the problem of a lack of trained manpower ended with the May 18 eruption. From then on, the USGS Administration gave them carte blanche. One respondent pointed out that there was a limited number of people with expertise in volcanism and it took some time for them to become available, even after adequate funding was no longer a factor. Those who were available did not at first have the necessary support staff to answer the telephone and handle more routine requests.

THE PROBLEM OF SCIENTIFIC ACCESS TO HAZARD ZONES

The shortage of manpower exacerbated the problem of scientific access to Mount St. Helens. The USGS was criticized for limiting scientific research, as well as for failing to release their own data on a timely basis (West 1980; DeMott 1980). As soon as a restricted zone was established around the mountain, the Survey was besieged by requests for access from researchers who wished to conduct studies there. The USGS scientists simply did not have time to properly evaluate the proposed research, nor did they see this responsibility as theirs since the closures were enforced by the state and USFS. According to West's account, some scientists accused the USGS of keeping sole rights to research within the restricted zone around the mountain.

> Faced with the delicate play between safety and the scientific right to know, the USGS has fumbled the ball, say the researchers, with the result that much important information is being lost daily in the rapidly changing environment. By excluding experienced vulcanologists, particularly researchers familiar with the Cascades, the Survey, some researchers contend, is robbing itself of expertise that may help evaluate Mount St. Helens' future activity (West 1980, 61).

This picture is at odds with the account of Nelson (1981), who quoted a scientist commending the USGS and said, " . . . they welcomed outsiders with something to offer. They helped provide clearances, and there was a great deal of cooperative effort and sharing" (Nelson 1981, 49). A similar account of USGS generosity and information sharing emerged from our interview with the Washington State Geologist who said, "The criticisms of the Survey holding back information are unjustified. The Survey had nothing to do with letting people into the mountain. That's strictly a DES and Forest Service show. If you follow the procedures you have no problem."

Whatever the initial frustrations and problems related to access, they were soon relinquished by the USGS. John Eliot Allen, professor emeritus from Portland State University and former president of the National Association of Geology Teachers, was one of the scientists seeking access to the restricted zones around the mountain. Because he was well regarded professionally, located nearby, and had the time, the USGS officials considered him an ideal candidate for the job of screening scientific requests for access. By April 20 he was issuing permits. The USGS officials were delighted. No longer overwhelmed by the requests, they could also avoid criticisms of keeping the area to themselves by turning the job over to an impartial committee headed by Allen. In the ensuing five months, Allen issued permits for studies in thirty-two areas of vulcanology by nearly five hundred scientists from fifty-five academic and twenty-three other organizations (Allen 1980). Clearly, there was a high level of scientific interest in Mount St. Helens as scientists from all parts of the United States and many foreign countries converged on the site.

The essentially unfunded, shoestring operation of Professor Allen provides a fine example of the kind of scientific cooperation and dedication associated with the Mount St. Helens eruption. Financing the work by means of a small fee charged for each permit, Allen carried on the operation almost single-handedly. Allen also had high words of praise for

> . . . the magnificent response of the amateur ham radio network participants. Hundreds of visiting scientists were accompanied by volunteer ham operators on their expeditions into the Red Zone, since they had to be in constant radio contact, and had no such equipment. Relay radio stations were continuously manned for many days to keep them in touch with events (Allen, personal communication, 1982).

After five months, the frustrations of dealing with bureaucratic rules revised five times by the USFS, as well as the lack of any financial support, led Allen, in turn, to relinquish his gatekeeper role. Thereafter, permits could be obtained at the USFS headquarters in Vancouver. This location was more convenient for scientists seeking access because a special trip to Portland was no longer necessary.

TIMELY DISSEMINATION OF HAZARD INFORMATION

More valid criticisms of the USGS than that of access to the area center around the dissemination of scientific information to other scientists and the public from the time of the earliest earthquakes. These criticisms are of two main types: the first reflects the lack of specialized personnel to serve as spokesmen or public information officers and will be discussed in the section dealing with the media; the second deals with the speed with which the Survey releases information which could be pertinent to emergency decision making.

The USGS has a well-deserved reputation for high quality scientific work which has been attributed to their regular publishing process—a careful, but slow peer review system. Its speed had been equated with that of the geological processes they investigate. "The Survey takes an unconscionable time to publish," said one geologist responding to our questionnaire as he described his experience of cooperative mapping work with them. "We would get done in a couple of seasons and the report would not come out for five years." He was quick to point out that "Bureaucracy slows them up—not individuals. [They] still don't know how to get a report out in a year or two instead of five or ten years." If this comment were true at the time it was made, it would certainly be refuted by the appearance within a year and a half of the massive and superb USGS professional paper on *The 1980 Eruptions of Mount St. Helens, Washington* (Lipman and Mullineaux 1981).

Still, this type of comment is not simply one individual's jaundiced view, but rather a part of the Survey's general reputation. For example, in a recent issue of *Science,* a comment on the new review process proposed for the Environmental Protection Agency (EPA) was that: "It is modelled on the peer review system at the United States Geological Survey which has the reputation of being the slowest to publish stuff in the world" (Smith 1981, 1346). To require such a review process for the EPA was seen by some as tantamount to withholding major sources of environmental information from the public. At issue here is not so much their regular publishing process, but how well the USGS responded to the need for public information during the Mount St. Helens hazard event. While the Blue Book was not published until many years after the initial fieldwork, the information was released as an open-file report much earlier. The open-file report contained the same information as the Blue Book and could have been quickly produced in quantity and distributed if precursory activity had occurred from 1976 on. A similar procedure has been followed in releasing information about such hazards as Mount Shasta and Mammoth Lakes. At Mount St. Helens, a concerted effort was made to adjust to the urgency of the hazard situation. The scientists appointed to present information to the public provided one—or two—paragraph daily updates and by August, 1981, the Survey had issued eight more detailed, bimonthly hazard updates (Rowley et al., 1984).

More detailed information from ongoing studies of the USGS scientists was difficult to obtain in a timely fashion. A representative from private industry said they hired their own consultants to gather and analyze data because they could not afford to wait. One non-USGS geologist said:

> I would like to have seen the Survey put out a not-more-than weekly report summarizing the results of all their different sorts of investigations. We have two tilt-meters on the mountain now. The Survey has four others. We get no reports from them because they are not allowed to give out information until it is published—an example of a fossilized bureaucracy inflexible under emergency conditions.

A geologist at Portland State University described the situation when the Mount Hood hazard watch was announced in July, 1980. His office was jammed with television personnel asking questions and he had no information from the Survey.

In an emergency situation, trained personnel are in short supply. In the future, special efforts to enlist the services of local geologists in the state government or state universities to share the task of interpreting scientific information for the public might be worthwhile. This would not only relieve the USGS of the total burden of interpretation, but would also make it more likely that all geologists would "speak with one voice." These types of arrangements should be agreed upon in advance rather than organized during an emergency period.

INTERPRETING SCIENTIFIC DATA

The scientists had to provide at least two broad types of interpretation. The first involved interpretation of their own monitoring activities in terms of potential hazards. The second was to explain in simple terms their own understanding of the geological processes. The two were interwined when explaining ongoing developments, explanations are absolutely essential to dispel the rumors that arise in situations of great uncertainty.

Interpreting their own monitoring activities in terms of potential hazards was difficult due to lack of experience with eruptions in the Cascade Range. None of the USGS officials who dealt with hazard assessment had ever had previous experience in appraising short-term hazards at an active volcano (Miller, Mullineaux and Crandell 1981). This lack of experience underlines the rarity of the event—the first volcanic eruption in the forty-eight contiguous states since the considerably milder eruption of Lassen

Peak from 1914 to 1917 (Decker and Decker 1981). The activity pattern for Mount St. Helens for the past 4500 years revealed some twenty eruptive periods of diverse durations and products. There were also statistics of eruptions in historical periods all over the world. Modern geophysical and geochemical techniques, and repeated visual observations from the ground and air are also important, but not generally carried out on most of the world's volcanoes. Thus it is no simple task to interpret the meaning of changes in total monitoring patterns, and especially to extrapolate to a short-term prediction.

Given all these uncertainties, it is not surprising that many different, well-qualified experts might develop widely varying, plausible scenarios regarding the outcome of the precursory activity at Mount St. Helens. This variability in scenarios was especially confusing for the public because many of the terms used to describe the situation were hard to understand (figure 13). The USGS tried hard to deal with the conflicting judgments as to the likelihood and magnitude of eruptions by contacting the sources of statements and warning and trying to resolve the differences (Miller, Mullineaux, and Crandell 1981). They felt that if the scientific information emanated from one authoritative source, the potential loss of credibility for all scientists would be avoided. This source was to be the daily press conferences organized by the USFS.

There is sometimes difficulty in conveying to the public the concept of gradational risk and the meaning of lines drawn around volcanic hazard zones on a map (Miller, Mullineaux and Crandell 1981). Our USGS respondents however did not feel they had any difficulty at public presentations in getting across why certain areas had certain risks based on the geological record. The great public interest, the use of maps with clear local referents, and their own credibility in a face-to-face situation probably helped make this communication effective. The Blue Book by itself, however, was probably not as useful for communication to nonscientists. One law enforcement officer compared reading it to "trying to learn the Russian language in a hurry," in spite of the deliberate effort to present the material in simplified form. The gap between lay persons and experts in understanding scientific terms is sometimes greater than both realize. The gap can, however, be bridged by face-to-face communication; as is evident in the following appreciative comment about a USGS interpreter: "I can't praise him enough. He took all the time I needed to make sure I understood what all the terms meant. He explained it exactly in a scene of great turmoil."

How much risk is acceptable is a question which must be considered in dealing with rare but potentially destructive natural hazards. It is difficult for the public to grasp the potential magnitude of the rarest events and thus it may be prudent to make this possibility known, even if it is not stressed as the most likely outcome. The Survey scientists were considering all possibilities, including one with a major landslide much like the one which did occur (Voight 1980); but, it is, of course, always easier in retrospect to see what was most likely. As the hazard assessment group indicated,

> There is the danger of losing credibility even for the warnings and hazard zones based on events known to have occurred before; at Mount St. Helens there was considerable opposition to closure of areas that were severely affected by prehistoric eruptions. If boundaries based on eruptions at other volcanoes were placed far enough from a volcano to rule out any significant risk much public criticism could be anticipated. . . . If less conservative boundaries were drawn closer to the volcano, severe criticism could also be expected if the catastrophic event did occur and lives were lost. The dilemma has no easy solution (Miller, Mullineaux, and Crandell, 1981).

The restricted zones eventually adopted were not as extensive as the hazard zones on the USGS maps (maps 7 and 8). The decisions on boundaries of the restricted zones were political, and the USGS officials were always careful to make it clear they regarded themselves as technical advisors, not decision makers (Miller, Mullineaux, and Crandell 1981). One aid to decision makers has been the recent attempt to place probabilities on certain events (Newhall 1981). The USGS has rarely provided this type of information before. They are only slowly beginning to recognize the importance of providing the public with an interpretation of hazard events in terms of a human rather than geological time frame.

In addition to assessing and interpreting for the public the likelihood of real dangers the geologists tried to dispel public concern over dangers that did not exist (Miller, Mullineaux, Crandell 1981). This task was done at public meetings, in response to telephone inquiries, and at press conferences. Examples of rumors, worries, or fears which cropped up were that the countryside from northern California to British Columbia would be destroyed by fast-moving lava flows, pyroclastic flows, or toxic gases; that lava was flowing down the slopes of Mount St. Helens; that glows were reported above the volcano at night implying the existence of molten rock within the crater; that Mount Rainier was erupting; that steam fumaroles around Spirit Lake a few days after the main eruption were another eruption; and that the "dam" blocking Spirit Lake might give way. A rumor, which persisted despite repeated denials at press conferences and meetings, was that the south flank of the volcano was bulging (Miller, Mullineaux, and Crandell 1981).

Figure 17 illustrates one mechanism by which rumors would begin at Mount St. Helens. Raw data transmitted by radio from the mountain

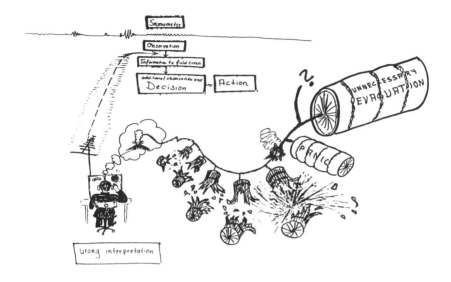

FIGURE 17. How Rumors Develop. From USGS, 1980.

were intercepted by amateur radio operators. Until the scientists assessed and made public statements about the significance of these data, there would be speculation about the meaning. Sometimes individuals would draw their own erroneous conclusions and there would be another rumor to dispel. The longer the delay between the original field report and the interpretation, the more time for speculation and the creation of rumors. This process shows the importance of continuous updating and timely interpretations of new developments. The daily press conferences played an important role in keeping such rumors at a minimum, although at times the USGS scientists felt their statements were misinterpreted by the media.

PROBLEMS WITH THE MEDIA

Dealings with the media presented problems to some USGS officials. There were complaints about being misquoted and having their information misrepresented and even flatly misstated. The daily press conferences, however, allowed for quickly correcting misunderstandings. Other complaints were that some members of the press entered the Red Zone without authorization and "their feelings about their right to know what was going on compromised the safety of those who were in there trying to find out what was going on." The USGS scientists contrasted their experience in passing on information in press conferences to attending community meetings. The people at community meetings, while sometimes angry over loss of business, would generally ask direct, forthright questions. They were very attentive, interested, and seemed to accept the geologists' explanations of the likelihood of various events based on past history of the volcano. On the other hand, representatives of the media were looking for stories. Many were seen as unknowledgeable about natural phenomena and they would ask "leading questions with a hook or razor in them," or set up second questions designed more to embarrass than inform. This behavior disturbed USGS scientists with no experience in such situations.

The responsibility for providing information regarding geologic-related hazards for state and federal agencies and the public was thrust upon the USGS by the Disaster Relief Act of 1974 (Shearer 1981). The new responsibility is one which requires special skills not generally developed by field-and research-oriented physical scientists, nor seen as a high priority by the Survey to date (Saarinen and McPherson 1981). As a result, direct communication with the public is an unfamiliar activity for many of those thrust into the new role.

The USGS did not anticipate being barraged by the media to the extent it was (Shearer 1981). The Geological Survey Public Affairs Office had no formal procedure for dealing with emergencies and had only five professional public affairs officers nationwide when called upon to respond to the events at Mount St. Helens (Rowley et al., 1984). As a result, Donal Mullineaux, in addition to his other duties, became chief spokesman for the Survey at most of the news conferences in March and early April. In addition to statements at the press conferences arranged by the USGS there was an intense demand for individual interviews with scientists. These requests could not all be accommodated by the USGS.

The demand for expert interpretations was so great that all the geologists from Portland State University, the closest university geology department, became "instant vulcanologists" and provided much information which was disseminated by the media. It was extremely difficult for the USGS scientists, charged with the task of hazard assessment, to find enough time, free of distractions, to do their job properly.

By early April, a proposal emerged from within the USGS Public Affairs Office that a full-time geologic spokesman be appointed to streamline the release of geologic information about the volcano. It was recognized that there were disadvantages to the use of technical people who knew little about dealing with the media and who were more interested in science than in news dissemination. These disadvantages, however, were considered less important than the need for technical expertise and credibility. This proposal for a full-time scientist as spokesman was shelved as news pressure subsided during the period of lesser volcanic activity in mid to late April. After the major eruption in May, the demand for news once more exceeded the USGS capability to respond. Finally, on May 20, a USGS scientist was assigned a full-time position as information scientist. By this time, the Federal Emergency Management Agency had taken charge of disaster information, and Tim Hait, who had a definite flair for this type of work, was appointed USGS information scientist. He worked very closely with the team of public information officers in the information center in Vancouver. A series of some seven other USGS personnel subsequently served as information scientists by the end of the year (Rowley et al., 1984). This job was still regarded a necessary nuisance rather than a prestigious position, for, as the people most involved state in their report, "As research scientists, most Information Scientists would have preferred the simple hazards of field work to the awesome battery of microphones, cameras, and poised pencils each day" (Rowley et al., 1984).

The USGS had still not grasped the importance of placing a specially trained person in charge of this public information function. The field scientists naturally felt frustrated in dealing with the media and were quite willing to rotate out and give others a turn, because they were not properly trained to handle the job. As one respondent put it, "You need a world-class PR man to deal with a world-class event."

This recital of events clearly shows that the USGS was far from being well prepared, with appropriate trained public information personnel, when overtaken by the events of Mount St. Helens. Only slowly did they come to realize that a full-time public information person was needed. Even then, they did not seek someone with the special training such a position might require. Instead of looking for someone who could combine communication skills or social science training with geological understanding, they fell back on what they could most easily provide, technical expertise. This expertise, they felt, would give the USGS more credibilty. This type of attitude is exactly what one might expect, for prestige within the USGS is clearly related to field research. A definite change in attitude will be necessary before the work of public information officers will be regarded as more important than an annoying but necessary chore (see also Saarinen and McPherson 1981).

A problem mentioned by some USGS respondents was a lack of public cooperation, particularly in two areas. The first complaint was that people simply ignored restrictions, more of a problem for the enforcement agencies. The second problem was related to people seeking special treatment in terms of relief from restrictions. One official remarked that it was "hard to get across the idea that the Survey does not establish boundary zones nor intercede with the Governor." The Survey geologists, in fact, strongly made a point of placing themselves in the position of technical advisors, providing the facts but leaving the decisions to those with the decision-making jobs. This type of attitude may be seen in the remark, "Never any political pressure on me. I'd just go back and use my map. You'll have to decide what level of risk you'd like to accept." The role of information source or technical advisor is also the way the USGS saw their relationship to the Forest Service.

RELATIONSHIP OF SURVEY SCIENTISTS TO THE USFS

All the USGS personnel were favorably impressed by the USFS emergency organization. This organization was based on their fire management system, and included methods of gathering and disseminating information. As one USGS member expressed it:

> They are uniquely qualified because of Forest Service fire fighting. It was logical for them to act as the central point. They had established the emergency center, involved the sheriffs, utilities, and Washington Department of Emergency Services and set up facilities for coordinating. They were beginning when we arrived but then we worked together hand-in-glove.

This smooth working relationship between the USGS and the USFS was spoken of appreciatively by all the USGS respondents. Another sample comment was, "Coordination with the Forest Service has been very smooth, almost as one agency."

By the time the first USGS official arrived, the Forest Service had already organized a meeting to develop a contingency plan, and had gathered the appropriate government and industry representatives. Mullineaux gave them a briefing the morning after he arrived and, from then on, the USGS provided the technical expertise, fed into the Forest Service Emergency Management System. The geologists would monitor and report on the volcano and the Forest Service would do the rest. "The way to put it," according to one USGS official, "was that we were consulting to them."

THE ASHFALL WARNING

In the introduction we included a quotation from the Blue Book which clearly and succinctly described the potential impacts of ashfall. This description was reinforced by map 9, which illustrated the zones where ashfall was most likely to occur, and figure 13, which depicted the relationship between thickness of the ash deposit and distance downwind from the volcano, as well as the frequencies with which deposits of various volumes might be expected. This information was excellent and was available long before the major eruption. It provided the basis for an effective USGS warning about ashfall.

Unfortunately, this excellent information was not communicated effectively to those in the ashfall zones. Map 14 shows the location of respondents who received the Blue Book before May 18, 1980. None of our twenty-five respondents from the ashfall zones of eastern Washington received it. Conversely, almost half of the respondents west of the Cascades, where the major warning activities centered, received Blue Books.

In later stages of the warning process, the USGS continued to provide excellent information but again failed to communicate this information to those in the ashfall areas. Thus, during the week of March 24–30, they arranged with the United States National Weather Service and the United States National Oceanic and Atmospheric Administration Air Resources Laboratories to receive upper air data from which potential ashfall areas downwind could be predicted and plotted daily by computer (Smith 1980; Miller, Mullineaux, and Crandell 1981, 791). Map 15 provides an example of such data plotted on a map. They provided an excellent means of illustrating hazard zones from wind-carried ash during eruptions.

Once again, the USGS did try to distribute their information, but did not follow through to the ultimate users or make sure someone else did. They provided the information to agencies represented in the Vancouver Emergency Coordinating Center (ECC), but these were mainly people drawn together by the USFS with very little, if any, representation from the potential ashfall areas east of the Cascades. The state Department of Emergency Services representatives were there and should have communicated this kind of information to all involved, but for various reasons failed to do so. By relying too much on others to follow through in the warning for the ashfall areas, the USGS contributed to the failure. They were most aware of the potential problems and they were charged by the federal government with the responsibility for warning the public about geologic hazards. To properly give warnings, the USGS must learn from this experience and do more than merely provide the hazard information. They must also deliver it to those who should use it, in a form the latter can understand.

CONCLUSIONS

The USGS served the nation well in the original selection of Mount St. Helens for detailed study. The distribution of their study results and personal contacts with other scientists led to a smooth and rapid relaying of messages from the geophysicists and foresters to the USGS individuals most knowledgeable and directly concerned.

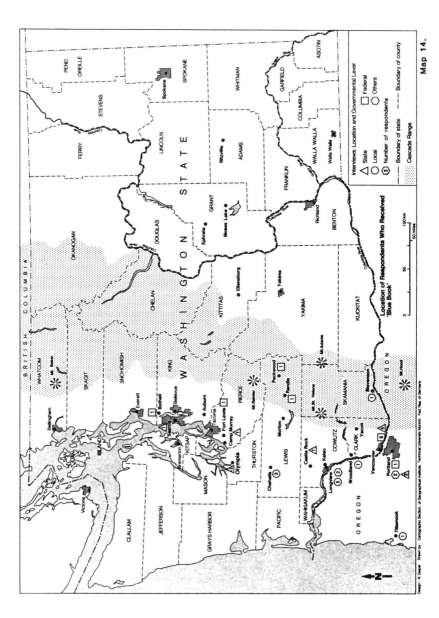

Map. 14. Location of Respondents Who Received "Blue Book".

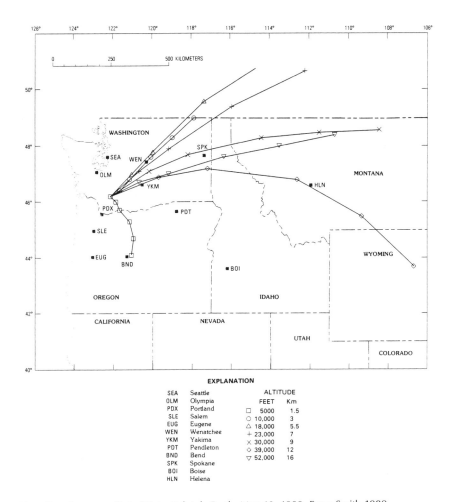

Map 15. Computer Plot of Potential Ash Track, May 18, 1980. From Smith 1980.

The USGS responded quickly and competently to the increasing seismic activity on Mt. St. Helens. As soon as it was apparent the earthquake swarm was probably a volcanic precursor, they sent in teams of volcanic experts to monitor the activity and provide hazard assessments. One weakness was the lack of support personnel and specialized public information officers to allow the scientists to devote full time to their more crucial hazard assessment activities.

To some degree, the initial lack of trained personnel was overcome by the exceptional dedication of those present and by farming out the problems of scientific access to the Allen Committee. However, this deficiency was never completely overcome. In the future, some mechanism should be developed to forge better links with locally based state and university scientists who could help in this respect. The USGS even made strenuous attempts to speed up the release of scientific information by preparing daily bulletins and bimonthly updates. This swift release of information could be extended to include more timely release of regular data from monitoring activities for use by other scientists.

A major weakness of the USGS warning was the failure to adequately inform eastern Washington about the potential problems due to ashfall. Although these hazards were clearly outlined in the Blue Book, and even though the USGS had arranged to enlist local people throughout the area to collect ash samples and the USGS and Weather Service had developed a computer program to make daily predictions of areas likely to be affected by ashfall should an eruption occur, there was never any special effort to make sure the people in eastern Washington were aware of the potential problems of ashfall. In the future, the USGS should include more specialized personnel to direct communication and to follow through, ensuring that the appropriate people receive and understand the information. By too rapidly relinquishing its warning role to other agencies, that did not understand the hazards as well, it contributed to this major failing of the entire warning process.

THE UNITED STATES
FOREST SERVICE _____

The United States Forest Service was one of the first agencies to become involved with the reawakening volcano, for Mount St. Helens is in the Gifford Pinchot National Forest. The Forest Service acted quickly and decisively and, through their own initiative, were soon playing a key co-ordinating role in the warning and response activities.

Because of their intensive involvement with the area, the Forest Service personnel knew Mount St. Helens was a volcano that could erupt. After the earthquake was felt on Mount St. Helens on March 20, one of them directly contacted Donal Mullineaux at the USGS, even before the seismologists sent word about the developing earthquake activity.

United States Forest Service personnel were well aware of the early warning activities of the USGS with respect to Mount St. Helens and this awareness helped provide the background for their decisive actions. One of our respondents reported personal contacts with Crandell and Mullineaux from the time the latter individuals began their studies of the mountain in 1970. From then on, the Forest Service was informed of each new development, such as the publication of the Blue Book and the original hazard notification in 1978.

THE FOREST SERVICE RESPONSE TO THE EARLY EARTHQUAKE ACTIVITY

One of the first agencies contacted by the University of Washington geophysicists was the USFS on March 22. All of our respondents reported being aware of the developments within a few days of the initial seismic activity. Most had received the information through official USFS channels, from the USGS, or from the University of Washington.

The first reactions to this information varied somewhat according to distance from the mountain. The nearest district ranger station exhibited a high degree of concern and immediately began working on a plan for evacuating the office. The next closest station indicated some concern, "we knew there was a good chance of something breaking loose there," and the respondent in the farthest district contacted felt "removed from it." The initial reaction in the Forest Headquarters in Vancouver appeared to be one of interest with some attempt to gain further information, or no concern at all. At this early point, only two people felt it was at least somewhat of a threat to public safety; most thought it was not serious.

Regardless of their initial reactions, the Forest Service was soon galvanized into action by the continued seismic activity. Most reported that they first took the warnings seriously in late March, after the first earthquakes occurred. "Within two days we came to the realization that we would have some event coming." From then on, the USGS and USFS were in such close contact that the respondents did not always remember whether they received information about harmonic tremors and the bulge through an official warning or not. By then, the USFS personnel were very involved in the event and all nine of our respondents had read or skimmed the Blue Book. Four reported having done so before the increased seismic activity in late March, the other five hastened to do so because of it. The important thing is that all were aware of the hazard assessment, had copies readily available, and made use of them when it seemed necessary.

The first type of activity following the receipt of warning information was to seek more information and to contact key people. Contacts were made with the USGS and the University of Washington seismic lab to seek further information, and with various "key people" in the Soil Conservation Service, the Corps of Engineers, Burlington Northern (who owned forested land on the volcano itself), Pacific Power and Light (who controlled major dams and reservoirs), loggers, the Skamania County Sheriff's Department, and other USFS personnel.

Within a few days, the USFS was taking the first actions to deal with the situation. On March 25 they closed the mountain above timberline after USFS observation flights spotted signs of avalanche activity. The same day they asked the Federal Aviation Administration (FAA) to set up a flight restricted area to control the "hundreds" of aircraft flying over the mountain. On March 26 Ed Osmond held a meeting at Vancouver involving some forty of the "key actors" to develop a contingency plan. With the eruptions of March 27, the Mount St. Helens District Ranger Station was evacuated, the logistics center was set up in Vancouver, and the first news briefing occurred.

No Forest Service respondent reported any problems making decisions based on the information available. Most felt the information as it was presented in the Blue Book was useful to them:

> "The information given us before the eruptions was practically what happened except for the lateral blast that took in more area than was anticipated."

Information singled out in the report as most useful were possible effects and areas of effects, and relative probabilities of ash direction and volume. The map of the possible area of effects made by the USGS personnel at the beginning of activity was mentioned as important in defining the area of closure. The feeling of the Forest Service about the information and its usefulness can perhaps be summed up by one of the USFS respondents:

> Predictions are uncertain; considering that, I felt comfortable with what was available. The Crandell and Mullineaux report was quite accurate, was done well, and they [Crandell and Mullineaux] were used as information sources for subsequent Forest Service actions, for example, closing the forest.

THE CONTINGENCY PLANNING MEETING

The USFS clearly asserted their leadership role in organizing the meeting on March 26 to develop the *Mount St. Helens Contingency Plan* (Osmond 1980). As they realized a volcanic eruption might be imminent, the Forest Service made contacts with Mount Baker-Snoqualmie National Forest personnel to take advantage of their experience when Mount Baker had a flurry of volcanic activity in 1976. The early contingency plan for the area was reviewed, as well as what had been learned about mobilizing efforts. Key individuals and organizations were contacted in forming a meeting to develop a contingency plan. Don Mullineaux, from the USGS, provided the geologic background for the assembled officials of federal, state, and local government, as well as of private industry. Figure 2 illustrates the basic organization evolved at that time, linking the county law enforcement officers, the major private industries, the state of Washington Department of Emergency Services, and the USGS and USFS. The initiative, organizational ability, and leadership capacity demonstrated by the Forest Service in arranging this meeting made them the logical choice for the leadership role in coordinating responses to the volcanic eruptions.

The general tendency to overlook planning for rare but potentially damaging events was evident with respect to Mount St. Helens; for, at this contingency meeting, for the first time, individuals representing many agencies and organizations began to think seriously about how they should respond individually and as a group. A good part of the effort was devoted to identifying problems with which they would have to deal, such as traffic congestion on particular highways, air traffic control, sightseeing, potential flooding, safety of personnel adjacent to the area, the complexity of the emergency decision related to volcanic activity, interagency communications, and the need to develop a range of geologic indicators and volcanic characteristics that would indicate the severity and potentiality of volcanic hazards.

By consensus of the group at the contingency plan meeting, the Emergency Coordination Center (ECC) was set up at the Gifford Pinchot Forest Supervisor's Office in Vancouver. This center would be the focal point for dissemination of information. The Forest Service was to take the lead role, and key agencies would be directly linked to the center by "hot lines" with twenty-four hour service. Those agencies needing direct links were the Skamania, Cowlitz, and Clark county sheriff's offices, and the state DES. The meeting was held none too soon, for the next day the first eruption took place.

The USFS also had connections with a number of businesses operating near Mount St. Helens. The top of the mountain was owned by a railroad (Burlington Northern), which also owns other forest land nearby, giving it a considerable interest in logging. Several other major lumber companies own land nearby (see map 7 for general location of private land holdings), and various utility companies operating dams, reservoirs, and a nuclear power plant as well. These companies were included in the Forest Service contingency plan, and provided the center with information about their organizational response plans and whom to notify for rapid warning. The motivation for aiding the Forest Service in this plan was strong, because no activity was allowed in the national forest until the plan was written— "While the emergency plan was being developed, everything was closed and through the development of the plan we maintained communication which got us back in."

Some of the major corporations developed contingency plans and Swift Reservoir was lowered to accommodate potential mudflows. This action, a result of the warnings, was useful because mudflows, of close to predicted amounts, did reach the reservoir even though the lake was not on the side of the mountain that was blown out.

WHY THE USFS TOOK THE LEAD ROLE

For a multitude of reasons, the USFS was the best prepared and most qualified agency to take the lead in coordinating the response to the volcanic activity on Mount St. Helens. We have already mentioned that the volcanic peak was located on their land and that, as a result, they were well informed and keenly interested in the reawakening of the volcano. In addition, they had the necessary resources to handle the coordination required, they had experience in dealing with hazards based on the model of fire control activities, they had the legal authority to act quickly on their lands adjacent to the mountain, and they had experienced public information officers to handle the necessary communications with the public.

The headquarters for the Gifford Pinchot National Forest in Vancouver, Washington, was well located for ECC activities and provided the necessary space for continuous face-to-face contact among the key individuals and agencies involved. In addition, the Forest Service had aircraft and support facilities necessary for monitoring activities on the mountain. A large and diverse array of personnel was available, as well as an emergency response fund which other agencies (such as the USGS) did not have.

Even more important than physical facilities was the factor of experience. Dealing with natural hazards (and forest fires) is a significant component of the work of our USFS respondents. Two-thirds of them reported considerable experience with hazards. The most important type of experience was that gained in dealing with forest fires.

The model adopted by the contingency plan for response to the volcano was that routinely used by the USFS in fighting forest fires. This system is flexible allowing them to use emergency funds and to draw in the extra personnel required for the emergency from other national forests. It is a military command type of organization which allows for quick emergency decisions by people accustomed to command. As an example of their ability to handle complex logistical problems in a rapidly changing situation, our USFS respondents pointed with pride to their actions in response to the eruption of June 12. As the ash cloud direction changed, they had to move their air operation from Portland to Dalles Port, to Salem, and then to Redmond, Oregon. With each move, the aircraft personnel and support facilities had to be shifted, all done without the loss of a single flight. Already established in the fire emergency model are relationships with the local law enforcement officers and a mechanism for dealing with the media through public information officers.

Because the eruption was in the area under USFS jurisdiction, USFS officials had the legal right to make decisions they deemed wise or necessary, and they had the support of local law enforcement officers to help back up the decisions. One respondent compared individual national forests to "minor fiefdoms" in terms of their autonomy and freedom from federal or state control. The military, command-type emergency operation, the legal powers, and the habit of making quick, forest-level decisions provided the USFS with a decisiveness which no other agency directly involved in the event could match. They performed well their perceived role as the "tough guys," willing to keep people out and able to take the heat these decisions generated.

Another major advantage for the Forest Service was the practice of using public information officers to deal with the media in emergency situations. As Mount St. Helens heated up, the Forest Service could call in additional public information officers. "They were able to get eight additional public information officers within a few hours after the May 18 eruption," according to one Forest Service public information officer we interviewed. Gathering all pertinent agencies to allow for verifying data, clearing up questions, and providing regular press conferences was invaluable. The face-to-face contact in the ECC speeded up decision making. The regular press conferences provided a single authorative news source for the media, helped control rumors, and thus provided informed responses to the changing circumstances in areas affected by the volcano. An additional motive for providing good public information was the awareness of the Three Mile Island fiasco, caused by the lack of an effective information center to deal with the hordes of reporters who descended on the scene demanding answers to difficult questions.

LIMITATIONS OF THE FIRE EMERGENCY MODEL

While the USFS fire emergency model was useful in providing general guidelines for the response to Mount St. Helens, it was not a perfect plan for dealing with the much more complex and extensive repercussions of volcanic eruptions. The Forest Service response was most successful in the areas closest to the mountain and with the agencies with which they usually deal. Most of the limitations of the model can be traced to the unusual circumstances of the rare volcanic event, which required responses well beyond the forest areas and with unfamiliar agencies.

The warning activities of the Forest Service were focused on the forest lands and areas immediately adjacent the places most likely to be affected by potential landslides and floods. A major concern, and rightly so, was with the river valleys, and especially the areas below the three major reservoirs on the Lewis River which had the greatest potential for disaster. The participants in the contingency plan meeting were mainly recruited from these areas. As was already noted, the only representatives from east of the Cascades (which received substantial ashfalls) were from Yakima County bordering the forest areas on the east. The natural tendency for the Forest Service was to be most concerned with the areas under its jurisdiction. Since the number of geologists in the Forest Service who could have provided independent assessments is limited, they relied on USGS personnel and the USGS report (Blue Book) which linked the greatest disaster potential to areas within or near their forest. Thus it was easy for the Forest Service to overlook the potentially disruptive effects of the ashfall further east, even though these effects were also outlined in the Blue Book.

Two USFS respondents commented on the failure of the contingency plan to include areas in eastern Washington where the ash was most likely to fall. Both mentioned expectations of a localized eruption:

> At the time we did that, we didn't expect an event of the magnitude that occurred on May 18, although the hazard assessment did indicate that which had happened before. We mainly were concerned with a fifty mile radius or counties contiguous to the mountain.

CLOSING ACCESS TO THE VOLCANO

The Forest Service had the authority to close the federal land to public access. The first closure was on March 25, when all areas were closed above timberline on Mount St. Helens. In making this closure, the USFS had an immediate jurisdictional problem with other landowners, including Burlington Northern which owned the top of the mountain:

> About the middle of March the Forest Service asked if they could close the mountain above the timberline. There were judisdictional problems, Burlington Northern owned the land and the Forest Service wanted to control it. The boundary on the Mount St. Helens closure was decided jointly with the Forest Service, Burlington Northern, and International Paper. At first it only involved people who understood the woods, then came a concern with people. Burlington Northern put out guards, which didn't work too well, then the sheriff took over.

Coordination with these landowners was quickly achieved and the closure was extended on March 27 to a set of Red (no public access) and Blue (limited public access) Zones on federal lands around the volcano. As can be seen in map 7, the Forest Service was able to establish a fair margin of safety (compared to the USGS hazard assessment—map 8) southwest and east of the mountain. To extend this closure area to the north and west required the cooperation of state and local authorities, as well as of private landowners (such as Weyerhaeuser Corporation).

The logging interests were reluctant to stop their operations and the restricted zones were defined in part by their property lines rather than geologically defined danger zones. Still, the private interests kept themselves well informed and made arrangements to evacuate their personnel whenever warned by the USGS and the Forest Service. In spite of the great risk, there was also great uncertainty as to when something might happen. Under these circumstances, it was very important that these large corporations were provided with interpretation and explanation of hazards. In spite of their reluctance to believe the worst, some of our respondents indicated that they made a conscious decision to rely on the USGS, and the personal contact was seen as important. The corporations wanted to keep well informed to protect their property, whether it consisted of trees, power plants, or reservoirs. In some cases, the major logging companies participated in attempts to keep the public out of the restricted areas. The loggers felt their personnel belonged there, but that the public posed a greater danger because of their unfamiliarity with the forest. It was very lucky for them and their workers that the eruption took place on a Sunday.

Cooperation with the nearby county governments was easier to achieve, and sheriff's deputies helped man roadblocks. The local division of the State Department of Transporation set up a roadblock on the Spirit Lake Highway (504) on March 25. Within the next three days, five other barricades were set up on roads leading into the area (see table 1). From the beginning, the authority for these closures was ill defined and pressure from various interests caused changes in the nature and location of the roadblocks. By April 4, the roadblock on Highway 504 had been moved five times, and manned by sheriff's deputies and troopers from the state patrol (see figure 18). After April 5, the state National Guard helped on the roadblocks.

There was a certain futility about the road closures because the governor had not closed the state lands around the mountain. The Department of Transportation had some authority to close the highways, and cooperated with the Cowlitz and Shamania county sheriffs in closing the main roads leading up to the mountain. However, the state land around the highways were not closed. People stopped at the highway barricades could bypass them, as one official noted, with legal impunity: " . . . prior to May 18, the roadblocks outside of Forest Service boundaries lacked legal authority to take enforcement action against those that by means of other routes, county and logging roads (private and state owned) bypassed roadblocks."

No state action was taken on further closures for a month, although Crandell outlined the potential hazards to the governor in a meeting on April 10. Finally, on April 30, the governor issued executive order EO-80-05, defining a Red Zone (no Blue Zone) around Mount St. Helens. However, examination of that executive order reveals that the closure area

Table 1.   Roadblocks Near Mount St. Helens, March 25-April 10, 1980

Road	Date	Location	Type
504/1	3/25	Camp Baker	Advisory only
2	3/27	County line	Manned by county
3	3/27	10 miles west of county line	Manned by county
4	3/28	Camp Baker	Manned by county
5	4/4	Junction W/505	Manned by state
503/1	3/25	Swift Reservoir Gate	Unmanned
N902	3/27	3 miles above Cougar	Manned by county
3	4/5	Jack's Store west of Cougar	Manned by National Guard
4	4/8	3 miles above Cougar	Manned by sheriff
5	4/10	Swift Reservoir Gate	Manned by sheriff
N818	3/28	Merril Lake	Manned
N73	3/28	Government Mineral Springs	Manned
Heally Road	3/28	West of Chelutchie	Manned

Source: Sorensen 1981.

was a verbatim copy of the Forest Service Red Zone established more than a month previously on federal land. No state land, apart from State Highway 504 near the National Forest boundary, was closed before May 18 (see map 7). After April 30, as one of our respondents observed, the area north and south of the highway was not legally closed to entry. It was senseless to continue manning the barricades, so a sign was put up and the police officers were removed on April 30. The governor took no more action to establish a state Red or Blue Zone until May 25, one week after the catastrophic eruption.

The interest generated by the volcano spilled over into the airspace around it, as people sought ways to bypass the roadblocks and found they could go over them. A new problem thus developed:

Volcano activity has never been a problem in the conterminous United States since the airplane has been around, and the interest from the news media, scientists, geologists, and vulcanologists has been, to say the least quite heavy. This has generated considerable air traffic in the area (Austin 1980, 1).

Fears that these aircraft could collide with each other or be damaged by material ejected from the volcano led the Federal Aviation Adminis-

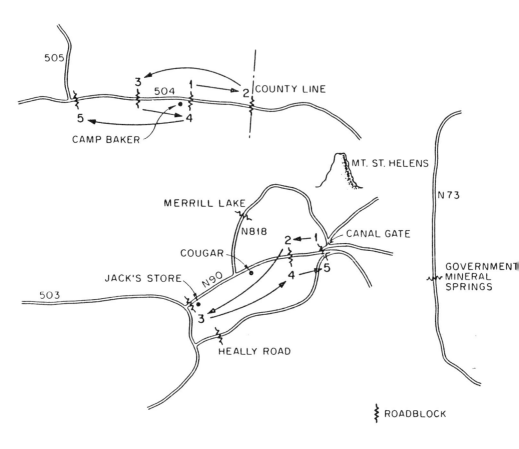

FIGURE 18.   Schematic of Changes in Roadblock Locations, March 22–April 10, 1980. From Sorensen 1981.

tration to establish a temporary flight restriciton area on April 1. To aid control over the restricted area, a special air traffic control section was assigned exclusively to Mount St. Helens, and special support facilities were established. Attention was also paid to providing public information: " . . . we have been informing pilots through the news media and other means, to stay out of the Mount St. Helens area unless they have official business there (Austin 1980, 1)."

Protecting the public from the potential hazards of the volcano was a multigovernmental problem. The USGS hazard map demonstrated threats to areas under several jurisdictions. The prompt action of the USFS in closing national forest lands was well supported by county and FAA efforts. On the state level, the initiative of the district personnel of the state patrol and Department of Transportation was not well supported by the government in Olympia. The resulting shape of the closure area made it possible for tourists and loggers to be quite close to the west side of Mount St. Helens. Both forks of the Toutle River, where the geologists had mapped the greatest avalanche and mudflow danger, were open to the public except for the highway. The failure to close state lands in the hazard area led to the mistaken belief by the public that those areas were safe, and to tragedy for those people caught in the eruption (no unauthorized people were killed in the USFS Red Zone).

The uncoordinated closure of land around the volcano, the exemptions granted to a few people (the most famous was Harry Truman, who refused to leave his home at Spirit Lake—and died there), some media coverage, and the tremendous attraction of the active volcano, were all factors contributing to the convergence of people around and into the closure area. This has been a continuing problem, as one respondent stated:

> The USFS, sheriffs, National Guard, and Washington State Patrol continually had problems with the public sneaking around control points, harassing security gate guards . . . Some with property were not understanding about being excluded. This hasn't changed since May 18. There are different types trying to get in; we have charged photographers, story hunters, and pseudoscientists, as opposed to tourists. This has increased because of the fame of the area, no longer simply a local problem. We've had Japanese, French, Germans, to mention a few . . .

Violations of the closure zone were common and the USFS was forced to "spend many, many hours of time dealing with them." Maintaining the closure was made more difficult, according to one respondent, by some entrepreneurs who even sold maps on how to get around the roadblocks.

The FAA controllers had problems in the air as well. An FAA patrol plane was kept in the restricted zone, identifying unauthorized intruders for citation. In one case, a pilot dove his plane right into the crater. One traffic controller said that even when the public pilots were cooperating by staying out of the Red Zone, they crowded around the edges, creating problems for controllers trying to avoid collisions.

The landowners, government and private, soon found that the tourists attracted by the volcanic activity created more of a hazard than the volcano itself was thought to be—and they needed to keep them under control. As one logger noted,

> We became involved with an aggressive public management policy. This was based on an assessment of hazards not based on the volcano directly, but a tremendous volume of people anticipated who are unaccustomed to dealing with the normal hazards of forests. We had a difficult time convincing other agency people that this was a hazard and should be mitigated.

A major problem was that the volcano attracted sightseers who behaved somewhat differently from normal tourists. As one respondent said: "Mount St. Helens was not the typical tourist site that people visit for a short time and then leave, people would stay for days or weeks waiting to see an eruption."

Aware that before the volcano awoke, "Spirit Lake and Mount St. Helens were getting 700,000 people a year," the industrial interests near the mountain expected a long-term problem dealing with people who wanted to see the area. Accentuating the problem before May 18 was the disbelief in the danger, inducing more people to take chances by entering the area and delaying coordinated agency action on public management until almost a week before the catastrophe.

To keep sightseers from getting too close to dangerous zones, the Forest Service opened two visitor centers at Ridgefield and at Lewis and Clark State Park (figure 19). At those locations the public could see the volcano, learn about the volcanic events, and be warned about the hazards. They could satisfy their curiosity without endangering themselves or worrying those charged with their safety. These centers have been very successful, and attracted nearly 400,000 visitors in the two months between July 15 and September 15, 1980 (United States Forest Service 1981, 48).

Some news media individuals created special problems by belittling the danger and the efforts to maintain the closure. In seemed to one respondent that some newspapers were playing a sort of game "to make the Forest Service and State Patrol look like idiots." Instead of trying to explain the need for the closures and the potential hazards behind them, some news stories did the opposite. According to another respondent:

> From the very beginning (March 27, 1980) the news media contributed to the problem by public broadcasts [for example], "You have a right to pass beyond road blocks to view the volcano," TV coverage of news media on the mount flanks, interviews with Harry Truman, with the latter two examples known to be in a restricted zone. . . .

News media people were also cited as the "worst offenders" in violating the Red Zone. When they not only violated the zone, but announced it in a news broadcast, many people could be led to question the effec-

FIGURE 19.   Sign for Visitor Center.

tiveness of the closure. An example of this kind of press activity includes a comment by one respondent about having to pick up several press people who hiked into the Red Zone after May 18 and were caught in the second (May 25) eruption. In another report, an FAA official said some newspeople were offering private pilots large sums of money to deliberately violate FAA rules and fly them into the restricted zone. Sometimes the news media could make trades with scientists with legitimate research needs—their resources in return for access:

> The press had a lot of resources, for example, helicopters. They would call up scientists and offer to take them up to the Red Zone. While the scientists are doing their legitimate work, the press goes all over. When TV news lands on the lip of the crater, the public wonders "Why not us?"

Access into the closure area has been a continuing problem. Red Zone permits were issued by the USFS, the State Division of Licensing, and the Allen Committee, and long-term blanket permits were issued for forest industries working near the mountains. We have already noted the frustrations of the head of the Allen Committee with respect to the five separate revisions of the bureaucratic rules for scientific entry. A Forest Service respondent explained that the USFS made no judgment on the validity of the research, but were concerned about the safety of the researchers.

Of special significance was the case of owners of property in the Red

Zone near Spirit Lake, who, according to Ota, Snell and Zaitz (1980), were feeling a "quiet rage" about the restrictions that kept them from entering the closure area to check their property or remove valuable possessions—

> Cabin owners worried about looting or that their summer places needed maintenance. They were angry, too, about having to pay taxes on property they could not use under the Red Zone restrictions. They had been sending letters to the governor's office demanding that they be let back in (Ota, Snell, and Zaitz 1980, V15).

On May 14, the governor allowed Boy Scout and YMCA officials to airlift about $100,000 worth of boats, camping equipment, and other property from their camps at Spirit Lake. By Saturday, May 17, other private property owners organized a caravan to the Red Zone barricades, protesting their restriction. Under this pressure, the governor instructed the state patrol to escort the property owners to their cabins so they could remove possessions (Ota, Snell and Zaitz 1980; Office of the Governor of Washington 1980). One of our respondents also noted that at 10:00 on May 18, another caravan of property owners was scheduled to be escorted into the Red Zone. That trip, however, was forestalled by the 8:32 disappearance of all property in the area. One can hardly help but wonder whether the decision to allow these property owners into the Red Zone (and also risk the lives of the Washington State Patrol escort) was made with any consideration of the scientific knowledge of the volcanic activity, especially the unprecedented speed of growth of the bulge on the north flank. The state's action seems particularly irresponsible since the USGS and USFS turned down these requests to enter the Red Zone, and, as one USGS official noted, "It was clearly pointed out that it was considered to be too great a risk, considering the monitoring data." As it was, the property owners' caravans missed the eruption by a matter of hours, not much in a scale of geologic time. Quite obviously, in retrospect, the safety of these caravans was a matter of luck, not good judgment.

In spite of the frustrations, the struggle to maintain road closures was seen as worthwhile by most Forest Service respondents, convinced their actions led to positive results. Most credited the closure of the forest with saving "a hell of a lot of lives," keeping an estimated 5,000–30,000 people out of the blast area. Coldwater Ridge was mentioned in particular. Being familiar with the area, USFS respondents could visualize the impact of the initial blast on curiosity seekers. For example, one respondent noted, "Coldwater viewpoint, where people would be, was levelled to bedrock."

FOREST SERVICE PROBLEMS IN PERFORMING THEIR ROLE

In response to an open-ended question about problems encountered in performing their role, Forest Service personnel mentioned (1) maintaining the closure of forest land in the face of political pressure and with no guidelines, (2) coordination with other agencies, especially before May 18, (3) lack of facilities, (4) lack of funding for some agencies, (5) the news media, (6) communications, and (7) difficulty in keeping abreast of events as they occurred. When asked about specific problems, a majority of USFS people cited lack of equipment or facilities, lack of public cooperation (already noted above), and lack of information. Needed equipment included communications equipment, aircraft and television for twenty-four hour surveillance of the mountain, breathing masks, and facilities to support both the Emergency Coordination Center and other USFS activities.

Information difficulties occurred because of a lack of communications equipment in some areas on May 18 (only a temporary problem for the USFS). In addition, sometimes the information was slow in coming, and it was difficult at times to gain helicopter access to assess damage. Also mentioned was the amount of misinformation coming from some sources. Valuable time was spent squelching rumors.

Several respondents also commented upon problems with the news media. These problems had two aspects: first, a lack of press support in maintaining the closure; and second, press harassment of key personnel as the latter tried to act in the emergency situation. The USFS had problems dealing with " . . . the continued pressure of the press on all parties—trying to do their job but continually hounded by press, who can be tenacious in digging out information—have to make sure it doesn't interfere with public safety."

This press problem seemed to be the worst at the disaster headquarters; in some other areas the news media left a favorable impression. In one ranger station: "We got along well with the local press—no problems. They always seemed to be pretty cooperative. We usually got them in one or two at a time, not in a mob."

Most Forest Service respondents felt coordination with other agencies was not a problem: "I felt there was generally good support; it (the volcano) was a threat to all of us—some problems of manpower and funding of certain agencies." The few interagency coordination problems which arose in the Forest Service view were "minor" and confined to the period before May 18. After the catastrophic eruption, the USGS respondents felt the problems were overcome and the working relationships led to friendships between people from many different agencies: "The disaster coordination was better than normal operations; now we talk about getting together socially."

The emergency situation seemed to stimulate a higher than usual degree of cooperation, and dampened interagency rivalry. The teams on flights to monitor volcanic activities routinely included Forest Service personnel who knew the area well, and geologists from the USGS. Similar teams received the radio messages back at the headquarters in Vancouver. This team concept facilitated more complete interpretations in the field and enhanced understanding of the messages sent back to the ECC. Familiarity between the Forest Service and the Survey bred respect rather than contempt. In the last chapter we described the USGS's appreciation for the Forest Service's efforts. The high regard was mutual. One Forest Service official commented that "we found out how good they are." Another said: "The USGS has been absolutely fantastic to work with all this time—top notch—excellent degree of cooperation."

Other agencies or organizations were also praised in terms of their cooperation. A district ranger spoke of the link with local authorities: "Most of our coordination was with the sheriff and we worked well together." There was initially some apprehension on the part of the Forest Service regarding the change of leadership as the Federal Emergency Management Agency began its activities following the federal disaster declaration. "We were apprehensive that the emergency center might change. We felt it should stay in place. FEMA came to the same conclusions; they had some super good people." The Forest Service did not understand FEMA's role at first, but were impressed at once by their ability to take charge "We actually benefited from their involvement," said a high-ranking Forest Service official. The Forest Service continued their monitoring and coordination activities while FEMA took over public information services which was moved to a new headquarters a few blocks up the street. Once the initial "turf protection problem" was settled, residual tensions may have remained but the coordination was smooth and, according to one of our Forest Service respondents, "I think they did a damn fine job—left a good taste in our mouth."

CONCLUSIONS

The USFS personnel are to be commended for the strong leadership role they displayed in response to the reawakening of Mount St. Helens. They took the initiative in organizing the pertinent individuals and agencies and developing a contingency plan for potential volcanic eruptions. The first active step in response to the developing volcanic activity was their closure of forest land above timberline. The USFS organized the Emergency Coordination Center (ECC) and provided facilities for it in their Vancouver, Washington, headquarters. There the Forest Service played the lead role in coordinating and assisting emergency response activities, in collecting and relaying visual data about the eruption, and in disseminating information to the public.

As a model for responding to the volcanic eruption, USFS personnel followed their own fire emergency plan. Fortunately for all concerned, the Forest Service had such a plan and considerable experience in applying it to fire emergencies, for there was little else to go on when the mountain first erupted. By and large the plan worked well, but it provided limited guidance for certain of the more complex and extensive aspects of the eruption. The Forest Service was used to dealing with their own forest areas and, like the USGS, they did not provide adequate warnings for the people in the ashfall areas east of the Cascades. This failure was in part due to the USGS emphasis on the areas of greatest disaster potential west of the mountain, and in part because of the Forest Service's focus on their own forest areas. Both organizations were correct in dealing first with the life-threatening problems, but failed to follow through in warning about ashfall.

The other major Forest Service problems were related to the coordination of many state and local agencies and to defining and enforcing the closure of danger zones for the general public. For this complex set of problems, their fire emergency model provided few guidelines.

THE STATE OF WASHINGTON DEPARTMENT OF EMERGENCY SERVICES AND THE STATEWIDE WARNING _____

In the state of Washington, the agency with the statutory responsibility for alerting the public about potential natural hazards is the state Department of Emergency Services (DES). As a result, they were recipients of all the USGS information on Mount St. Helens from the original hazard notification, and most of our respondents in the agency said they were aware of the full range of information provided. This chapter examines the DES and statewide efforts at warning and coordination of the emergency response. Also briefly examined are the roles played by the National Guard and National Weather Service.

THE DES REACTION TO THE FIRST MOUNT ST. HELENS HAZARD NOTIFICATION

When first informed by the USGS of the volcanic hazard on Mount St. Helens, in December 1978, the director of the state of Washington Department of Emergency Services thought Mount St. Helens was "waking up." She immediately began to make plans for evacuating the Toutle and Lewis river valleys. Consultations with the USGS and state geologists clarified the immediate situation, assuring the DES director that no eruptions were likely in the near future. However, it was decided the DES should arrange a briefing from the USGS to determine how imminent an eruption might be and to what degree the state should be concerned. State DES representatives had previously been briefed about the USGS hazard notification system in a regional meeting in Portland, Oregon, in December 1977.

In January 1979, Don Nichols, head of the USGS Geologic Hazards Warning and Preparedness Program, came out to Washington to brief the representatives of a large number of state agencies, as well as many locally based federal agency personnel, about the volcanic risk. Nichols described the meeting this way:

> At that time, I passed out copies of Bulletin 1383-C [the Blue Book] and the Baker Professional Paper and told them that although these were the two volcanoes most likely to erupt in the near future, we did not, at that time, have any evidence of an imminent eruption of either one, but that response plans, including evacuation plans, plans for lowering of reservoir levels, and other measures were certainly in order (Nichols, personal communication, 1982).

This briefing made the potential hazard seem less immediate than the earlier notification. Although the early DES response tends to be seen as an overreaction, it did at least alert a large number of state officials to the hazard potential of Mount St. Helens.

DES REACTIONS TO THE REAWAKENING OF MOUNT ST. HELENS

The DES was first notifiied about the signs of renewed activity on Mount St. Helens on March 24, when they were called by Don Mullineaux and Clem Shearer of the USGS. Those DES people who did not talk to the USGS scientists directly learned of it soon after through their own agency. In the weeks that followed, they also received warning information from the University of Washington seismologists, from the Newport Observatory, from state geologists, and from the amateur radio network. It is important to note that the DES was under a different director than the one who "overreacted" in 1978.

The main reaction of DES was to contact all the people on their emergency planning list. "We were like a funnel for information from state to local," explained one DES respondent. State and local people were contacted, mainly those listed in the Washington State Emergency Service Contingency Plan of April 1980. This list included all state agencies thought to have emergency responsibilities, as well as local government officials and representataives of emergency services organizations in the adjacent states of Oregon and Idaho, and in British Columbia in Canada.

Their own contingency plan was developed and continually improved, and DES representatives were involved in the development of the contingency plan of the USFS. In both these contingency plans, the focus of attention was in the six counties closest to the mountain: Cowlitz, Clark, Skamania, Lewis, Yakima, and Klickitat. No other counties are listed by name and many DES respondents said they really thought Yakima and Klickitat counties were unlikely to be affected. Although information on Mount St. Helens went by teletype to all county emergency services directors in the state, it was never keyed directly to them and, as will be developed in a later chapter, was not thought relevant to the concerns of eastern Washington. The county emergency services directors were employees of the counties, not the state DES, and, according to its director, there was not much coordination between the two groups.

In addition to funneling information to the local communities and developing contingency plans, the state DES had representatives involved in delimitation of the Red Zone, serving on the Mount St. Helens Watch Committee, and acting as liaison with many state agencies. From the start of the ECC (Vancouver), the DES were considered part of the team.

In their own contingency plan, the DES worked out the emergency response procedures they would follow in the event of a major eruption. These are detailed in their plan and include lists of volunteers, duty officer procedures, activation of the emergency operating center, standard operating procedures for the communications room, for public information, for air traffic control, and for ash observation and sampling, and other emergency activities.

In spite of all this advance preparation, from the early warning information to the intensive preparations following the first eruption in late March, the DES was still in such a state of disarray on May 18 when the major eruption occurred that their warning to the local communities was delayed for nearly two hours.

PROBLEMS SEEN AS IMPORTANT BY THE STATE OF WASHINGTON DEPARTMENT OF EMERGENCY SERVICES

The state Department of Emergency Services was plagued by many problems which negatively affected their role in responding to the volcanic eruption, according to our thirteen respondents from that agency. Virtually all agreed there were major problems in the lack of equipment or facilities, the lack of funds, and the lack of manpower in their agency. These deficiencies all resulted from years of neglect, and reflected the general level of concern about emergency planning in the state. Still seen as important, but not at the same level, were problems of lack of information and lack of public cooperation, mainly related to the political pressure and the public clamor to get into restricted areas. While "keeping the public out of the Red Zone has been a real nightmare," in other instances the public displayed "unbelievable cooperation."

Still other problems identified were lack of coordination with other agencies, and the media. The former problem mainly related to their dissatisfaction with the Federal Emergency Management Agency, who did not come to Olympia as DES thought they should, but instead made their headquarters in Vancouver. Elsewhere there were comments about excellent cooperation with other state and federal agencies.

The media also received high praise in general, but were criticized about unprofessional conduct by some who sought sensationalism, violating the Red Zone, creating rumors, and playing people off against each other. Other DES respondents were piqued about the exaggeration of the disaster, which they felt was bad publicity and might cause economic losses for the tourist industry. Many of these problems are not directly pertinent to the main role of the DES.

The General Problem of Neglect of Emergency Planning
in the State of Washington
The major problems identified by our respondents from the DES are the result of years of emergency planning neglect in the state. The state has been relatively disaster free, and some respondents spoke of the "disaster will never happen to us" syndrome, which had led to a neglect of disaster planning. Many DES respondents pointed out that Washington has no state disaster fund for emergencies, and one put this deficiency in perspective, asserting that they were "one of the two or three states in the Union without an emergency fund." Some help did arrive after the May 18 eruption. One reaction to this belated largesse was: "You can't go from the dark ages to the space age in a short period of time."

The DES headquarters in Olympia are a clear symbol of the relative power and prestige of emergency operations in Washington. They are housed in World War II-type barracks, and the equipment within was described as of about the same vintage: "antiquated equipment," definitely "not state of the art communication equipment." A clear lack of confidence in the agency may be seen by the preparation of other government agencies of the state of Washington for the impending eruption. Instead of following the lead and direction of the DES, a new Mount St. Helens Watch Committee was established. The director of DES, a recent political appointee rather than a hazards professional, became the deputy chairman of the Watch Committee. The chief of the Washington State Patrol became chairman. These actions were regarded by one DES respondent as showing a "complete lack of confidence in the agency" and "like a slap in the face."

Many large state agencies, some housed in large prestigious office buildings with thousands of employees, such as the state patrol, the National Guard, the Department of Transportation, the Department of Social and Health Services, and the Department of Ecology, were represented on the Watch Committee. The DES, in contrast, had only twenty-one employees. According to a DES representative on the committee, other agency representatives felt that, "We have no problem taking orders from the State Patrol but we'll be damned if we'll take orders from DES." The DES role became public information dissemination rather than warning and coordination of state and local community efforts.

The exact authority of the Watch Committee, and its role in the chain of command between the governor, the DES, and the other state agencies was unclear. Perhaps this is best illustrated by the contradictory responses of two of the governor's staff members to a question about the role of the Watch Group in relation to the DES—one said the Watch Group was subordinate, the other said the DES was. The former elaborated on what may have been the ideal case by saying the Watch Group was: "to work with DES; it was subordinate to DES in its particular area. DES used this as a resource group." Another member of the governor's staff considered the Watch Group an advisory body reporting directly to the governor, which is borne out by the order establishing the committee: "The Chairman of the Watch Group will report to the Governor on the Group's activities as often as the situation requires."

The mobilization of state agencies into a standing committee, with the director of the DES as chairman, would have done much to establish the DES role and responsibility as the lead agency in organizing the state's emergency response to the subsequent eruptions. As it was, the appointment of the chief of the state patrol as chairman and the failure to place it under the DES probably undermined the DES leadership role in the emergency response. An alternative view, expressed by several of our respondents, was that the Watch Committee was established to provide leadership the DES was failing to demonstrate. One state official said, "The obvious lack of leadership and establishing a chain of command within their organization was embarrassing. The lack of respect by other agencies was due to their own mismanagement practices not a Watch Committee." Another federal observer felt the confusion in the state organization was an indication of a general lack of leadership in the state:

> Professional expertise was not the issue; the issue was leadership ability. The leadership issue goes far beyond DES. It ultimately must reside with the Governor. . . . The Governor's orientation . . . was toward maximizing federal aid and avoiding state responsibility. The confusion and lack of direction within DES was a symp-

tom of a fundamental problem in government in the State of Washington.

The Lack of Funds and Equipment

The lack of funds was basic to the lack of manpower and equipment. To deal effectively with a disaster of the magnitude of Mount St. Helens requires funding and a staff prepared for the worst case. Without funds it is impossible to acquire or maintain a state of the art warning system. Despite all their problems, one DES respondent insisted the "agency performed well considering the budget."

The NAWAS system, or National Warning System, is an example of the type of equipment used by the DES and of local attitudes toward emergency planning. The system in Washington consists of a hot line telephone with direct connections to county emergency service representatives around the state. When the system is activated, an alarm bell rings in each of the locations included in the warning network. This NAWAS system has existed for two and a half decades. According to a Federal Emergency Management Agency (FEMA) representative who inspected the system, it was not well regarded in Washington. Placards with information on how to use the warning system were not posted, and local people regarded it with attitudes ranging from "humor to total disrespect." When the May 18 eruption occurred, the system failed to operate and this failure was repeated on May 25, though when tested after each of these events it functioned well. The failure seemed to be based more on the attitudes toward it than on the physical characteristics of the system. After the system failed for the third time on June 12, the FEMA person inspecting the USFS setup found

> There was a paper folded and jammed between the striker and the bell, and people furtively glancing around when asked if the bell went off. It's strange that the bell is always unoperational just when needed and not when tested. There is an attitudinal state that doesn't take the phone seriously—laughs at civil defense.

NAWAS was only one of several warning systems. Others included the regular telephone services, the Law Enforcement Teletype System (LETS) which sends teletype messages to each law enforcement office around the state, the Emergency Broadcast System (EBS) whereby a conference call alerts area radio stations who in turn broadcast the warning information, and the Radio Amateur Civil Emergency Services (RACES) which helped provide visual surveillance was well as information on weather and seismic activity to DES headquarters at Olympia. It was a message from Gerald Martin, one of the radio amateurs on this network, killed in the eruption, which provided the DES with their first information on the May 18 eruption. In spite of all these systems, the DES did not get their warning out until nearly two hours after the eruption on May 18.

A major problem reiterated by many DES respondents was the lack of an adequate emergency operating center. The room was described as too small for a major operation, as having poor facilities and no back-up equipment such as a dependable emergency broadcast system; so, the DES had to rely on facilities of the Washington State Patrol located in an adjacent building. One respondent estimated that 99 percent of DES communication was by phone. In a time of crisis the lines become jammed, as in the pandemonium following the May 18 eruption. At this point, many members of the DES became firmly convinced of the need for dedicated lines such as those installed later connecting the DES in Olympia to the USFS-USGS headquarters in Vancouver.

The Manpower Problem

Despite all the problems with equipment, the more serious problem was probably the lack of manpower, especially of trained personnel, which in part helps explain their high level of concern about the lack of information. A major emergency like the Mount St. Helens eruption requires more staff members than a small agency like the DES can muster. One respondent described trying to warn forty different agencies by himself via telephone. It took him three or four hours to do this and many had already heard of the eruption before he called. To some degree, this manpower problem can be overcome by the use of volunteers or by designating persons from other agencies to serve in temporary emergency capacities. The moral support provided by the arrival of staff members from emergency planning agencies in Oregon, California, and British Columbia was gratefully acknowledged by DES respondents. Other local volunteers were also available, but they were not always well trained nor was there enough time during the crisis situation to train them further; and the real shortage was in trained personnel.

The size of the DES staff made it hard for them to provide twenty-four-hour service on a sustained basis, as is required in a disaster event of the magnitude of the Mount St. Helens eruption. For more specialized tasks, the same person had to remain on duty for the entire emergency period. One such person said, "I was on duty for the first 24 hours straight and I did not go to bed for the first three or four days after the 18th." Such experiences underline the need for cross-training personnel so each specialized person would have a counterpart to provide relief in a sustained situation. The bedlam of the posteruption period also indicates the importance of a contingency plan, for the demands at that time preclude any possibility of planning.

People with enough geological training to interpret developments were lacking in relation to the Mount St. Helens eruption. The DES was dependent on interpretations from outside, and many comments indicated frustrations when immediate confirmation was not forthcoming and when uncertainities in the available data gave them something less than the exact time, place, and magnitude preferred. The inability to quickly grasp the significance of geological events led to delays, as the following comment indicates: "Using up our warning time making decisions has been our biggest problem since Day One." One means of overcoming their own lack of geological expertise would have been to ask the help of geologists employed by the state.

WHY THE MAY 18 WARNING WAS LATE

A lack of information was cited as the reason the DES warning for the May 18 eruption was not forthcoming until nearly two hours after the event began. All accounts agree that the DES received their first warning of the eruption through the amateur radio network from Gerald O. Martin, a volunteer ham radio operator, a volcano victim who died in the line of duty. He was last heard from at about 8:32 A.M., May 18, via a radio transmission from his motor home parked west of Coldwater Peak, eight miles north of Mount St. Helens. Martin's last message, according to a DES respondent, was "The whole north side is giving way. It's consuming the USGS people and it's gonna get me." This message was sent to Reid Apgar who coordinated RACES. From him it was sent to the DES duty officer, who in turn called up DES personnel to report for duty because of the eruption.

When the closest DES employee arrived at the headquarters there were already two others there, including the director, but the warning procedures outlined in the contingency plan had not yet been activiated. The recent arrival asked about initiating the warning procedures but was told not to worry about it and to call the state agencies about an eruption in progress. Those already present had been at the office to make arrangements for a second contingent of Spirit Lake homeowners to go in to take care of their property. Before leaving to take the caravan of property owners in and out, they were checking on the state of the mountain with the ECC at Vancouver. As they were about to hang up (at 8:36 A.M.) with "a clean bill of health," the person at the ECC said, "Wait a minute, something is happening at the mountain." The person on the phone checked emergency communications with the amateur radio network—"All I could hear was that something was happening quite a bit bigger than in the past." Meanwhile, the line to the Forest Service headquarters was still open and the duty officer was calling people in. Twelve minutes later (8:48 A.M. by the

Forest Service log), the Forest Service person passed on the latest information about the eruption to the DES official still waiting at the other end of the open line.

Over an hour later the statewide warning had still not gone out. DES officials said they were still waiting for "official" confirmation from the USGS and the Forest Service. One DES official described his dilemma: "You're sitting here without good information. All lines jammed. We were getting bits and pieces. Experts are gathered and haven't given their analysis. What the hell do you tell them with you don't know?" By the time the DES sent out their first warning to all counties through the LETS system, the only system that worked that day, there were five DES officials present at their headquarters. By then (10:l5 A.M.), according to their own log, they had received a flash flood statement from the Seattle Weather Service (9:10 A.M.), a plume trajectory report from the Seattle Weather Service (9:30 A.M.), information about ash at Cispus Environmental Camp (9:15 A.M.), and information about floods and evacuation on the Toutle River (10:00 A.M.). The first report on ash was from Cispus Environmental Camp. The director called and said, "It's dark as hell. We have two inches of ash on the ground and I've got kids here." This was an hour before the DES warning went out, and already the eruption was in the news. According to one DES respondent, "Our best source [of information] was the media, radio and TV."

In contrast to the DES officials, who felt they did not have enough information to activate their warning system on the morning of May 18, the National Guard acted immediately in response to the same information. They based their plans on a "worst case scenario plus 50%." They were particularly aware of the problem of ashfall. For example, the following message was sent to all units on April 3, six weeks before the major eruptions:

> If Mount St. Helens erupts, it may produce a heavy ashfall. If you are in the area receiving heavy ashfall, you will observe the following events: 1) It will get very dark, even though it is daylight elsewhere, 2) Visibility will be reduced to what would occur in a heavy sandstorm or blizzard, 3) If you are in a vehicle, the ash will clog the filter of your engine and the engine will die, 4) Radios and televisions will not work for two hours. You will be protected if you seek shelter under a roof; if you are in a car, remain there until the ashfall ends. The ash looks like dust refined at Yakima Firing Center, except it is grey in color.

The above quotation exemplifies how the DES could have used the geological information. If the preceding message had been sent to all outlying state and local agencies on the various communications networks, one might suppose the areas on the east side could have been better prepared to cope with the ash when it appeared.

At Camp Murray, the first official news was received from the DES at 9:40 A.M. on May 18, more than an hour after the initial eruption. This is how it was recorded in the Washington National Guard log,

> The latest quake to date has occurred at 0832 hours. A major eruption is in progress; flame and fire coming out of mountain. The largest ash plume to date has occurred (100 times larger than any to date), the north side of the mountain is very unstable; a flash-flood watch has been issued for Skamania and Cowlitz County rivers. (This is only a "watch" and not a warning at this time.) The environmental center at Cispus reports the sky went completely black and now has a ½ inch of ash on the ground, and this was in a matter of seconds. People are leaving the upper reaches of the mountain. We are now in the process of notifying Federal, County and State agencies. As far as activating the National Guard, "This is not an activation call at this time." It is just an information call (Log, Camp Murray, May 18, 1980).

Based on that "information call" which preceded the first official warning by thirty-five minutes, the helicopter troop at Yakima was called at 9:45 and ordered to "immediately" return to Gray Field (Fort Lewis). The timing was quite close, for the USGS isochron map of the time of ash arrival indicates the ash reached the Yakima Firing Center sometime between 9:45 and 10:15 (Sarna-Wojcicki et al. 1981). As it was, nineteen helicopters were able to escape Yakima (sixteen from the Washington and three from the Wyoming National Guard); according to one respondent, six helicopters did not get out of Yakima. At 10:30, the chief of the state patrol requested the helicopters for search and rescue work. By 1:20 P.M. that Sunday, a Tactical Operations Center was established at Toutle, and the first search and rescue missions began. For the next three days the National Guard, plus six helicopters from the Air Force Reserve and one from the Coast Guard, bore the main burden of the search and rescue (SAR) operations around the mountain. In a total of twelve days of SAR operations, the National Guard flew 397 sorties and picked up 124 of the 197 people rescued (Washington National Guard, Executive Summary 1980).

ASSESSMENT OF THE STATE DEPARTMENT OF EMERGENCY SERVICE RESPONSE

Clearly, the state Department of Emergency Services was a neglected, underfunded, ill-equipped agency not fully prepared to deal with a hazard event of the magnitude of Mount St. Helens. More important than any lack of equipment was the lack of efficient, well-trained personnel and, especially, the leadership needed to implement the contingency plan developed prior to the eruption. Because they had the major responsibility for warning the public, this problem was serious, with roots extending beyond the DES to the long-term neglect of emergency planning in the state. No state emergency planning agency can be expected to be always fully manned, prepared, and posed to handle rare, high-magnitude events easily. On the other hand, with reasonable equipment and well-trained personnel, these agencies should have the flexibility to expand with the help of trained volunteers and personnel from other agencies, and to have a clear sense of priorities so that the most essential task, a timely warning, is accomplished.

The DES in the state of Washington did not really provide leadership and coordination before the major eruption (instead they simply funneled messages back and forth). In part, this failure occurred because they, like most people in Washington, did not really think the eruption would be of the magnitude that took place. Although the event scenario was clearly outlined in the Blue Book, they did not, for whatever reasons, do their job effectively. Surprise about the magnitude of this event may be understandable in the general public, but it is not acceptable in an agency formed to protect the public from just such events. Their business is to know what to expect and to take appropriate actions to mitigate the worst effects.

The DES failed to warn those affected by mudflows and floods in time. They, like the USFS and USGS, also failed to warn the people east of the Cascades about the ashfall. Their lack of geological expertise contributed to this failure, but as one DES respondent complained: "I can recall no real discussion of excessive ashfall, or ashfall like it was, or where it would fall, or the consequences. Then when it fell, we got all the adverse publicity. Why didn't you tell us it was coming."

Although there was no emphasis on ashfall in public statements about an impending eruption, the topic was discussed in the Blue Book and in the DES contingency plan. The importance of a timely warning was illustrated by the Washington National Guard in Yakima. Before an official warning about the eruption was issued, the DES were contacting state agencies about what had occurred. This unofficial message reached the Washington National Guard at 9:40 (they were first alerted, however, through the news at 9:00) and was relayed to the base at Yakima at 9:45, soon enough to allow nineteen helicopters to get away just before the ash cloud arrived. Had they waited for the official warning from DES which arrived at 10:15, it would probably have been too late to beat the ash; and, as a result, the search and rescue operation may have been much less successful, for it was the National Guard that picked up the bulk of the people rescued around the mountain.

RECENT CHANGES IN THE STATE OF WASHINGTON DEPARTMENT OF EMERGENCY SERVICES

To finish on a more positive note, we can report that the major eruption of Mount St. Helens did stimulate a great deal of concern about emergency planning at the state level. The DES respondents without hesitation all answered "yes" to the question "Are you prepared to deal with any future eruptions?" One answered wryly: "We've had several to practice on." Not only did they all feel they had learned from the experience, but there was also more support forthcoming for better equipment and facilities. There is now a new director of the DES, and one respondent seemed to reflect the new morale as he said when referring to the warning failure on May 18: "It wouldn't happen again. We have a new director with a new direction and new emphasis. He has unquestioned support to do what needs to be done." Today's effective DES organization contrasts favorably with the DES that existed at the time of the eruption. Interestingly, most of the personnel are the same.

THE WARNING ACTIVITIES OF THE NATIONAL WEATHER SERVICE

Although a federal agency, the National Weather Service (NWS) was also important in warning the people in Washington State. These warning activities provide a dramatic contrast to those of the DES in terms of efficiency and dispatch. The National Oceanic and Atmospheric Administration (NOAA), within which the National Weather Service is situated, has the responsibility for issuing flood warnings. The National Weather Service found itself concerned with the possibility of flooding caused by a volcano rather than a storm as is usually the case. This distinction was not lost on the personnel. As one noted, the problem was " . . . not a normal flash flood situation, based not on atmospheric conditions but geologic. As a warning agency, the National Weather Service had the network and took over the task of warning." A secondary concern of the NWS was to monitor the extent of ash plumes, primarily because of the dangers to aviation.

Planning began immediately after the first earthquakes in March. By March 27, the Seattle office had a preliminary plan including contacts with the other major Weather Service offices in Portland and Olympia, the River Forecast Center in Portland, and the Washington State Hydrologist. Subsequent heavy earthquake activity provided "practice" for issuing flood warnings, revealing a major problem. Initially, flood forecasts for the volcano area were issued by four NWS offices: the Seattle headquarters for Washington State, the Portland Weather Service Office at the request of the USGS, the Portland Fire Weather Office which is responsible for Gifford Pinchot National Forest, and the Olympia Weather Service Office which is in close contact with state agencies. This diversity created a fear that contradictory information might be sent out, therefore the plan was revised so that the Seattle office assumed the sole responsibility for issuing warnings. In addition to assignment of authority, the NWS plan included a notification list, prewritten warnings for the teletype, and other procedures for warning. Through a computer connection with Washington, D. C., a model was available that produced forecasts of the direction and speed of a possible ash plume, which they were prepared to transmit on receipt of information about an eruption.

NWS Response to Eruptions
The eruption of Mount St. Helens was not predictable, in the usual sense, for the personnel of the National Weather Service, and so they depended on someone else to tell them of the mountain's activity before warnings could be issued. On May 18, at 8:45 A.M., the Weather Service received a call from the FAA, telling of a pilot report of smoke and lightning in the cirrus clouds above the volcano. This report was confirmed through the NAWAS system at 8:50. At 9:00, the following flash flood watch was issued for the area around Mount St. Helens:

> THE NATIONAL WEATHER SERVICE HAS ISSUED A FLASH FLOOD WATCH FOR SKAMANIA AND COWLITZ COUNTIES WITHIN 20 MILES WEST AND NORTH OF THE BASE OF MOUNT ST. HELENS.
>
> A FLASH FLOOD WATCH MEANS FLASH FLOODING IS POSSIBLE WITHIN THE WATCH AREA. PERSONS IN THE WATCH AREA ARE ADVISED TO BE ALERT FOR SUDDEN RISES IN STREAMS, RIVERS AND TRIBUTARIES . . . AND TO BE READY FOR QUICK ACTION IF FLASH FLOODING IS OBSERVED OR A WARNING ISSUED.
>
> A FLASH FLOOD STATEMENT WILL FOLLOW SHORTLY WITH ADDITIONAL DETAILS.

The above statement had been prewritten and stored for quick dispatch. Almost immediately, NWS personnel began working on a more detailed statement which was sent out at 9:10:

> A FLASH FLOOD WATCH IS IN EFFECT FOR THE SKAMANIA AND COWLITZ COUNTIES WITHIN 20 MILES WEST AND NORTH OF THE BASE OF MOUNT ST. HELENS.

APPARENTLY A MAJOR ERUPTION HAS OCCURRED AT
MOUNT ST. HELENS.

AN ERUPTION MAY PRODUCE MUD FLOWS AND RAPID
SNOWMELT CAUSING POSSIBLE FLASH FLOODING IN
THE AREA.

DETAILS FROM WITHIN THE AREA OF CONCERN WILL
LIKELY BE SKETCHY BUT THERE HAVE BEEN REPORTS
OF THE PLUME REACHING TO 60 THOUSAND FEET. . . .
RADAR ECHOS REPORTED BY WEATHER RADAR AS
WELL AS NEARLY CONTINUOUS LIGHTNING OVER THE
MOUNTAIN. PERSONS WITHIN THE WATCH AREA ARE
ADVISED TO TAKE PRECAUTIONS AND BE PREPARED
FOR QUICK ACTION IF FLASH FLOODING IS OBSERVED
OR A FLASH FLOOD WARNING IS ISSUED.

These first two warnings were primarily targeted to the river flood
plains immediately around Mount St. Helens. At this point, little information was available about the magnitude of the eruption. Using their
prepared plan, at 9:30 A.M. the weather people transmitted a probable
plume trajectory forecast based on wind speed and direcitons at various
altitudes:

. . . . MOUNT ST. HELENS PLUME TRAJECTORY
FORECAST . . . .
. . . . PLUME EJECTION ABOVE MOUNTAIN
TOP . . . .

PLUME TRAJECTORY OF ASH IF EMITTED FROM MOUN-
TAIN WILL GENERALLY BE TO THE EAST NORTHEAST
THRU NORTHEAST TODAY THROUGH MONDAY.

ELEVATION	WIND FROM	SPEED	PLUME GOES TO
12000 FEET	240	15	NORTHEAST
18000	240	20	NORTHEAST
24000	250	35	EAST NORTHEAST
30000	260	40	EAST NORTHEAST
40000	260	60	EAST NORTHEAST
50000	260	20	EAST NORTHEAST

At this point, the plume forecast was vague because of sketchy information. One NWS official noted, "The only error was 'if' rather than
'is'," for the prewritten statement had not been modified to reflect the
eruption. Problems interpreting these data occurred since the height of

the ash was not known and, therefore, calculating the time of arrival from the point of origin was not possible. By the time the necessary information was available and the necessary calcuations were computed, large areas were already hit (for example, Yakima at about 9:30). At 10:00 a better statement about the plume was issued, targeting specific cities likely to be hit:

BASED ON DATA FROM ERL TRAJECTORY MODEL . . .
PLUME AT LEVELS FROM MOUNTAIN TOP TO ABOUT
40000 FEET WILL TRAVEL NORTHEASTWARD. THERE IS
THE POSSIBILITY OF THE PLUME PASSING NEAR TO
THE FOLLOWING TOWNS IN EASTERN WASHINGTON . . .
YAKIMA ELLENSBURG WENATCHEE EPHRATA PASCO
OMAK AND SPOKANE ALSO OTHER URBAN AREAS IN
THIS GENERAL REGION.

By 10:20, more information about the mudflows led to upgrading the flash flood watch into a warning of imminent danger:

A FLASH FLOOD WARNING HAS BEEN ISSUED FOR SKA-
MANIA AND COWLITZ COUNTIES WITHIN 20 MILES
WEST AND NORTH OF THE BASE OF MOUNT. ST.
HELENS.

A FLASH FLOOD WARNING MEANS FLOODING IS IMMI-
NENT OR HAS BEEN REPORTED. PERSONS IN AF-
FECTED AREAS SHOULD TAKE IMMEDIATE ACTION.

A FLASH FLOOD STATEMENT WILL FOLLOW SHORTLY
WITH ADDITIONAL DETAILS.

Somewhat later in the morning, satellite pictures came in showing the extent and speed of the ash plume. This data enabled the transmission of a plume update at 11:30:

SPECIAL WEATHER STATEMENT ON SATELLITE LOCA-
TION FOR MOUNT ST. HELENS PLUME.

BASED ON 1045 PDT SATELLITE IMAGES . . . THE MAIN
PORTION OF VOLCANIC PLUME IS MOVING EAST
NORTHEASTWARD AND COVERED AN AREA FROM THE
MOUNTAIN TO JUST SOUTH OF PASCO ON ITS NORTH-
ERN BOUNDARY. THE TOP OF THE CLOUD APPEARS TO
BE MOVING ABOUT 60 MPH.

Capping off a busy morning, the NWS at 12:00 expanded the flash flood watch area to the junction of the Toutle and Cowlitz rivers. This expansion was based on observations by people in Cowlitz County:

> THE NATIONAL WEATHER SERVICE HAS ISSUED A FLASH FLOOD WATCH FOR THE TOUTLE RIVER BELOW THE TOWN OF TOUTLE TO THE JUNCTION OF THE TOUTLE AND THE COWLITZ RIVERS.

> THE TOUTLE RIVER BELOW THE JUNCTION OF THE NORTH AND SOUTH FORK IS RISING RAPIDLY. THE READING AT NOON IS 5.7 FEET. THERE IS NO FLOOD STAGE ESTABLISHED AT THIS POINT BUT THIS IS STILL BELOW FLOOD PROPORTIONS.

> A FLASH FLOOD WATCH MEANS FLASH FLOODING IS POSSIBLE WITHIN THE WATCH AREA. PERSONS IN THE WATCH AREA ARE ADVISED TO BE ALERT FOR SUDDEN RISES IN STREAMS RIVERS AND TRIBUTARIES . . . AND TO BE READY FOR QUICK ACTION IF FLASH FLOODING IS OBSERVED OR A WARNING IS ISSUED.

> A FLASH FLOOD WARNING REMAINS IN EFFECT FOR AREAS WITHIN 20 MILES OF THE BASE OF MOUNT ST. HELENS INCLUDING THE TOWN OF TOUTLE.

Through the remainder of the day, the NWS monitored events, issuing flood warnings for the rivers near the volcano and travelers' advisories for the ashfall areas in the east. These NWS bulletins went directly to state and local officials as well as to the public (via news media), providing almost instantaneous warnings of unfolding events. The NOAA Weather Wire is a direct line to the media as well as to other weather offices via teletype. Another link is the NOAA Weather Radio, a special band on most news radios. In addition, the NWS used the NAWAS system to contact state and county points. For his role in responding to the volcanic events of May 18 at Mount St. Helens, Paul Goree, in charge of the warnings from the Seattle office that day, received a special citation.

Interestingly, even in the National Weather Service where the plume trajectory forecasts were issued, the flood problem was by far the major concern. Ashfall was seen as important merely in terms of its effect on the aviation industry. "We did not think of fall-out. We did not think it had the potential for damage," explained one Weather Service respondent. In March, a National Weather Service meteorologist was quoted in a Spokane newspaper as saying that there "should be no actual ash fallout" in Spokane (Warrick et al. 1981). So even though timely warnings were being issued about the direction of the plumes from the volcano, the public still had not been prepared for the event.

Chapter 5

THE RESPONSE OF LOCAL OFFICIALS: WEST OF THE CASCADES

The areas immediately adjacent to Mount St. Helens and especially those to the west along the major river valleys had the greatest disaster potential, and did eventually sustain the greatest amount of damage in the major eruption of May 18. Because of this great damage potential, most of the warning activities were focused in Cowlitz, Clark, Skamania, Lewis, Yakima, and Klickitat counties, especially the first four. The more intense warning activity west of the Cascades can be seen on map 14, which indicates the location of respondents who received the Blue Book prior to the May 18, 1980, eruption. All these respondents are in or west of the Cascades. From here, the sample of twenty-two discussed in this chapter were selected. They include such local officials as law enforcement officers, mayors, county commissioners, town council members, emergency service personnel, Red Cross representatives, and a scattering of other individuals from other city or county offices and businesses drawn into the local response to the volcanic activity.

The discussion so far has focused on federal and state agencies which played very important roles in the warning activity related to Mount St. Helens. In this chapter and the one immediately following, we will trace these warnings down to the local level to try to determine how they affected the response to the eruption. In this chapter, we are concerned with the local officials in the areas immediately adjacent to the volcano and to the west, while the following chapter examines the ashfall areas east of the

Cascades. Warning activities were mainly directed towards people west of the Cascades while those in the east were largely overlooked. Of interest, then, is the effect of this difference on the responses in the two areas.

PRIOR EXPERIENCE AND EXPECTATIONS

Most local officials interviewed said they had some previous involvement with natural hazards. Such experience was related to floods, snowpacks, ice storms, and even an earthquake (a former Los Angeles resident). Most felt they had a moderate amount of personal experience with hazards. They also felt their agencies had had a moderate rather than a considerable amount of experience.

The local respondents tended to know that Mount St. Helens was a volcano and could erupt. It was general community knowledge and, from time to time, reminders appeared in news reports or articles, the most recent in conjunction with Mount Baker. But only one person in the sample thought there was any likelihood of an eruption, and he took a long-term view: "It probably would eventually, . . . not necessarily this century." Nobody thought there was any serious danger. "If you wrote a contingency plan before, you would have been laughed out of town."

WARNING PERIOD

Only five of the local officials we interviewed west of the Cascades received their first volcano warnings through official channels. Four of those were in Cowlitz County, where sheriff's deputies received word on March 24 or 25 from the USGS-USFS and transmitted the information to the others in that county. In all, three local officials in the west side sample were warned directly by the USGS-USFS and participated in the contingency planning meetings in Vancouver (these were all sheriff's department employees). Most of the others received their first information on the increasing volcanic activity from news media sources, the earliest being a March 23 television report on the earthquake activity, the latest occurring in late April.

Upon receipt of the first warning information, most respondents did not seriously consider it a threat to public safety. The only individuals who considered it a very serious danger were in Cowlitz County, but two of those said their reaction was in assuming the worst for purposes of planning, e.g., "If the police don't stay paranoid, nobody does."

Those who did not think the threat was serious cited a lack of information—"There was no official information; therefore no consideration," or the low population density—"The scattered population around the mountain reduced the worry," or doubted that anything serious would happen:

> We were alert to the fact that it was a great potential there but in the backs of our minds we were saying nothing would ever happen.

> It was more of a geological curiosity than a threat. I figured on lots of smoke, some lava, and then it would go back to sleep.

Reactions to the first warning information ranged from curiosity to dismay to skepticism to action. There was a distancing effect in the initial reaction. One official said his first thought was, "I'm glad it's sitting back where it is in the forest. I just hope to hell it doesn't reach this far." Only six respondents reported taking any sort of initial action, mostly information seeking or planning activity. Much of that initial response settled into watching without further preparation.

In this initial warning period, the most internal communication among local areas took place in Lewis and Cowlitz counties. There was some excitement, some uncertainty and, according to one Lewis County official, "everyone talked with everyone." At this time, only a few respondents reported making contacts outside their own counties. Cowlitz was the only Washington county in which officials reported initiating outside contacts. Most of this interaction was over the development of the Red Zone, including contacts with the state DES for the delineation of boundaries, and Weyerhauser, the USFS, the Washington State Patrol and other state agencies to plan how to keep out the public. Aside from receiving warnings, no county DES personnel reported any contact with the Washington State DES nor did any report interactions with other counties. Each county appears to have operated on its own, without consultation with its neighbors. The USFS, in bringing together the sheriffs of Clark, Cowlitz, and Skamania counties, provided a real service.

The concentration and penetration of the USGS hazard warning activities in certain counties may be seen in table 2, which indicates how many respondents reported receiving each official warning. Nine of our twenty-two respondents from this general area said that before May 18 they had received a copy of the Blue Book (map 14). In addition, each of the official USGS warnings: the hazard watch on March 27, the notice of harmonic tremors, and the notice of the bulge were received by most of our respondents with city or county hazard response responsibilities. Several respondents reported personal contact with USGS officials who explained the hazards. Also cited as an important contribution was the hazard map prepared by Crandell, "then we knew what we were up against."

Table 2.   Number of West Side Local Respondents Who Received USGS Warnings (22)

	Warning			
County	*March-May* *Blue* *Book*	*March 27* *Hazard* *Watch*	*April 3* *Notice of* *Harmonic* *Tremors*	*April 30* *Notice* *of the* *Bulge*
Cowlitz	5	3	3	3
Lewis	3	3	4	4
Clark	–	1	1	1
Skamania	1	–	–	–
Total	9	7	8	8

ªThe number in parentheses refers to the total number of local west side respondents who answered this question. This figure does not include Red Cross or business respondents.

Not all respondents were contacted nor convinced. The police chief of Castle Rock and the mayor of Morton, for example, reported receiving no warnings from the USGS, nor did Red Cross representatives. This oversight suggests the USGS warning activities, though intense, may not have been entirely systematic in coverage. Other warnings were received by local officials as well. About half reported being warned from other sources, including the Washington and Oregon DES and USFS.

Local officials on the west side did many things in response to the warnings. These activities mainly involved planning—developing evacuation plans, manpower allotments, or warning networks, as well as informing the public. Most of the activity was in Cowlitz County. A warning and evacuation plan was developed for areas of potential danger; one respondent said a plan for the Toutle and Cougar areas was ready before March 27 (using volunteer fire departments and school districts). A telephone notification system was developed, with linkages to the USFS-USGS headquarters in Vancouver and to residents in the danger areas (one respondent felt this phone system was unreliable and, considering later problems with overloaded phone lines, perhaps was correct). Related to this planning was informing and preparing the public for disaster. As one person emphasized, "A lot of effort went into education about what might happen and how people should respond." Another county activity involving a great deal of effort was the closure of access around the mountain. A protective zone was set up by the county, in cooperation with the USFS, before the state acted to establish its own "closure" area. Access control required establishing and manning roadblocks, and also traffic control for sightseers. Activity in the other counties ranged from information seeking, warning, and planning, to actually evacuating about sixty people from the vicinity of the mountain on March 27.

Some of those taking no action felt there was nothing they could do in advance; they could only wait for the event to occur: "There isn't a great deal to do that you can plan . . . As far as the city is concerned we're not going to evacuate; all you can do is batten down the hatches and watch it come." In other cases, there was inadequate information about the potential danger and how to deal with it. One person reported his organization did not do anything "until the mountain blew. We really had no idea of the potential of the mountain."

WHEN AND WHY WARNINGS WERE TAKEN SERIOUSLY

Not surprisingly, the first local respondents to take the warnings seriously were closest to the mountain, in Skamania and Cowlitz counties. The event leading to a serious reaction in most cases was either the seismic activity or the March 27 eruption. One person also cited a March 28 meeting with the USGS people; considering their maps and the "personal observations and theories behind those maps" led him to believe the situation was very serious. More local people considered the continued seismic activity in April a serious harbinger, while a couple more were convinced by the growth of the bulge on the north flank. Two others were not convinced it would be a serious problem for them until May 18, when the mountain erupted.

Several comments by respondents indicate the difficulty of convincing people the event was likely to happen:

> A situation like this is very difficult to assess. Flood hazards have recurred enough that we understand it and can assign a probability of one in a 100 years, but who can comprehend a one in 32000 year mudflow? I was aware of the capability of that happening, but the odds were so low that I didn't believe it would.

In addition, it was important to interpret the likely events for particular places:

> I wanted to know how much damage it could do in our county. We are 14 miles from the mountain. There was no problem communicating, they broke it down and explained it . . . Questions we couldn't answer we would refer to Vancouver headquarters and they would respond; sometimes they would say "we don't know." If anything they were conservative—didn't want to get people excited. We wanted to know the worst.

Other people wanted to know the nature of the risks and the potential of severe earthquakes or various types of eruptions. One respondent said the most useful information was presented in " . . . the charts and maps outlining potential flooding, mudflows, pyroclastic flows. Mullineaux and Crandell used these maps in talking to people, making them aware of potential effects."

Several people said they did not have problems with the information because of the quality of the USGS information (all these respondents were in Cowlitz County), "The USGS information was outstanding; whatever they told us came true; they were pretty well right on from the beginning. Without them we'd have been in really tough shape." Apparently, those in direct contact with the USGS were able to obtain satisfactory information:

> "The information provided by the USGS could not be improved upon. I felt we had all the information the USGS had and immediate notice when conditions changed." The direct contact with USGS officials helped make the information meaningful for local officials who, in turn, tried to educate the local population about the risks and develop contingency plans.

DEVELOPMENT OF LOCAL CONTINGENCY PLANS

About half the officials surveyed said they were involved in contingency planning, mainly at the local level, for warning, evacuation, maintenance of water or sewer systems, flood control, roadblocks, and coordination of response. Two people included in the USFS plan reported they assumed roles of warning and evacuation. One of these stated that according to the USFS plan, "We weren't supposed to do anything in our county except look for ashfall. We went ahead and expanded it . . . planned for blast activities and alerting systems." In Cowlitz County, response plans had already been developed in case of problems with the Trojan Nuclear Power Plant and in some cases these were adapted for the volcano.

In spite of this high level of activity and motivation, some coordination problems remained. Sometimes, several contingency plans emerged which could lead to rivalry rather than cooperation. According to one county DES director, plans he had developed in cooperation with county departments and school districts in some areas were later superceded by the sheriff's department. Three of our respondents were involved in the USFS *Mount St. Helens Contingency Plan*, attending meetings in Vancouver and providing some input. One of these was very critical of the local involvement in this plan, especially in the failure to develop an adequate search and rescue plan before May 18. This lack of preparation was, he thought, because "each county felt that they could handle their own problems," and only "later realized that we needed coordination." The result was that

"We had our own plan but we did not realize what the other counties were doing."

Oddly, one group not represented in the USFS planning process was the Red Cross. Involvement of the local Red Cross chapters seemed to depend on their own connections to county government. In one case, the county Red Cross director took on more than he was responsible for:

I assisted with the sheriff's warning and evacuation plans, found sources of power for life-sustaining machines, made a survey of people who would need assistance and a survey of four-wheel vehicles, made arrangements for transport to the hospital. I also wrote up evacuation plans for nursing homes and day care centers—which had not been done before.

At other places, the Red Cross directors were not warned at all. One respondent was rather cynical about the local warning system, referring to it as a "joke." He stated further:

The only warning I received officially about the possibility of an eruption was on May 18, when the DES director (county) called me and told me the volcano *may* erupt when it was *actually* erupting at the time—I could see the plume from my home.

RESPONSE TO VOLCANIC ERUPTIONS

Most of the local officials intereviewed west of the Cascades said they acted in response to one of the volcanic eruptions; most of these were involved in the emergency caused by the May 18 eruption. There were many different activities reported, including actions related to protection of people and property, information transmission, cleanup and repair, and coordination.

Seeking and Transmitting Information

Activities related to information included information seeking, public information, and communications. Discovering what had happened was an immediate problem for some. The telephone lines were jammed so that some people could not even be notified that the eruption had occurred: "I found out about 10:00. The sheriff called. There had been numerous attempts to call me and my phone did not ring, probably because the phone lines were jammed."

In other instances, those with information on the eruption had trouble relaying it. The town of Morton is some twenty-five miles north of Mount St. Helens, and was hit within a few minutes by falling debris. "The first fall was mudballs," according to one official. Immediately after this began, "The chief of police called the county DES and said there was an eruption, and they told him there was nothing happening." The silence in the official channels of information was apparently loud enough to drown out the report of a responsible eyewitness.

Other people were trying to obtain information on the effects and dangers, especially those concerned with evacuation who needed to know areas in danger, escape routes, places of safety, and who needed help. Information from the Toutle-Spirit Lake areas was "spotty and garbled," and sometimes the official information was incorrect: "We got a call that Toutle would be covered by a 200 foot wall of water. It was false, but confirmed officially, so we evacuated." This particular report was corrected shortly afterwards.

Another important task was transmitting information to the public—first alerting them, then the continuing task of reassuring them that they were safe. In some areas, the warning system did not work. In the relatively isolated area of Morton, the local radio did not broadcast the news of the eruption until 11:15 (according to one informant); by then the people in Morton were all too aware of their situation. After the public was alerted, some officials had to spend a great deal of time keeping down panic and spiking rumors, e.g. of floods and poisoned gases. According to one DES director,

> The single most bothersome thing was the public near panic, their willingness to grasp rumors rather than seek reliable information. My office was swamped by calls, which I alleviated by having a direct channel to two local radio stations . . . Even when there was nothing going on, because when nothing was reported, people believed the worst.

This need for reassurance by the public led to telephone lines being jammed, and some people were concerned with maintaining the ham radio communication network as an alternative. Hams, according to one respondent, were the primary communications link between the emergency operations center and the Red Cross shelters and evacuation centers.

Protection of Lives and Property
Most of the activities of May 18 were centered on the protection of lives and property. This action included creating roadblocks, evacuation, pro-

viding supplies and shelter, and search and rescue. The roadblocks around the Red Zone had been in place since the closure was established, but when the May 18 eruption occurred and the danger of flooding along the Toutle and Cowlitz rivers was made apparent, more roadblocks were necessary. The USGS had warned of the danger of mudflows in the Toutle Valley, and the county and state law enforcement and highway officials knew what to expect and what to do.

The actions of the local units of the state patrol stand as a fine example of how early warning and planning can help in an emergency. On May 18, state patrol officials in Vancouver knew about the eruption within fifteen minutes. Troopers were immediately dispatched to block eastbound traffic on state highways 504 and 505; also, officers were standing by to block the Toutle River bridge on Interstate 5 when mudflows should threaten it. When the first mudflow reached the Toutle River bridge about 11:00 A.M., the bridge was closed and north-south traffic was detoured through Astoria, on the coast, until 2:00 that afternoon. The other two mudflows forced closures of the bridge intermittently until 7:00 A.M., May 19. In addition to blocking the roads, the WSP personnel were also (as they were before the eruption) helping sheriffs maintain order among the crowds of people trying to get in or out of the threatened area. The danger also forced evacuation of people in the river drainages. Another group taken to safety were the families of the search and rescue volunteers. As one informant said, "I feel it's best to overreact regarding families so that volunteers can operate in confidence."

The people evacuated or stranded because of blocked roads needed shelter and supplies and this activity was also important for some local officials as well as the Red Cross. About a dozen shelters were set up for people evacuated from Cowlitz County areas, although they were not all used at the same time. People tended to stay in their shelters on a temporary basis, moving in with friends or relatives in safe areas, or moving back home after the danger was over; during the most use it was estimated some 300–400 people were at the shelters. A related activity was "burglarizing" a storage building for shelter supplies, because the person with the key could not be located. There was also some activity by police in protecting evacuated property from looters.

Search and Rescue Activities
A major activity in the area around the volcano was the search and rescue (SAR) operation. It became quickly apparent to the sheriffs of Cowlitz and Lewis counties that they did not have the resources to rescue people impacted or threatened by the eruption; both independently requested military assistance. This help was provided by the National Guard (see chapter 4) and some air rescue units of the Army, Air Force, and Coast

Guard. Forest Service personnel were also involved in the SAR, but they also had to contend with a multitude of other responsibilities and were not able to devote more than a small part of their resources to search and rescue (Kilijanek 1981, 61). The SAR effort was also aided by a mobile control tower furnished by the FAA. Affectionately known as "Moby Dick," this control unit arrived at Kelso airport at 11:00 P.M., May 18 (after being held up at the Toutle River by mudflows). On Monday morning the tower was operating, handling about 230 SAR missions that day. Two days later, the threat of flooding forced the tower to relocate to Toledo, where it continued to operate (Shake 1980, 7).

The SAR was generally a picture of confusion, as coordination systems worked out by people on the spot became disrupted when newcomers arrived and began to operate with their own ideas of what should be done. Originally, the sheriffs of Lewis, Cowlitz, and Skamania counties, as well as the Forest Service, were coordinating the response. The National Guard and other military units came in on the afternoon of May 18 and began their helicopter searches, dividing search areas into sectors which would allow each military unit to control its own resources independently of the local organization. Attempts were made by the three sheriffs, the USFS, and the state DES to develop a control system, but the military units were not involved in the discussions, and tended to ignore the civilians. The DES effort was hampered because the SAR coordinator for the state was also in charge of the Emergency Operations Center at Olympia. By Wednesday, heated discussions finally brought the National Guard and military air rescue units under the control of the local officials (who were legally in charge from the beginning); however, the disaster declaration by President Carter that day brought fresh soldiers from the Ninth Army Division, stationed at Fort Lewis. Most of the officers of these new units had not had any previous contact with the SAR people and were not accustomed to responding to the authority of county sheriffs. The result, not surprisingly, was more confusion. (For a detailed description of the search and rescue, see Kilijanek 1981.)

Assessment of Damage, Repair and Clean-up Activities
The public works people in Lewis and Cowlitz counties had another set of problems—finding out what areas were damaged or covered in ash, and developing a set of priorities for repair and cleanup. The extent of ashfall in eastern Lewis County on May 18 was hard to determine; it was a new experience and one official felt, "people exaggerate." There were also questions about whether or not the ash was harmful and how to deal with it. Mostly these questions were answered by experience.

In Cowlitz County, the volcanic ash presented a minor problem compared to other effects, especially the mudflows and floods. Because of the poor visibility of that Sunday in May, not until May 19 did an air photo reconnaissance reveal the extent of the damage to county property—two bridges (of a total twenty-seven destroyed), ten miles of road (another 170 miles of state, USFS, and private roads, as well as 18 miles of railroad were also destroyed), one water supply source destroyed by mud, and parts of other water and sewer systems damaged (see Schuster 1981, for more information). Not until Thursday, May 22, could the public works people really begin to work—"There was much waiting to get information, to assess the damage."

The State Department of Transportation at first could do little beyond call in personnel and set up barricades and signs for the prearranged roadblocks and the detour through Astoria. After the third mudflow, highways 411 and 504 were kept closed because of the damage and efforts began to clean the mud from the roads and under the bridges. After May 25, the Department of Transportation was also involved in ash cleanup on the west side.

All the west side counties received some ash, if not on May 18, then on May 25 or June 12, and all were involved in efforts to deal with it. Perhaps the hardest hit community west of the Cascades was Morton, cut off from the outside by a heavy ashfall on May 18.

> You couldn't drive it in, it was bad. A mass attempt at evacuation would have people dead on the highways. We had 150 people (stranded tourists) in the fire hall, got water in from deep wells that hadn't been exposed (the ash contaminated the city water supply), got food supplies from the stores, and we had to get masks, flares, cots, and other supplies from Chehalis-Centralia.

Lewis County received enough ash on May 18 that the entire public works department was mobilized to clean it up. The second fall on "Ash Sunday" (May 25) hit them before they had finished. In all, it "took 100% effort from our department for three weeks" to clean up. In Multnomah County, some foresighted individuals sent equipment and personnel to help Yakima and also to gain experience in dealing with ash. This action may have helped them when the winds of June 12 brought ash into the Portland-Vancouver area—not totally however. In Portland they soon discovered that "It was a different kind of ash there. Theirs was like a beach sand and ours was real fine."

Another ashfall problem was the potential of damage to the Portland sewer treatment plant, forcing them to dump raw sewage into the Columbia River for six days. "Ash Sunday" hit Cowlitz County when they were totally involved in cleaning up the damage of the May 18 floods and mudflows. The Cowlitz Department of Public Works management felt they could only continue to clear roads of mud and repair damaged water and sewer systems, "considering ash as a secondary nuisance." The ashfall added to problems that might have made many lose faith. According to one official,

> Our ash came down with a rain and stuck to everything like mortar. It had to be broomed off or physically washed off, but all major water supplies were in critical danger; the Cowlitz River was filled with mud. We had to use water trucks and could only do about five miles a day (there are 550 miles of road in the county). The public became very impatient.

Coordination of Response and Recovery
Another set of activities engaged in at the local level was coordination of response and recovery. This work was primarily carried on by the county commissioners and DES directors. Some of this effort involved getting equipment. As one DES director noted, "Usually I tried to connect people who needed things with people who had them—vehicles, radio equipment, portable power plants, water purification units. . . . " The county commissioners were especially involved in the disaster recovery. As one said,

> The commissioners were involved in all aspects [of recovery] from seeking federal and state aid to dredging and diking. We were also involved in helping individuals, relocating, evacuating, feeding animals, clearing roads.

The Corps of Engineers became involved as information came in about the mudslides and flooding. At first, they pulled in their contractors and tried to obtain further information. Engineers were dispatched to areas needing assistance and an emergency operations center was organized. After the eruption, the Corps supervised the large scale recovery operations in the Toutle-Cowlitz-Columbia rivers. This operation involved getting their own dredges to work, locating and contracting for others (figure 20), building catchment dams and sediment ponds on the Toutle River to catch ash (figure 21), and cleaning out the Columbia River to reopen it for navigation. A major concern was to remove mud and ash to increase the capacity of the streams, and to lessen the likelihood of floods. Resources were also directed toward building catchment dams to reduce runoff, especially down the Toutle Valley.

A Feeling of Accomplishment
The local respondents felt their actions had positive results. Many thought they contributed to public safety and comfort, and smaller numbers also noted the public is better informed because of their efforts; these officials

FIGURE 20.   Dredging on the Cowlitz River.

had become better prepared to respond, and the damage has been cleaned up. The actions thought to yield the most positive results were in establishing the roadblocks and shelters, and in the ash cleanup. Those involved in the weeks of maintaining the roadblocks seemed to have a certain sense of vindication, most strongly stated by one of the law enforcement officials: "We think we saved three to five thousand people's lives." An equal number felt the ash cleanup protected people by alleviating a potential health hazard and a definite traffic hazard. Those who worked with sheltering and relocating stranded travelers and evacuees from the danger zone also felt a sense of reward: "We made lives a lot more comfortable, helping people locate each other." Another official thought the shelters reduced the traffic hazard.

> I felt that the actions as far as setting up receiving centers for stranded motorists were helpful in keeping them off the highway where there were extremely hazardous driving conditions. They kept people from getting panicky, provided information.

Other positive activities mentioned were the warnings "that saved people in the Toutle area," the flood control actions, the mud cleanup, and crime prevention. The positive results also included the development of "a better rapport" between government and citizens, and also a sense of accomplishment: "Productivity was high during the first two weeks; we used all our equipment all the time. The fulfillment for a lot of people was

FIGURE 21.   Catchment Dam on the Toutle River.

tremendous, they were really able to accomplish something." In some cases, this euphoria was short-lived, as one Department of Public Works supervisor noted,

> The first two weeks were exciting—rules and regulations were thrown out, things were done and problem solving occurred which was exciting to engineers. Now the red tape is back. We've overregulated ourselves when it comes to a disaster.

MAJOR PROBLEMS IN RESPONDING TO THE ERUPTION

Table 3 indicates that local officials west of the Cascades experienced many problems they felt affected their response. Lack of equipment or facilities, funds, information, manpower, and coordination with other agencies were reported by half or more of the respondents.

Lack of Equipment or Facilities
The problem mentioned by the most people was lack of equipment or facilities. This need was especially felt when trying to deal with the ash. The need for personal protection in cleanup or search and rescue activities was reflected by complaints about the lack of face masks or self-contained breathing apparatus. The need for mechanical help and protection was demonstrated by requests for air filters, tank trucks, and flushers for re-

Table 3.   Major Problems of Local Officials West of the Cascades (22)

Problems	Percent Respondents
Lack of Equipment or Facilities	72
Lack of Funds	61
Lack of Information	55
Lack of Coordination with Other Agencies	55
Lack of Manpower	50
Newsmedia	33
Lack of Public Cooperation	22
Political	22

moving ash. There was a good deal of improvisation and borrowing, as demonstrated by Morton where they needed tankers and street washers: "We converted a fire truck to a street washer and borrowed one from a lumber company. Congressman Bonker got us a surplus Forest Service tanker."

The local search and rescue (SAR) people also needed equipment, notably four-wheel drive vehicles, helicopters, and communications equipment. As a worker noted,

> We are based more for vehicle SAR work; we're not set up for air search and rescue. We need communications equipment and full backpack gear for field workers, including air masks. Equipment wears out quickly (in the ash) and much of this is personal property which should be reimbursed.

The only other equipment need mentioned was a temporary water purifier to replace one lost at Toutle, but that problem is best discussed under interagency coordination.

Another problem related to equipment was quite the opposite—people volunteering things or contractors looking for work. In Cowlitz County, aside from the need for a water purifier, one respondent noted, "We have enough equipment, but we found volunteers or contractors looking for part of the action. There were even minority contractors who demanded it." Cowlitz County was swamped with donations. The Red Cross and Salvation Army received large quantities of clothes and food, and a large number of breathing masks were donated by a firm in Massachusetts and flown in free of charge by an airline. There were donations reflecting a concern for animals—forty acres of standing hay were donated to the local humane society (which they could not harvest), and one official commented on receiving "about a hundred 50-pound sacks of dog food that were stacked up in the courthouse." In another case, a fire department outside the county volunteered a fire truck to help "and after the news of federal assistance, they sent me a bill for $35.00/hour."

Lack of Funds

After equipment, the next most common problem was lack of funds. In no case did lack of money hamper the immediate response, the necessary things were done regardless of the cost; only later did cost considerations affect the recovery work. According to one public works employee, "At first we didn't worry about money; now we do." The response was financed on the local level by diverting money from other accounts, leading to inadequate funding for normal programs. As one official noted,

> Cowlitz has been an affluent county, we didn't have some of the problems of other counties with front money, but some programs are affected. Many expenses aren't eligible for FEMA reimbursement, for example, overtime, management costs. People devoting full time to Mount St. Helens can't make up time for abandoned projects.

Help from the federal and state governments was slow in coming, and wrapped in red tape. This was no surprise to some because, according to one respondent, "We're still waiting for our money from the 1977 flood." Comments about FEMA control of recovery funds centered on their "overdemand of documentation," lack of qualified personnel, and slowness—

> They came in with millions of dollars and then they sent inspectors to haggle over unit cost. They sent out people that are not qualified, with their rule book in their back pocket. They're infatuated with the goddamn process rather than getting the job done . . . FEMA is geared for paper work, not for getting the job done. Part of the problem may be that they have a nucleus of people but have to hire retreads and unqualified people in the case of disasters.

The local officials had to spend a great deal of time dealing with the federal damage survey inspectors, many of whom were not FEMA professionals but borrowed from other agencies. In one example, "I had two DSR (damage survey report) inspectors from the Corps of Engineers in my office for three to four days, plus more time on the phone with them, involving hours of administrative time."

Another problem was in the uniqueness of the volcano situation— how to classify the damage. In Cowlitz County, one official was told everything from May 18–25 was considered flood damage, from May 25 on was ash damage. In one case, a portable power generator operating because of flood damage to the Toutle Fire Department was damaged by ash on May 25. The official had to send out two damage survey reports. The way reimbursement funding was tied up in federal regulations was a source of cynicism to some. One person speculated that "It probably cost FEMA $10,000 for the administrative cost of cutting my expenses by $7,000." For others, it was a source of bitterness:

> Morton had no indebtedness at all going in, but our budget for the year has been spent. To begin with, we were promised 100% reimbursement on cleaning, but when we got around to the federal people coming down and explaining what was going to be allowed it got pretty bleak. We lost the engines on two police cars and one dump truck, and the roof on the city hall was finished off by ash (it was well worn before), and the feds won't reimburse us. We were the first and hardest hit, and we were alone.

Even in those areas in which federal reimbursement was allowed it was slow to arrive. A newspaper article (Johnson 1980) illustrated the problem in Castle Rock. The town had submitted claims for $134,000 and had received no money three months after the damage was done.

Lack of Information

Information was reported as a problem by over half the local respondents on the west side. Most of these complaints were about the speed with which information came from the Vancouver headquarters. As an example, one DES director reported that the warning for the May 25 eruption was not received until three hours after it occurred. Other problems with lack of information ranged from receiving no information at all to inadequate information about how to deal with ash and mud. One engineer reported his concern with lack of knowledge about the structural characteristics of the mud and whether or not things could be rebuilt on top of a mudflow. There were also concerns about the sources of information. One official discussed problems in gaining information useful to people management from the scientific data he was given. Two others commented on the information being sent out by the state DES on the teletype; one felt "The state teletypes were almost a joke to begin with. Some of the suggestions, were too obvious, such as don't walk toward the volcano."

Some respondents reported problems in decision making based on the information that was available. Lack of information was the main problem specifically mentioned by several people who depended on the NAWAS and state DES system:

> . . . we had State DES send out a teletype asking what actions would be taken, and I sent a note saying the actions taken would

depend on the answers to our questions. They referred us to a bulletin which we already had.

Of importance was speed of information transmission. One respondent felt the time taken by the scientists to assess the data was too long, and what was needed was " . . . a little less interpretation and a little more instant, raw data. On the May 18 eruption, everybody heard it, but it wasn't confirmed until 1½ hours later." In another case, it was noted that information through the official channels often moved more slowly than to members of the press, who " . . . often have it before our office, which puts us in an embarrassing position because we don't watch TV all day." Lack of information also led to the circulation of rumors discussed previously, such as floods or poisoned gas.

On the west side, the Red Cross had problems obtaining information about the emergency response. In one case, a director was told to set up a shelter in a town that was being evacuated. In another situation, an official helping the sheriff with missing persons had an extra problem because communications between the military and the sheriff in the search and rescue operation were so poor that "nobody told us where the rescued people were."

Coordination with Other Agencies
A problem related to several of the above was the lack of coordination with other agencies, also cited by more than half of the local respondents to this question. Although no problems of coordination were mentioned on the local level, a sizeable number said there were problems in coordination with the state and a somewhat smaller group found problems with federal agencies. Coordination problems with the state of Washington were reported with both the governor and the DES. Some of the local officials felt communication with the governor was poor, and that she was making assumptions about the area without talking to them. Attempts by one local official to have a liaison person from the governor's office come to Cowlitz County resulted in failure. A similar situation occurred with the state DES. Several people in Cowlitz County commented on the DES attempt to control the operation from Olympia without sending representatives to the area of activity—even after the county commissioners requested a meeting. One respondent drew a contrast between dealing with the state ("a complete breakdown; we can't get any answers") and the Corps of Engineers ("We have daily contact, just like USGS") and commented, "Of all the problems we have encountered, dealing with our own state has been the most perplexing."

A related problem was in obtaining assistance from the Washington National Guard. Requests for National Guard help were sent to DES, and according to one respondent, " . . . it was slow, if it came at all." Another person complained about the "bureaucracy".

It took three days to actually get troops into areas we had requested. In the past we requested and used them in floods. Now we seem to have to sit down and have meetings; there must have been a change in policy. We needed to establish more specific detail of what they were to do before they were released, such as how many people at each point? That was hard to do when they were to be sent to the east end (of Lewis County) and assigned tasks by deputies.

Coordination problems with the federal agencies centered around FEMA rules and military assistance. Obtaining military help from the federal government was contingent on proving that all state and local resources, including those in the private sector, were committed. One person mentioned problems in obtaining Army helicopters because there were civilian ones available, even though their cost was very high. Another respondent, whose request for Army search and rescue troops was denied felt that FEMA's lack of familiarity with local needs was partly to blame. This person went on to say, "I find it unacceptable to be denied the use of the country's troops in time of a disaster." Some local people felt the delays, denials, and demands for justification of requests by FEMA were interfering with their ability to respond to the emergency. As one respondent put it,

We have a lot of problems with FEMA. We felt they were interfering with our effort by not providing the resources we needed. We got delayed 6–8 hours on needed equipment, helicopters and radio equipment to coordinate with the helicopters. We felt they had no right to interfere, to check on our requests. We felt our requests were credible. There were some hard feelings between FEMA and local officials. They should coordinate, not direct our efforts.

The locals who reported problems with FEMA felt that adherence to rules hurt the emergency response to a totally unique situation. One respondent contrasted the inflexibility of FEMA with the problem-solving efforts of the Corps of Engineers: "FEMA was upholding their regulations about what they would allow but this situation is different. The damage survey report people are contrasted by the Corps of Engineers who were willing to try to help find answers."

To illustrate problems of both the unique aspects of the volcanic effects and the FEMA regulations, a couple of people in Cowlitz County mentioned the difficulty in obtaining a water purification unit to temporarily replace a lost reservoir. On May 18, the water supply at Toutle was knocked out by the mudflows, and something had to be done to supply the 250 people there with water. According to the respondents, the National Guard set up a water purification unit on Silverlake but it failed to operate. In searching for others, they found the Army had several units at Fort Lewis (about 70 miles away), but these were not to be used because "local resources were determined not to be exhausted." According to one official,

> A civilian unit was available from the private sector. There was a unit available in Orgeon but the cost was $950/day which was too much to service 250 people . . . . Senator Hatfield put on political pressure to use that unit.

Two other units were located through the California Office of Emergency Services who sent them to Toutle for no charge but shipping. But the county public works people found, "We didn't have the technical expertise available to work the system." Apparently because of the availability of these systems in two other states, the Fort Lewis equipment was never released for use. The county had to haul water into Toutle in milk trucks, which was "very expensive," until they could drill a well. A further problem with the wells illustrates an unexpected effect of the volcanic eruption and underscores the risk run by not having water purification units quickly available. According to one respondent,

> We drilled a mediocre well and using salvaged equipment were able to build a temporary water treatment plant. A second well had a high phenol count, so we drilled a third well, which also had a high phenol and iron content. The scientists speculate that hot mud formed phenols which leaks out into the groundwater. This was a problem of new unexpected nature—the phenols were instantly formed.

If these reports are correct, FEMA's lack of flexibility in a unique situation led to results that were neither cost-effective nor rapid, and, in the case of the fast phenol development in the wells, were potentially dangerous.

Another area where coordination problems approached dangerous levels was in the search and rescue operation. The fragmentation of authority, resources, and planning, as well as lack of knowledge of other agency roles, made organizing the SAR difficult. With separate units flying on independent missions, the airspace was unsafe.

Coordination problems in the SAR were intensified because of civilian-military rivalry and lack of understanding. Even communications were difficult. As one officer noted, "The military operates on different frequencies, speaks a different language." There were even problems in comparing maps and map coordinates. The Army maps, using a military grid based on meters, did not match Geological Survey or Forest Service maps using the rectangular land survey system based on feet and miles.

Lack of Manpower
The local officials also reported problems with lack of manpower, especially trained people. This shortage was felt acutely by those maintaining the roadblocks, "We have dedicated staff for particular purposes but not for continuing emergency situations."

Maintaining the roadblocks for weeks with a limited number of deputies put a strain on all the sheriffs' departments in Lewis, Cowlitz, and Skamania counties. They were able to augment their personnel with people from other counties, the state patrol, other state agencies, and finally the National Guard. The National Guard, however, had a drawback because they were not allowed to man a roadblock alone, a deputy sheriff was required to be with them. The county DES directors also had manpower problems, finding

> . . . a lack of trained manpower capable of going into emergency situations, a lack of manpower even here in the Emergency Operations Center. It's hard to transfer people from other agencies to answer phones because they are not familiar with what you do.

Another experienced a similar situation: "We used a lot of volunteers, but to coordinate them I had only myself and my secretary. I put in 123 hours the week after May 18, 90 hours the week after that." In both cases, the county DES manpower situation reflected that of the state DES, where a lack of trained staff (or reserves) overwhelmed them.

Problems of Public Cooperation
Public cooperation was not seen as a major problem by the respondents in the areas west of the Cascades. In general, the public reaction was described as "super," "fantastic," "great," and "pretty damned good." One person found that during the ash cleanup there were "many volunteers, they were in more of a hurry than we were. They donated manpower and machinery.

The problems of public cooperation concerned public access to the Red Zone. As one person stated, "The deaths resulted from people breaking the restrictions." In addition to dealing with people breaking into the Red Zone were, according to one respondent,

> . . . extra pressures by people who had cabins near Spirit Lake. They got media attention and got the governor to make exceptions

to her executive order which had us take some people to Spirit Lake on May 17 to check their cabins.

This informant noted the attitude changed after the May 18 eruption, saying there was "20% cooperation before the eruption and 80% cooperation afterwards." The long hiatus between the eruptions of March 27 and May 18 tended to lull expectations that anything more disastrous would happen. According to one report, the prevailing mood was far from standing in readiness for catastrophe.

> In early May, the reports about Mount St. Helens were so commonplace that one began to develop an attitude of "let's get on with the show." Entrepreneurs began "milking" or taking advantage of the mountain's activities for all they could. Local populations were lulled into either a smug secure attitude, or one of "festivity." Mountain watches, professional and casual alike, partied in the small town and resort located at the base of Mount St. Helens. A sense of "bravado" prevailed (Anderson 1980, 1).

One official described the Red Zone situation as "like hand-to-hand combat at the barricades." Curiosity, economic pressure, and disbelief in the danger were all contributing factors in people's movements into the closure area. One person was especially aware of problems with the logging industry,

> The people who want to work there get angry . . . . If they were kept out and there's no eruption, they get anxious to get in and make money . . . . Many people cannot comprehend that a twenty year eruption period would change the lifestyle of people dependent on the mountains.

Other respondents were sympathetic to the problems of people with jobs in the Red Zone; one felt their protests were justified. Another noted the success of a union-backed program to have loggers wear masks and maintain safety precautions in ash danger areas as an example of cooperation. Another official felt "the spirit of the people was very noteworthy," and that the biggest problems were with "'the ten percent that is curious and wants to go in, but they're not malicious or vandals." This respondent also talked about the convergence phenomenon, "The roadblocks became camping sites. They would gather there to see Mount St. Helens. But they were cooperative; for example, when asked not to have fires, they didn't."

Problems with the News Media
Many west side respondents said they had problems with the news media.

There were reports about newspeople violating the Red Zone and arrests being made. Five of the six people reporting these problems were in Cowlitz County. This problem was especially present after May 18 when the newspeople "descended here in droves," and "called from all over the world demanding to talk to a commissioner or DES person." This demand for interviews took valuable time away from emergency response activities, several officials felt, and another mentioned that the media were given priority for helicopters, even over local official use. According to one official, "At meetings there wasn't even space for the participants because the media had all the seats. Meetings became too large to be problem-solving and participatory. The presence of the media interfered with the operations."

Perhaps the most blatant act by a newsperson was posing as a DES worker. In this case, however, the respondent who mentioned this impersonation felt, "She didn't do anything wrong and she was an asset while she was working." The biggest complaint about the news media was their tendency for exaggeration, "making the news rather than reporting it." Comments were made about newspeople misinforming, editorializing, and misquoting in their reports. One official thought the news activities were obstructing information flow between the officials and the public.

> Our role is to keep the public informed, but the media was interfering with the transmission of information for the public and the decisionmakers. The information that came out of the media was not consistent; there was some editorializing. Their role is informing, not inciting, and I don't think it always turned out that way.

One of the Cowlitz officials noted that part of the problem was in the local officials' lack of experience in dealing with the press. "This is a small area and there are no PR men in the area." This respondent subsequently suggested the county hire a public information officer.

CONCLUSIONS

In the areas immediately adjacent to Mount St. Helens and in the river valleys to the west, there was a concerted effort to warn people about the potential danger of a volcanic eruption, particularly after the reawakening of the volcano in late March, 1980. Although the initial tendency of local people was to discount the hazard, a significant number of them were persuaded by the repeated warnings about the ongoing volcanic activity. A high proportion of our respondents remembered receiving warnings either directly from the USGS or from other agencies. Indeed, many local officials became actively engaged in warning activities themselves as they realized what might happen.

The importance of several separate warnings as well as face-to-face contact with the experts is illustrated by the events on the west side of the mountains. Here, where the bulk of the warning activity was concentrated, there was an active response. Many contingency plans were developed which contributed to the evacuation of people from the river valleys. Road-blocks were set up and patrolled, keeping large numbers of people away from danger zones and thus helping to reduce the death toll.

In spite of the many warnings some people remained unconvinced, and contingency plans did not fully prepare the population for the magnitude of the event which occurred. This is evident in the lack of coordination between the various counties and the lack of equipment or manpower available to overcome the many diverse problems facing the people in the immediate vicinity of the volcano.

It would, of course, have required an exceptional contingency plan to take in stride the test of fire the west side residents experienced. Mudflows, ashfalls, floods, and search and rescue operations in the blast zone and beyond resulted from the May 18 eruption. While still reeling from these blows, many communities were once more subjected to additional ashfalls on May 25 and June 12.

The public and the officials responded energetically to the volcanic events and gained a great deal of confidence and experience, which they felt would better enable them to handle any future eruptions. A major lesson reinforced by the volcanic eruptions is the great importance of developing good contingency plans well in advance.

Residents on the west side of the Cascades are living in a different set of circumstances than what prevailed prior to the eruption. A familiar, local landscape was totally transformed, and to this sense of loss is added the uncertainty of future eruptions. The long-term economic impacts, however, may become balanced, with a loss in lumber compensated for by an increase in tourism.

Chapter 6

THE RESPONSE OF LOCAL OFFICIALS: EAST OF THE CASCADES

On May 18, people east of the Cascades were taken completely by surprise when a cloud of ash darkened the sky and ash began to fall. They were surprised in Yakima an hour after the eruption began, and even in Missoula, Montana, though the leading edge of the ash cloud took some six hours to get there (map 4), and nine hours may have elapsed before ash began to reach the ground (map 11).* Why the warning system failed and the consequences of this failure are described in this chapter.

The sample on which the description is based was selected from city and county officials in the ashfall areas of eastern Washington. The sites range from Ritzville, where the heaviest ashfall was experienced, to Moses Lake, Yakima, Spokane, and Ellensberg, where lesser but still substantial amounts of ash blanketed the ground (maps 5 and 10). The twenty-six individuals interviewed were in critical leadership positions for responding to such an emergency situation. They included state patrol and transportation officials, county sheriffs and directors of emergency services, as well as city police, and fire chiefs, superintendents of public works, health officials, a city manager, and a county commissioner. Because of their roles,

---

*Map 4 was based on NOAA satellite photographs and the times correspond to the arrival of the plume on the fastest moving wind layer. The ash would not be visible from the ground until much later, thereby preceding the first ashfall used as the base for map 11. At Spokane the leading edge of the plume arrived at 11:45 A.M. The ash cloud was visible from the ground at 2:00 P.M. and ash began falling at 3:43 P.M. (Sarna-Wojcicki et al. 1981).

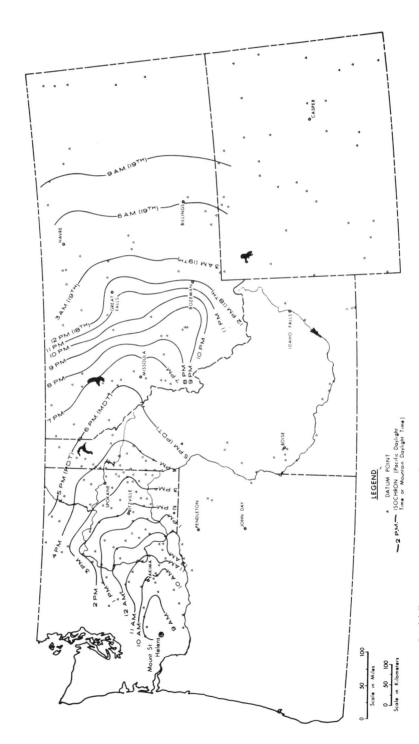

MAP 11. Time of Ashfall, May 18, 1980. From Warrick et al 1980.

these people should have been the first in their communities to receive official warning information about the eruption of Mount St. Helens; so, although the sample is small, it was strategically selected to include those one would expect to be the best informed about and most involved in the emergency response.

PRIOR EXPERIENCE AND EARLY WARNINGS

Natural hazards are relatively rare in eastern Washington, and it is not surprising to find that 60 percent of the respondents had very little or no experience in dealing with such events. In spite of this inexperience, there was usually an individual such as a sheriff or director of emergency services in each community whose job had provided some hazard experience. Among our sample, the most common previous hazard experience involved floods, but also included dealing with snow and windstorms, tornado warnings, hazardous materials, a cave-in, mountain rescues, and a toxic allergy bloom.

Mount St. Helens was known to be a volcanic peak by most of our sample, and all the respondents had some idea an eruption was imminent because of the intensive media coverage from the time of the early earthquake reports in March to the major eruption in mid-May. The importance of the continuous media coverage in enhancing awareness of Mount St. Helens was evident. Different individuals first became aware of the eruptive potential, and began to take it seriously, at quite different stages. Events mentioned by respondents and thoroughly covered by the media include the early earthquake swarm, the first steam eruption, and the development of the bulge. Other respondents, who could not remember exactly when they first became aware, did mention the media as their source of information.

The main official source of warnings, the state DES, was mentioned as a source of information about an imminent eruption by only three respondents. All of these were in offices where the Washington DES teletype messages were sent. "We got teletype messages every day," said one, who also remembered kidding with Lewis County about keeping the volcano in their own area. At the time, he did not think there was a serious threat to Yakima County for, "I didn't realize that 1900 feet of the volcano would fall on us."

Though interested, curious, even fascinated by the developments at Mount St. Helens, the local officials east of the Cascades did not think it posed any threat to their communities. No one we interviewed considered it a serious threat to their area. Spontaneous comments in response to the question reflect their feelings about the remoteness of the volcanic peak, for example:

My reaction was probably that I'm glad I'm not near there. I didn't think the problem would reach us. The immediate area around the mountain [is] in trouble but not us. We didn't know how to react. We had no information on what it might do.

Consequently, none of the respondents we interviewed took any action, even though all had heard about the potential eruption of Mount St. Helens. Given their distance from the peak, from 80 to over 200 miles, this inaction is understandable, for as one expressed it, "no one told us it would dump on us."

THE FAILURE TO WARN ABOUT ASHFALL

The eastern Washington ashfall area was overlooked in terms of official warnings. None of our respondents remembered receiving the original USGS hazard notification or an official communication about the hazard watch. None knew of the Blue Book before the May 18 eruption. Not even those in the city or county departments of emergency services knew of the publication, and one such official said, "I received nothing that indicated it would be hazard to this area." Another stated that even on the morning of May 18 they were not advised. They were told the volcano had erupted, nothing more. They did not know the ash was coming until it started falling. None of our respondents were involved in the development of contingency plans before the May 18 eruption. Many helped prepare such plans in the months that followed, so later eruptions reaching these areas are likely to find the population well prepared.

The lack of official warnings, the lack of direct references to their locality in information bulletins on Mount St. Helens, and the great distance that separated them from the peak made it easy for local officials in eastern Washington to discount the hazard, and helps to account for their surprise and unpreparedness for the ashfall. When asked at which point they began to take the warnings seriously, over half our respondents indicated it was when the ashfall began, as in the following reply, "When I saw that big dark sucker coming at me. At that point we knew something was going to happen but we didn't know what."

The same type of pattern was seen in the four study sites of Warrick et al. (1981). This group did a quick response study in four communities affected by the May 18 ashfall—Ellensburg, Ritzville, and Cheney, Washington, and Missoula, Montana—and concluded that: "The initial warning about ashfall issued by the Washington State Department of Emergency Services had absolutely no utility at any of the community study sites" (Warrick et al. 1981, 103). No one interviewed was aware of the existence of volcanic hazard maps. No one took preparatory action as a result of the warnings.

Nor did the media prepare people for what was to come. A content analysis of the major Spokane newspapers by Anderson (1983) reviewed 152 articles on Mount St. Helens and/or volcanic hazards for the period March 20 through May 18, 1980. Only eight articles suggested that ash in the past had fallen as far from the mountain as Spokane. Three explicitly discounted ashfall as constituting a serious hazard, and the others qualified it so as to give no hint of a real threat. "At no time were Spokane and its environs set in the content of risk; the hazard was viewed externally as a remote one that might only affect areas closer to the mountain, such as the Yakima Valley" (Warrick et al. 1981, 62).

A similar pattern was seen for other sites remote from the mountain. In Ellensburg, which lies well within the ashfall zone indicated on the USGS volcanic risk maps, there were stories of historical ashfalls. In spite of this history, residents did not expect risk to their communities (Warrick et al. 1981, 103).

The totally unexpected and unprecedented nature of the event is seen in the disbelief expressed even as it came. "I couldn't believe it," said one. "I still did not know it would get dark," said another, who said she had, an hour in advance, heard a radio report with much information on the eruption, and with a warning about a large cloud moving northeast and maybe some ash.

The surprise and dismay in response to the ashfall was much greater than it should have been, for the potential effects of ashfall were clearly described in the Blue Book as stated in chapter 1. An even stronger indication of the total lack of preparation for the ashfall hazard is that surprise and dismay continued all day long in each successive area affected. Although the state DES sent out teletype messages at 10:15 A.M. and again at 1:38 P.M., neither message was keyed to particular counties (see appendix A).

On the east side of the volcano, there was little expectation there would be much effect from an eruption. Yakima had about one hour before the ash reached it. One Washington State Patrol respondent was at home when he was notified about 9:00 that an eruption had occurred. He made no connection between the eruption and the huge cloud beginning to darken the west, "I saw a black cloud coming that I thought was probably a rain cloud . . . . There was also a severe lightning and thunderstorm which threw people off." When the ash cloud hit, "it went absolutely dark when it had been a bright, sunny day," and traffic problems began immediately, compounded by the "unblievable number" of people who "went out to go driving in it and got caught." The confusion was great and it was not until about noon that roadblocks were set up on Highway 12 and Interstate 90. The Yakima Department of Transporation (DOT) was in a similar state of confusion, almost in isolation because "the phone lines were so plugged up nobody could have gotten through." Efforts to contact local personnel or other districts failed. "It wasn't until Wednesday that we were able to make our important calls. The four lines we had were lit up all the time with nuisance calls; we couldn't call out."

At Ritzville, about 100 miles northeast of Yakima (as the ash flies), the first warning about the ash came around noon when a local DOT official "walked out the door and saw it coming." The Ritzville DOT people collected their roadblock signs and waited until orders came from Davenport to close Interstate 90. With the ash already falling around them, and visibility at "zero," four DOT workers set up the barricades at 2:00 and manned them until the sheriff took over at 7:00 P.M.

Even those in county departments of emergency services failed to see any connection between ashfall and their area. In Spokane, the Department of Emergency Services first learned of the approaching ash cloud when the sheriff heard from Fairchild Air Force Base that it was coming. This warning was about 1:30 or 2:00 in the afternoon. The 1:38 P.M. teletype message from the state DES did not provide suggestions for closing the roads, and no action was taken before the ash started falling at about 3:43. By then, considerable ash had accumulated further west and traffic westbound from Spokane would soon be stopped by it.

At Missoula the ash did not begin to fall until about 6:30 P.M., local time (Sarna-Wojcicki et al. 1981). Still, not one of the four key emergency response officials—county health officer, civil defense director, county sheriff, or city police chief—learned about the ash from an official warning source (Warrick et al. 1981). By then, it was close to nine hours since the eruption began. Confirmation of the hazard was primarily through telephone calls to the sheriff's office in Spokane.

> The first few hours of the emergency were marked by confusion and a lack of useful information about the nature of the ash and effective ways of dealing with it. In short, despite the long lead time, Missoulians were caught quite off guard (Warrick et al. 1981, 87).

The general public also learned of the eruption from unofficial sources, according to a telephone survey of 1464 eastern Washington residents by Dillman (1981). He found that the major source of initial information about the eruption came from another person (51.9 percent), followed by radio (33.6 percent) and then television (12.2 percent). As late as three hours after the blast, over half his eastern Washington respondents had not yet learned that an eruption had occurred. For many people, the huge black cloud was their first inkling of the event.

The intensity of activity immediately after the eruption is indicated by the entries in the official USFS log. Immediately after the eruption, entries were recorded so constantly that some forty-five pages of log were completed before the end of May 18 and another thirty-six before the end of the following day. Clearly, such a busy time is not the proper period in which to make plans for the emergency. Plans have to be laid out well in advance so that the procedure is clear and can be followed through. The importance of advance planning can be seen in the lack of warnings on May 18 to the eastern Washington counties subject to heavy ashfalls. The concern at the Vancouver, Washington, headquarters was with events developing around the mountain. Only a few of the scores of items logged mention the ash cloud drifting eastward. One of the frustrations of people in the heavy ashfall areas was the lack of response from western Washington to their plight.

Those first hit by the ash also failed to warn others about the coming cloud. For example, State Department of Transportation or Washington State Patrol personnel at Yakima, hit at about 9:45, could have given about three hours warning time to Spokane, and thousands of travelers heading into the ashfall area could have been diverted rather than stranded when the ash hit. Part of the explanation seems to lie in the incomprehensibility of the conditions, making a sudden warning without advance information (as was sent, for example, to National Guard units in the area, including Yakima and Spokane) hard to accept.

Other reasons for the failure to pass on the word were the communications problems already cited by the Yakima Department of Transportation official, and the overwhelming nature of the local problems. One official emphasized that the local emergency situations required a great deal of effort: "When the ash hit Yakima, the people there were so involved with their own problems that they failed to warn others."

MAJOR IMPACTS OF THE ASHFALL

As may be seen on map 5, appreciable amounts of ash fell on four states, with the greatest concentration in the eastern Washington counties of Adams and Grant. Roads were blocked, people were stranded, communities were isolated. It did become dark during daylight hours, just as the Blue Book predicted. All normal activity came to a standstill. The people in much of eastern Washington were faced with caring for thousands of stranded motorists, with a clean-up problem of massive dimensions, and with the possibility of major crop losses. To make things worse, there was very little information as to what had happened, how people would be affected, or how long it might last.

In a well-written personal account of his own reactions, Dillman (1980), a sociologist from Washington State University, outlined his experience and feelings day-by-day for the first week, before things began to get back to normal in Pullman, Washington. In a later paper he stated:

> It is hard to overstate the uncertainty that prevailed in the hours
> after the eruption, especially after ash began falling and the out-of-
> doors became pitch black over much of Eastern Washington. No
> one knew how long the darkness would last. It was unclear how to
> deal with the ash and whether contact with it should be avoided.
> The near impossibility of driving due to poor visibility, became evi-
> dent to all who attempted to drive (Dillman 1981, 5).

The most immediate effect of the ashfall was on transportation. Visibility was reduced to zero, so there was almost no possibility of driving.
This condition continued after the ashfall stopped, for the fine ash was
easily stirred up by vehicles. One respondent said it was "like living in a
cloud for the first three days." In addition to creating visibility problems,
the ash could immobilize vehicles by clogging the engines. Consequently,
soon all the roads in the entire region were impassable, and transportation
by railroad and air were also impossible. The result was a drastic but
temporary curtailment of travel, much like the effects of a major snowstorm
(Dueker et al. 1980).

Thousands of travelers were stranded by the ashfall. Map 12 shows
the locations and numbers of those registered at Red Cross emergency
shelters. Many more unrecorded travelers were temporarily stranded with
friends and relatives, checked into motels on their own, or were sheltered
in smaller communities not tallied by the Red Cross. Anderson (1983)
estimated that over 10,000 people were stranded. Although even a small
amount of ash could cripple our modern technological society, apparently
the largest numbers of people were stranded in the areas of heaviest ashfall
from Ritzville to Moses Lake. There they remained until the roads were
cleared. In some cases, the large numbers of stranded travelers severely
strained the available services of small isolated communities.

The road closures effectively shut down schools, businesses, and government offices for the period required to remove the ash. In Spokane,
even the police and fire departments only attempted to respond to life-or-
death emergencies in the immediate aftermath. A state of emergency was
declared, and everyone was asked to stay at home by the county sheriff.
Movement of cars was limited and strict speed limits imposed to avoid
stirring up the dust. Fears arose with respect to the health effects of breathing the ash and concerns were expressed about its effects on local water
supplies.

Many of the worst fears about business losses, health hazards, or
agricultural losses did not materialize. All merchants did not go broke
because of a loss of business. The losses of the first few days were often
made up quickly, and some businesses, such as taverns, did better than

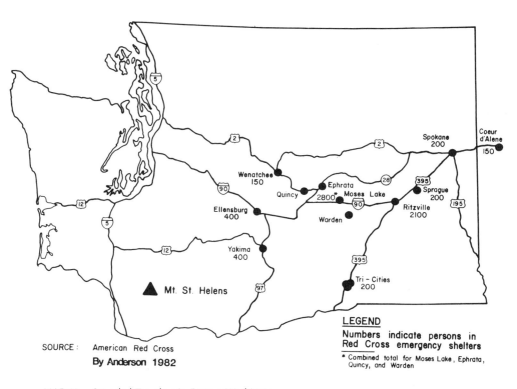

SOURCE :   American Red Cross

By Anderson 1982

LEGEND
Numbers indicate persons in
Red Cross emergency shelters
* Combined total for Moses Lake, Ephrata,
Quincy, and Warden

MAP 12.   Stranded Travelers in Eastern Washington.

normal. New fears developed about the potential loss in tourist revenues and some local chamber of commerce offices prepared vigorous publicity campaigns to overcome this possibility (figure 22).

Eventually, acute fears of silicosis faded as the small, temporary increases in the number of hospital admissions for pulmonary disorders soon returned to normal (map 13). Some questions about long-term effects remain unanswered, including the psychological effects of living with the constant grit and dust. Apparently, in the immediate aftermath, many symptoms of poor mental health were held in abeyance. After some delay,

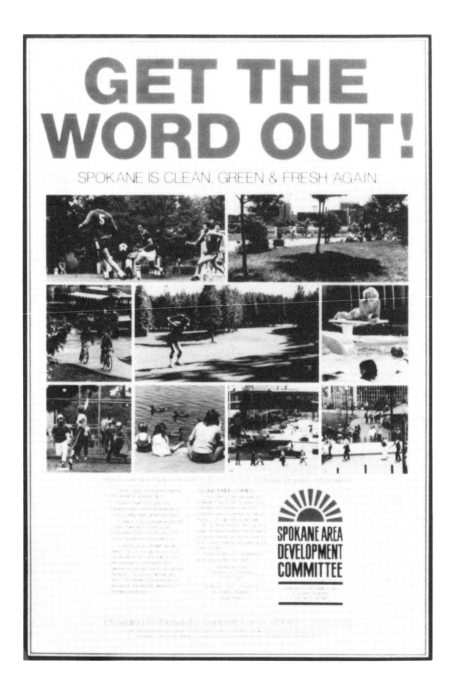

FIGURE 22. Example of Anti-Ash Publicity.

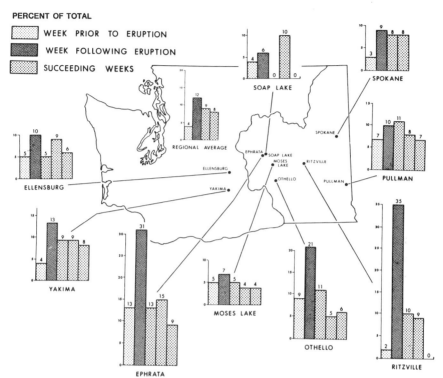

From Anderson,1982, adapted from FEMA Technical Information Bulletin 8,June 21,1980.

MAP 13.   Weekly Hospital Admissions for Pulmonary Disorders.

however, they began to appear, often in terms of dealing with the bureaucracy (State of Washington, Division of Mental Health 1981). There
was also expected to be long-term health impacts for people working in
the ash—"The Center for Disease Control will be following them around
for the rest of their lives." Mental health impacts were reflected in increases
in child and spouse abuse, and crisis line phone calls. For long-range mental
health, "The biggest single contributor will be repeated ash falls."

The crop losses in eastern Washington were less than originally expected (Cook et al. 1980), amounting to approximately 7 percent of the
normal crop value. The wheat, potato, and apple crops were normal or
about normal, although alfalfa hay was severely damaged. The effects varied
locally according to types of crops and livestock. In the case of wheat, a
major crop in the area of heaviest ashfall, the ash may even have increased
yields in some fields by slowing evaporative loss from the soil surface (figure

23). Increased costs of production were caused by the abrasive effects of ash on machinery and increased tillage to incorporate the ash.

FIGURE 23.   Ash "mulch" in wheatfield.
Photo by T. Saarinen.

RESPONSES TO THE ASHFALL EMERGENCY

The lack of warning and consequent failure to develop contingency plans, coupled with the ash-induced isolation, forced individual communities to improvise and depend on their own resources for emergency action. This response may be seen in the actions of local officials from twenty-six different jurisdictions in the ashfall areas of eastern Washington (Kartez and Kelley 1980). Only a third of the jurisdictions surveyed reported using an existing countywide emergency preparedness plan as a basis for action and almost half reported no use at all of such a plan. The most useful sources of assistance during the first week of emergency response were individuals' "own observation and judgement," followed by the "news media," "other cities," and "other counties." State and federal government were ranked last. Most local emergency operations appeared to be formed by adapting of existing local organization rather than the result of implementing formalized pre-emergency plans. Central aspects of the local response were acquisition of emergency resources and communication with citizens.

The effort to clear the highways of ash was slow. The fine material was hard to handle and would blow back with the slightest breeze. The equipment was not designed for ash removal and a great deal of improvisation was necessary, as well as frequent stops for maintenance work. In addition, great numbers of stranded motorists had to be rescued.

Plowing priorities were established to facilitate rescues of stranded motorists, and to evacuate small isolated communities. State highway maintenance workers took a three phase approach to opening cross-state traffic on the margin of the fallout zone. Local highways serving small communities, where many motorists were stranded, were opened up so that motorists could be convoyed to the edge of the zone. Finally, the major Interstate, I-90, which goes through the heart of the fallout zone, was opened—one week after the eruption (Anderson 1980, 2).

Despite their initial sensitivity to volcanic ash, communities were surprisingly resilient, demonstrating a remarkable capacity to "bounce back" to normal (according to the quick response study by Warrick et al. 1981). The diagram shown in figure 24 explains the findings of Warrick et al (1981). It illustrates three main generalizations: that community systems were quickly and drastically impaired by the ashfall regardless of the depth;

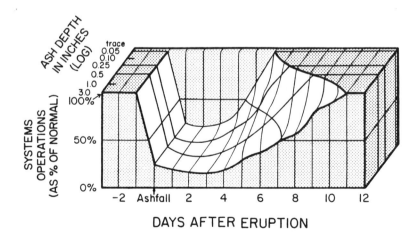

DAYS AFTER ERUPTION

FIGURE 24. Generalized Disruption Surface from Volcanic Ashfall. From Warrick et al. 1981.

that recovery time was directly related to ashfall amounts; and that all sections in the ashfall areas approached normalcy rather rapidly, within a couple of weeks. This quick recovery was made possible by outstanding local responses throughout the region, for there were many difficult problems to solve.

RESPONSE PROBLEMS IDENTIFIED BY LOCAL OFFICIALS

The major problems in dealing with the emergency response to the ashfall are described in terms of answers to our questions about specific problem areas. Table 4 indicates that local officials east of the Cascades tended to have more problems dealing with the eruption than the aggregate sample. Much of this added difficulty could be attributed to the lack of warning and advance preparation by respondents east of the Cascades.

Table 4.   Problems in Responding to Mount St. Helens' May 18 Eruption (East Side Local Officials)

	Percent Perceiving the Problem	
Problems	*East of Cascades* *n = 20*	*Aggregate Sample* *n = 130*
Lack of Information	80	58
Lack of Equipment and Supplies	60	48
Lack of Funds	55	48
Lack of Coordination with Other Agencies	55	41
Lack of Manpower	45	37
Lack of Public Cooperation	5	25

A lack of information was considered a problem by 80 percent of respondents east of the Cascades compared to 60 percent for the total sample. Similarly, more respondents in ashfall areas had problems related to a lack of equipment or supplies, of funds, of coordination with other agencies, and of manpower. In contrast, they did not have the problem of a lack of public cooperation—quite the contrary. When asked whether public cooperation was a problem, they asserted the opposite and paid glowing tribute to the outstanding performance of the public in response to the crisis.

The Problem of Lack of Information
The most important problem identified by public officials east of the Cascades was a lack of information. Comments from the respondents indicate

that better information was needed before the major eruption, on the day of the eruption, and in the immediate aftermath of the eruption. Their complaints centered on the information flow from higher to lower levels of government. They had few complaints about information dissemination at the local level.

Before the eruption there was a lack of good warning information specifically linking ashfall possibilities in particular counties with the general information of developments at Mount St. Helens. This lack of early warning was noted by several respondents. The few who were aware of the Blue Book by the time of the interview in the summer of 1980 felt it would have been useful to have had that information in advance. Others stressed the need for information on how to handle the ash and what to do. "There is a need for prior planning, otherwise [you] just play catch-up" was one comment. Another added: "Before the eruption we didn't know what was needed. Didn't even know what ashfall was. The information we got was rather skimpy. I saw the cloud and thought it was rain."

When the ashfall began, "We didn't know what was going on, how long it would last, or the hazard factor of ash." One respondent pointed out that even on the day of the ashfall no teletype message arrived until 10:15, and he had ashfall by 12:30. The next bulletin he received arrived at 1:38, was the first which provided some instructions as to what to do, and he complained that it made no mention of what ash could do to a car. The instructions provided in the 1:38 bulletin were an exact copy of, "What To Do When a Volcano Erupts," as listed in the *Mount St. Helens Contingency Plan* more than a month earlier (see appendix A).

After the eruption, many communities east of the Cascades were completely isolated for different lengths of time. Many respondents spoke of the difficulty of getting information out or in at this time. This problem may be seen in such comments as,

> We were isolated for 10 days, had trouble getting information out to tell the extent of our problems, or getting people in.

> For several days the state was not relaying information to us. Finally we got a ham operator to get information from the mountain to us.

The local communities often took the initiative in seeking out information, in particular on how to proceed with ash cleanup, and whether fears of medical effects were valid or not.

The lack of information on ash characteristics led to developing an experimental approach in learning how to handle ashfall cleanup. Although some respondents stated that they talked to people in other cities and counties about how to deal with ash, for the most part the cleanup seemed to start with trial and error. Advice from other areas may not have worked in any case since the consistent and physical characteristics of the ash varied from place to place. Yakima's ash was like sand, that in Spokane was more like talcum powder, while other places had other grain sizes.

> The big difference was in particle size—it ranged from coarse beach-like sand to dust less than ½ micron in dimension. The coarse material, deposited within 85 miles from the mountain, was easiest to clean up. It was not very dusty—much like our sand used during the winter as abrasives on ice and snow-covered roads. The talc-like volcanic ash deposited four inches deep, 200 miles east of Mount St. Helens, was a horse-of-a-different-color (Anderson 1980, 3).

The snow removal plan for each community was often the starting point, but ash did not behave like snow. Instead, it often fluffed up and then slowly settled back after the sweeper or other mechanical implement had passed. Generally, after a day or so of experimentation, the communities evolved their own techniques. These usually involved wetting the ash and then blading it off. This technique worked well on paved roads but for gravel roads other methods might be needed. Once a method was developed, cleanup became a matter of time, manpower, and equipment, for the scope of the job was daunting.

Many respondents mentioned the development of unnecessary fears about the potentially negative medical effects of ash because of a lack of information. The delay in determining the medical effects also provided a climate favorable for breeding rumors. A health department official from Spokane explained:

> We were in the precarious position of representing a million people in the fallout area, trying to say something about the health risk. We didn't have the answers. We called all over the world. We had an expert from Tulane University come in and put at rest the health risk of silicosis.

For such officials, the frustrations of not having the correct information were great, especially in light of conflicting lab reports and the lack of a single spokesman to coordinate the information. Under these circumstances, it was safer to be on the conservative side by recommending staying inside, minimizing activity, and having the highest risk people wear respirators.

Problems Related to the Magnitude of the Clean-up Task
Several of the major problems cited by local officials east of the Cascades

could be attributed in large part to the scope and magnitude of the ashfall clean-up operations. Close to half the respondents said that shortage of manpower, lack of funds, and lack of equipment and supplies posed problems. These figures could have been much higher had there not been a tremendous public response helping with the manpower problem, a short-term disregard of the costs in order to do a necessary job and an influx of equipment from neighboring counties and private contractors to fill the gap. In spite of such efforts, there were still problems in each category due to the size of the event, a fact reflected in such comments as,

> So much work to do. There isn't any city with that much equipment.

> Ritzville allows a thousand dollars a year for snow removal. How can you fund something like this?

> We were working seven days a week, twelve hours a day; the people were getting tired.

The Lack of Manpower
The lack of manpower was, to a considerable degree, overcome by an outstanding effort by the people in the region. This cooperation may be seen in such comments as: "We have an excellent volunteer response." "We spent a lot of money on overtime."

A certain pride in coping under stress underlies the laconic comment, "We did what we could with the people we had." In spite of the general willingness of people to exert extra effort and work longer hours, witnessed in all sorts of jobs and in the individual cleanup of homes and neighborhoods, clearly there was a manpower shortage. This problem shows up in such comments as:

> We were overtaxed. Nine deputies worked twenty hours per day.

> All the off-duty people responded to the need but they were overworked; put in overtime without replacements. I had all the people from other departments I could possibly scrape up. I needed people with training and ability to make decisions.

Many respondents made comments about people being overworked, particularly since they had their own residential clean-up problems after their work on the job. As the cleanup continued, the number of local volunteers began to drop off. In Moses Lake an official said: "We got 60 National Guard from Spokane by Thursday; by the following week we had 300. The cleanup would not have been possible without them."

The Lack of Funds

Lack of funds was not a problem with which people concerned themselves in the immediate aftermath of the ashfall, but it began to assume greater importance as the dimensions of the cleanup became apparent. In the beginning most communities made local decisions to work with the problem. This attitude may be seen in such comments as: "When you're in that situation you have to spend whether you've got it or not." "We spent money anyway; things had to be done." The result of this type of decision was expressed by one respondent as, "We spent part of the regular budget; will not be able to spend more on construction."

Many respondents gave rough estimates of the magnitude of the cleanup costs incurred, and indicated that these costs were beyond the means of their community. An example of the heavy costs involved may be seen by the work of getting the county roads back in operation. In the heavy ashfall areas, this required blading off the ash and, in the process, losing the gravel already there. Thus, new gravel had to be spread over the entire length of all the small county roads to bring them back to former standards. A truckload of gravel may be relatively inexpensive, but when this figure is multiplied by the large number of truckloads needed per mile of road, and again by the miles of road in these rather large counties, the costs could run into millions of dollars. Even with generous federal reimbursements the communities had huge bills to pay. The comment "we need all the help we can get" from one official would apply to many communities.

As the agency responsible for disbursing federal disaster funds, the Federal Emergency Management Agency (FEMA) became the target for many disgruntled local officials. Some problems may have arisen because local people were not aware of what types of expenditures were reimbursable; others said problems occurred because the eruption was "a new disaster for FEMA; they're not used to this kind of clean-up." There were also complaints about reimbursement delays. The most outspoken, however, were those disgusted by the red tape involved in claiming expenses. The flavor of such complaints may be seen in the following remarks:

> I'm disappointed with the Feds. In some areas I don't think they were fair. We only put in for expense incurred. The Feds replaced the engine lost but disallowed maintenance.

> I don't expect much from FEMA's phoney little regulations; they will pay for replacement filters but not for improvements to filter more efficiently.

Lack of Equipment

Many different problems were described under lack of equipment. First of all, shortages of many different types of equipment were noted by different respondents. These ranged from hoses, to wet the ash, to heavy equipment, for moving the ash from the streets, to masks, respirators, and protective clothing. Another type of problem was ash damage to equipment.

Several respondents said a major problem was damage to their vehicles due to ash. Thus, one respondent in Moses Lake said "We lost six of our seven cars." Ambulances, police cars, fire trucks, and other vehicles needed in the emergency situation were often damaged by the ash, particularly in the early stages before the abrasive effects were understood. Later many of these problems were overcome, but only by dint of extra preventive maintenance. Many ingenious filtering devices were invented and installed (figure 25).

FIGURE 25.   Jury-Rigged Ash Filter.

The major problem described under lack of equipment was the shortage of machines to physically remove the ash from the streets. While only a small amount of ash was sufficient to shut down traffic, the deeper the layer the longer the clean-up time, and the greater the need for extra equipment. The magnitude of the problem can be illustrated by Moses Lake, where five pieces of such clean-up equipment are sufficient for regular needs. At the height of cleanup, sixty pieces of equipment were being used and a total of seventy to eighty-five pieces of equipment were used during the emergency. One official there explained the key role of the Corps of

Engineers in locating much of this equipment for the community. Some pieces came from contractors in more distant places such as California and even Indiana. Some communities initially isolated from a local pool of contractors with suitable equipment could benefit from such a broad-scale system of contacts.

Other problems discussed by respondents under equipment shortages stressed the general lack of preparation for the volcanic eruption. There were inadequate supplies of masks, poorly equipped cars and communication equipment inadequate to deal with the emergency situation. These problems could have been avoided with a little advance preparation.

Lack of Coordination with Other Agencies
The lack of coordination with other agencies was rated as a problem by over half the respondents east of the Cascades. Although there was some variation from community to community, suggesting the important role played by certain individuals, the general picture was clear. The state, particularly the departments of Emergency Services and Transportation, was given a poor rating, and various federal agencies were also cited as being unresponsive to local needs. In contrast, the cooperation among local agencies was seen as "great," "fantastic," and problem free.

Some respondents were blunt, making such comments as "the state bungled it," "the state fell down," or "I believe the people at the state didn't know what to do." Others were somewhat more emphatic, as in the comment:

> If they [State of Washington, Department of Emergency Services] had an idea of how to handle the problem, or what it would be, they would have been more prepared. But how do you prepare for something you have no idea of? The state needs to set up a better communication system, to provide information and receive information.

Much of the criticism was directed at the failure to provide a better warning of what to expect, but, in addition, there was much criticism of the failure to provide good information in the immediate aftermath of the ashfall. Many respondents described the total isolation of their communities following the May 18 eruption, as noted above in the section of lack of information. "We couldn't coordinate with any agencies outside the city. We were almost isolated. The teletype was the only direct contact with the outside," said one Yakima official. Another complained, "A very serious delay in the city being able to gain assistance from national forces. Equipment in the military center 11 miles from the city was conveyed away from Yakima while other equipment came in." A Spokane respondent said: "The state agencies tend to forget that the east side of Washington exists. They were confronted with a traumatic disaster on the west side so I can't blame them for directing most of their effort there, but they should have let us know what was coming."

A major problem was the failure of state agencies to promptly close the highways. This delay resulted in many more stranded motorists than necessary. An extreme case was Ritzville, where a local population of 1800 had to look after 2000 stranded motorists, most coming from the east several hours after the iniital eruption. A Ritzville respondent explained that: "My biggest problem was getting the interstate closed. Some people in Olympia were not happy with me for closing the interstate. I forced them to do so." Later there were conflicts related to opening the highways, with some difference of opinion between local and state officials as to when they should have been opened.

Help did eventually come from the outside. "No one here for at least a week; then everyone helped." Some irritations remain. A Yakima official trying to prepare for future ashfalls told of a lack of cooperation from the military: "I have tried to get a letter of agreement saying we could use the Army equipment, if necessary. They say they can not do it."

In contrast to complaints about coordination with state and federal agencies was a strong tendency to take pride in their own efforts and to heartily praise the cooperative behavior of local officials, as in the following comments:

No help from the state, as if they weren't there.

We did it ourselves.

Espirit de corps developed among people: the sheriff was magnificent.

Great community pride was also expressed for the response of the public.

A Superlative Public Response

A striking feature of our interviews east of the Cascades was the response to the question regarding public cooperation. Overwhelmingly respondents said there was no problem, and went on to emphasize that the public cooperation was "fantastic," "super," "tremendous," "excellent," "admirable," and "great." "Never saw anything like it," "it brought the community together," and "caused people to unite in a fashion that you rarely see" were typical descriptions of the local response. Great pride was generated among populations which persisted in the face of great difficulties. This feeling reached its most extreme form in comments from some of the hardest hit communities:

The majority of people here are proud we got through something others haven't and probably never will. I shudder to think what would happen in larger centers with three inches of ash.

The independent attitude of the people enabled them to handle it. People in other areas would have committed suicide. They wouldn't have been able to cope with it.

Specific instances of extraordinary public cooperation were cited, as by the hospital manager in Ritzville who described the response to the danger of roof collapse on some public buildings because of the weight of ash.

The sheriff's office put out a call for volunteers to clear Hawthorne School roof. Over a hundred people were immediately available. They came over here and cleared the roof (of the hospital) in two hours. They cleared over 32 dump truck loads from the hospital roof.

Clearly, the high solidarity often noted in the immediate aftermath of disasters was present in the ashfall areas after the May 18 eruption of Mount St. Helens. This solidarity is confirmed by a survey by Anderson (1983) in Spokane County, in which "sense of community" was seen as the greatest positive effect of the ashfall.

CONCLUSIONS

The very general information about Mount St. Helens sent by teletype from the state Department of Emergency Services, and the tremendous media coverage of the volcano's awakening did not serve as effective warnings for people in the ashfall areas east of the Cascades. Although interested, even excited and fascinated by the drama of these natural events, they could see no connection between such distant developments and their own communities. What was lacking were definite references to local risks and reinforcement of these dangers by credible informants.

As a result of the lack of warning, there were no contingency plans developed and no other preparations for the possibility of ashfall. Surprise and dismay were the initial reactions, and only slowly did the public and local officials come to realize exactly what had occurred; too slowly to prevent the stranding of thousands of travelers as the transportation system was stopped by the ash.

The communities in eastern Washington were isolated from each other and lacked good information. To overcome this, local officials responded with energy, ingenuity, and flexibility; and outstanding public solidarity helped to overcome some of the shortages of equipment, manpower, and funds. The immediate emergency was over within a couple of weeks, but residents must continue to cope with the long-term physical and emotional effects of ash in their areas.

The May 18 eruption of Mount St. Helens was clearly a peak experience for the people directly involved and exciting for people throughout the nation and the world. It serves as a forceful reminder of the power of nature and the importance of having plans to deal with such natural events. In the process of dealing with this massive emergency, a great deal was learned which is being incorporated into local contingency plans. This information should be compiled to provide a check-list of adjustments and preparations which could be used by other communities subject to volcanic eruption.

Chapter 7

THE ROLE OF THE FEDERAL EMERGENCY MANAGEMENT AGENCY AND OTHER FEDERAL AGENCIES

On May 21, 1980, President Carter declared the state of Washington a "major disaster area" due to the eruption of Mount St. Helens. This declaration immediately mandated a major role for the Federal Emergency Management Agency (FEMA), for this agency is responsible for coordinating the efforts of all federal agencies involved in presidentially declared disasters. Traditionally, the FEMA disaster response is triggered by declaration of the president, following a request for assistance by the governor (FEMA 1980). The federal participation normally takes the form of helping rebuild affected areas and contributing to the payment of emergency costs. Following a declaration, the president designates a federal coordinating officer (FCO) who becomes the chief federal administrator of the disaster response. In the case of Mount St. Helens, most of the FEMA personnel came from Region X, with headquarters at Bothell (near Seattle), but the federal coordinating officer came from San Francisco.

Because FEMA normally becomes involved after the disaster has occurred, it is mainly concerned with response rather than warning activities.

In the case of Mount St. Helens, because of repeated eruptions and other unusual aspects, FEMA did actually become involved in warnings as well as in responses to the eruption (Cogan and Lodato 1981). Its activities are described in this chapter. In addition, we include discussion of several other federal agencies that played significant roles in response to the eruption.

PRIOR EXPERIENCE AND EXPECTATIONS

All FEMA respondents said they had had considerable experience in dealing with natural hazards, and the FEMA agency, although relatively new, has also had considerable experience. Most FEMA respondents were aware of the potential for an eruption at Mount St. Helens; some personnel had received the Blue Book or the 1978 hazard advisory that included Mount Baker and Mount St. Helens. No one, however, felt there was any likelihood of an eruption. As one said, "I can't say we were very worried about Mount St. Helens before March 27. We were watching Baker since 1975."

Most FEMA respondents found out about the activity on Mount St. Helens in March, soon after the first earthquakes. One received the news from the state DES and the rest found out through official FEMA channels. Although this news generated some interest among the FEMA respondents, most were not concerned. One felt it could be somewhat serious locally, but—"I didn't feel any great disaster would occur. The most likely possibility was local disturbances, maybe some evacuations. I didn't expect problems in the Columbia and Cowlitz."

One other possible reason for the lack of concern among FEMA personnel was their involvement in other disasters. FEMA people are often shifted from disaster to disaster in the United States. Several respondents were working on the Los Angeles floods and could not afford to concern themselves with Mount St. Helens—"I was so wrapped up in what was going on in Southern California that I was not keeping up with it."

Only one person reported taking action in the warning stage—helping the USGS-FS develop a warning system and public information plan. A NAWAS drop was installed at the Forest Service headquarters so they could warn the counties, and the FEMA people tested the warning system about a month before the disaster. This informant reported concern with the USFS ability to transmit the warning information because of their inexperience and because "the scope of their attention was limited to the forest."

THE FIRST FEMA INVOLVEMENT

The first FEMA official to become involved in the May 18 disaster was a public information officer asked to help the DES in Olympia a few hours after the eruption began. On Monday, May 19, another was asked to help the state prepare a request for a presidential disaster declaration. Also on May 19, the first FEMA official arrived at the Emergency Operations Center in Vancouver. The next few days were spent getting organized. On May 21, the president declared a national disaster and designated Robert Stevens of FEMA to be his representative as federal coordinating officer. At first there were some problems in taking control. One respondent noted, "There was some healthy skepticism with respect to us; but we were not going to manage, just coordinate." This person also said that although most federal agencies know FEMA's role, the USGS and USFS were in-experienced in disasters and did not understand what FEMA was going to do; so they were somewhat reluctant to give up control. This reluctance was overcome by the fact "that Mr. Stevens' proximity to the president made his role readily identifiable." Once FEMA became established as the coordinating agency, much of the actual control of the area around the mountain, access to the mountain, and warning activities was left to the USFS Vancouver headquarters. FEMA concentrated on consolidating all federal and state public information operations into one disaster infor-mation center, the development of a technical information network for dissemination of volcano-related information, the direction of military assistance, provision of protective masks and housing the local people, and the direction of the disbursement of disaster assistance funds. The search and rescue operations remained under the control of the sheriffs and others (see Kilijanek 1981).

FEMA PUBLIC INFORMATION ACTIVITIES

The public information effort led by FEMA was particularly impressive. Their goal was to "provide accurate, timely flow of information to the public," and to provide a central clearing house so that all agencies were "speaking with one voice." FEMA's role was to establish a central infor-mation facility for all agencies beginning on May 23; this disaster infor-mation center was staffed with a large number of public information officers from a wide range of agencies. It operated twenty-four hours a day, seven days a week and routinely handled calls from newspeople all over the world, as well as gave two press conferences each day for the large number of newspeople in Vancouver. The magnitude of this operation was unusually large for FEMA; one official noted, "We spent a great deal more effort and resources on public information than has ever been spent before".

Another unprecedented FEMA activity was the creation of the tech-nical information network, a group of experts from federal, state, and private organizations who developed a series of papers discussing various aspects of the volcanic effects. Whether this idea came about as a result of comments by President Carter, his scientific advisors, or an internal memo circulated by a member of the FEMA staff (as one respondent said), apparently there were a great many unknowns stemming from the eruption—

> The scope of the disaster, the short- and long-term social and economic impact of the eruption, and the possibililty of future eruptions were so poorly understood and so vitally important to so many people that no facet would be left unexplored (Kerr 1980, 18).

To help dispel some of the uncertainty, the technical information network was established. Through the month of June 1980, some thirty-three Technical Informatin Bulletins were issued, covering such topics as flood hazards, impacts on wildlife and plant communities, and volcanic ash effects on children, insects, livestock, and machinery (for a complete list of bulletin titles see appendix C). According to one respondent, "The public got the benefit of what was known as soon as it was known." This rapid information dissemination from the information center and technical information network was thought to have controlled rumors, reassured people, and kept people away from the hazard areas.

THE FEMA ROLE OF COORDINATING AND DISPERSING FEDERAL DISASTER ASSISTANCE

FEMA also had the task of evaluating and responding to requests from local and state agencies for federal assistance (including military) in the emergency response. FEMA regulations mandate that local and state agencies take the lead in disaster response, federal aid is supplementary and only to be used if state and local resources are exhausted or inadequate for the task. As one respondent said, "The federal government assumes the state and local governments will succeed in their response, federal aid is only to supplement them."

The magnitude of the Mount St. Helens eruption was simply far too great for state and local agencies to cope with alone. This incapability is seen in the high percentages of respondents who cited the lack of funds, equipment, and manpower as major problems. Extra costs such as personnel to man roadblocks, equipment rental to clean up ash or dredge streams, and the long hours of overtime put in by state and local officials severely strained or exceeded the budgets of many agencies. FEMA personnel had to determine the validity of local and state requests, and direct federal support.

When county and National Guard search and rescue operations were shown to be inadequate for the task, FEMA had the authority to order units of the regular Army and the Air Force to provide additional help. The search and rescue operation at Mount St. Helens could have benefited from a strong FEMA coordinating role; but, FEMA involvement followed the disaster declaration, the disaster declaration followed the eruption by three days, and by the time the full force of the military could be diverted to the search and rescue operation on May 22, all the survivors had been rescued. The units operating from May 22 to May 30 recovered 23 victims, no survivors.

FEMA also administers Disaster Relief Act funds for family grant and temporary housing, as well as local government recovery. Federal money was used to partially fund response efforts by state and local agencies and to reimburse those agencies for expenses and damages incurred in the emergency. To determine which requests for reimbursement were valid, a number of damage survey teams were created from personnel in the Corps of Engineers, Federal Highway Administration, Environmental Protection Agency, and Bureau of Reclamation. Under FEMA direction, these teams were sent to evaluate and document requests for disaster relief assistance. Once these requests were approved, they were processed for reimbursement to state and local governments. This reimbursement was to cover 75 percent of the eligible costs. The state and local governments were to pay the other 25 percent.

The work undertaken by the Corps of Engineers was probably the most significant form of federal assistance in terms of funds dispersed, but most of their activities belong to the period of disaster recovery and are not within the scope of this study. Other significant expenditures were for restoration or repair of major civil works such as highways, bridges, water supplies, sewage-disposal drainage and flood control systems, as well as for aid to individuals and families for damage to homes, farms, and equipment (Schuster 1981).

PROBLEMS OF FEMA OFFICIALS
IN RESPONDING TO THE EMERGENCY

In table 5 may be seen the major problems in responding to the emergency as identified by our FEMA respondents. Lack of information and lack of coordination were most often cited, followed by political problems and a problem related to the NAWAS system.

The Problem of Lack of Information
The problem cited by most respondents was lack of information, both about volcanic impacts and about assistance needs on the local level. One

Table 5.   Problems of FEMA Officials in Responding to the Mount St. Helens Eruption (5)

Problems	Percent Respondents
Lack of Information	80
Lack of Coordination	60
Lack of Funds	20
Lack of Public Cooperation	20
Lack of Manpower	0
Lack of Equipment or Facilities	0
Others:	
Political	40
Warning System	40

person felt there was a "tremendous amount of missing information—not because the USGS wasn't giving any information they had." The unknowns in this case were many, including the effects of volcanic ash on health, agriculture, and machinery, and how to deal with it. One person who had experience with Hawaiian volcanoes said it was "worthless in this situation." The unprecedented nature of the disaster can perhaps be summed up by the following quotation: "There has never been an eruption like this in a civilized society. We were flying by the seat of our pants in this operation." The lack of information, one felt, began at the warning stage,

> There was a real problem about the direction and speed of the ash-fall; the counties and states in the path of the ash were not warned. I don't think anybody pictured that ashfall would be a problem. Either the scientists didn't expect it or they didn't communicate it forcefully enough.

Another area where FEMA officials felt they lacked information was in verifying requests for local assistance. A FEMA official stated that verification of resource needs requested by local governments was the responsibility of the state DES. Instead of doing this job the latter merely passed on the requests. One noted that although requests for money came in quickly, information about those request was slow, and, "The damage survey teams have a great deal of trouble obtaining information from the applicants, they are often not cooperative. This holds up the assistance process."

Problems in Coordinating with Other Agencies
Aside from the problems of cooperation in local government requests for disaster assistance, the only other reported problems in cooperation were with the state government. On the federal level, most felt cooperation was

excellent. As one respondent said, "This disaster was one of the best examples of interagency cooperation." One person reported difficulties in communicating with the governor, but he felt this was because of "some breakdown in the communication between state agencies and the governor"; another bluntly stated that "the governor was getting very bad information.

Problems with the state first surfaced when FEMA had to decide where to locate the disaster field office. Although the state wanted them to locate the office in Olympia, the federal effort was headquartered in Vancouver because it was "close to the action." The Forest Service and Geological Survey were operating from there in already established facilities and it was easiest to continue the operation from there. The state DES director, however, objected to the Vancouver headquarters and refused to leave Olympia, even when the federal coordinating officer personally asked him to come to Vancouver. The result was the "state agencies resisted staffing" in the disaster field office, even when FEMA "provided every opportunity for the state to cooperate at Vancouver." The DES personnel sent to Vancouver were few and low level, according to one FEMA informant, and official connections with the DES were (according to another respondent), "so poorly coordinated that it was three days before we knew there was a DES person working in the public information office issuing statements."

According to another FEMA respondent, this one, "untrained" public information officer was the only person sent by the DES to handle requests from all over the world for information about state operations. Although public information officers from other state agencies were promised, apparently they were never sent, and this one person worked through the time of major demand "until she suffered from stress and fatigue," and had to quit. The DES then replaced her with one other person.

Whether this reluctance by the state to locate in Vancouver was due to a wish to better organize state resources, or, as one FEMA respondent thought, because of "fear that we were usurping their role," it affected the response. Communication between the two headquarters was often blocked by jammed telephone lines, and distrust between the major coordinating agencies certainly did not help the emergency. This bottleneck also affected federal coordination with local agencies. As one FEMA respondent said, "We were supposed to go through the state. We had no direct contact with locals, since the state was overburdened and understaffed."

Local requests for assistance had to go through the state DES before they were sent to FEMA; because of the difficulties in communcation there were often denials and delays (see discussions by local officials). Some FEMA respondents had very strong feelings about the problem of coordination with the state DES. One felt "the DES Olympia operation was a deliberate slap in the face of reality." Another bluntly stated, "Deaths resulted from the lack of coordination."

Public Cooperation

The only person reporting problems with public cooperation was involved with the damage survey reports. He felt local public officials displayed a " . . . lack of understanding. Maybe they don't want to understand. There is a tendency to blame somebody in a disaster."

For the immediate emergency response, however, no problems were reported with the public. As one respondent put it, "Generally the public responded fairly well to the information provided them. The majority stayed out of the Red Zone and got to disaster assistance."

Availability of Funds, Equipment, and Manpower

Lack of funds was initially a problem, according to one respondent. FEMA's expenditures in other emergencies had reduced the available funds, and "since Hurricane Frederick, we were operating on a shoestring for awhile." Congressional appropriations in the wake of the May 18 eruption allowed FEMA to budget for a large-scale response. There was little problem after that, except, as another FEMA official noted, "It is taking us longer to get money into the hands of local governments." For the immediate emergency response, FEMA officials reported no financial problems; in fact, one public information officer said, "I was given a blank check," enabling him to set up an operation to cope with the worldwide press demands.

Another problem was with the NAWAS warning system. This was partially an equipment problem, but in the eyes of the FEMA officials it seemed more of a personnel problem. This failure has already been discussed in chapter 4.

Another FEMA official felt the Forest Service personnel lacked the experience to handle NAWAS or any major warning system; he went on to comment that "the Forest Service was given responsibility for warning and they blew it." The above statement should not be seen as an overall FEMA conclusion; another agency respondent said that "the USFS did an excellent job providing warning around the mountain. For warning beyond that the USFS had neither the full responsibility nor the experience to do the job. This was properly a DES job."

In general, FEMA respondents reported they were able to obtain all the manpower, equipment, and facilities they needed. One reason cited for the more than adequate number of personnel available was the system of "reservists" set up by FEMA, consisting mainly of retired people available on short notice for temporary employment. Another reason is FEMA's authority to ask other federal agencies to provide personnel in the case of an emergency. This use of other agency people led to problems in disaster assistance evaluation. According to one official, "we don't always get the kind of people we want," which he referred to as a "hellish problem" in the Mount St. Helens emergency. This lack of trained, experienced damage survey evaluators has left FEMA open to criticism from local and state agencies about red tape and delays in distributing disaster assistance funds.

Political Problems
Several FEMA officials were concerned about political problems. According to one; "Mount St. Helens was the most frustrating experience in my career. There was a lot a politicking going on. That smokescreen has a negative impact. The politicking causes raised expectations that are unjustified."

Aside from the large political question of who was in charge (which FEMA officials seemed to feel was answered with the appointment of the federal coordinating officer), the main political problem centered around the disbursement of disaster assistance, involving unreasonable requests for equipment or funds. In part, some FEMA officials felt they were being used as scapegoats and to further political careers. One respondent discussed the case of a "sheriff running for office," who requested a military helicopter for an activity outside the search and rescue operation in which he was involved (he apparently wanted to monitor the mountain himself, feeling the USGS was not sufficient). This request was in violation of federal policy in two ways—the activity was outside the scope of the life saving search and rescue operation, and local commercial helicopters were available, "but the sheriff didn't want to pay for them." This type of request is seen as the result of a misunderstanding of the federal role, based on a less formal working arrangement in previous small-scale search and rescue operations. The attitude was discussed at length by one FEMA official:

The sheriffs are accustomed to getting immediate federal support for search and rescue operations. They have a different arrangement directly with the Department of Defense, which does not exist in this type of situation. The Department of Defense, in supplying helicopters at that time, really violated one of their basic precepts— that federal resources cannot be used unless there is a threat to health or safety, a threat to life. We had 20 or 30 helicopters in there, we pay for it all. We respond to requests from the state for any type of federal support. The state has to certify that it is beyond the ability of state and local government and that no commercial resources are available.

This misunderstanding of the federal role extends into disaster assistance funding. As noted by one respondent,

The perception is created that everyone is going to be made whole, which is wrong if you read our law. It is clear that federal aid is supplemental to local and state aid; it is not an indemnification program to put everyone back to pre-disaster.

This respondent went on to note that the state of Washington had balked at providing state funds to match the federal 75 percent share of assistance,

The State of Idaho has accepted that responsibility, the state is paying 15% and the locals 10% for their 25% share. Washington has not done that. I don't know that I ought to be the guy to comment on that, all I can say is that the governor has given no indication of wanting to do that.

Ultimately, the state of Washington did appropriate over $4 million to assist local governments with the local share.

The FEMA officials were stung by the criticism of their handling of disaster assistance funds, the complaints of red tape, hard documentation requirements, and slow processing. But as one person said, "We are charged with accountability of tax money. The eligibility rules can't make everybody happy; we attempt to reduce it but we can't eliminate it as long as we have accountability."

This mandate of accountability in spending public funds was complicated in the ashfall area, especially in differentiating between legitimate losses to ash damage and those caused by human error:

Relatively little damage by ash is found to be verifiable. The state patrol sustained more damage than any other agency, and most was human error. Properly filtered machinery should take little damage; what passes through is below engine tolerances and there is no problem.

There is, however, an awareness among FEMA officials that there may be too much regulation in situations like Mount St. Helens, and that rules on eligibility for assistance funds may be too stringent. One respondent discussed this: "There are odd rules of eligibility, some that don't make any sense. We have requested of headquarters that they waive some of the rules, such as not being able to pay for fringe benefits."

Relations with the Media
There were no problems with the news media reported by FEMA officials.

One public information officer reported "excellent cooperation," and went on to say, "It was probably the best, most responsible coverage of an ongoing disaster situation I've ever seen." Another official felt the quality of the press coverage was due in great measure to the quality of the public information operation—

> The press was quite responsible in general, but some measure of that belongs to FEMA. By providing ready access to the press, nobody has to wait long for information, and there was enough news that they [the press] didn't have to make news.

There was also an awareness among FEMA public information officers of problems with the news media on local and state levels, stemming from inadequate public information operations. One comment about the state operations was:

> We had a clear dichotomy in the public information office between state and federal; it's almost as though they were separate operations. Adequate support and sound policies in managing public information are important and useful, and the federal/state contrast should show this.

CONCLUSIONS

The Federal Emergency Management Agency played an important role in the response to the Mount St. Helens eruption, but only after the major eruption of May 18. When the state of Washington was declared a "major disaster area" on May 21, FEMA became the lead agency for the federal government. Although it had not been deeply involved in early warning activities related to the reawakening volcano, the agency and its personnel had a great deal of experience in dealing with disasters.

FEMA quickly and firmly took responsibility for coordinating the disaster response. They amplified and extended the public information system by bringing in representatives from a vast array of federal agencies to a new Disaster Information Center, set up a few blocks from the original one developed by the USFS. This public information operation was soon the largest ever developed by FEMA. Meanwhile, the Forest Service and USGS continued with the hazards assessment and monitoring activities as before. In addition to coordinating the response of federal agencies, FEMA also administered the program of disaster assistance and was in charge of search and rescue operations, although arriving a little late for proper discharge of the latter responsibility.

A major innovation was the creation of the technical information network, a group of experts from federal, state, and private organizations who worked closely together to develop a set of Technical Information Bulletins on all aspects of volcanic effects. This information was important because of the unprecedented nature of a volcanic eruption in a modern technological society and the many unknowns which had to be addressed. It would, of course, have been invaluable to have had such information before the May 18 eruption. Even so, it did help overcome the major problem of a lack of information.

There were some problems of coordination and some political problems related to the location of disaster headquarters and the disbursement of disaster assistance. The initial skepticism of the Forest Service regarding the FEMA takeover was overcome rather quickly, but less harmonious were the relations between FEMA and the state DES. The state of Washington DES wanted the disaster relief operation centered at Olympia, but FEMA felt they should locate at the center of action and information in Vancouver. The resultant lack of coordination with the state may have led to delays and lack of understanding with the local people as well.

The role of disbursement of disaster assistance placed FEMA in conflict with some local officials who felt the bureaucratic rules and regulations were too rigidly applied. This mandate of accountability of public funds given to FEMA placed the agency in opposition to public perceptions that everything would be made whole and returned to predisaster conditions. In the case of the volcanic eruption, this problem was exacerbated because the usual bureaucratic rules did not always fit the unusual circumstances. Furthermore, the large scope of the disaster required the rapid training of inexperienced personnel to apply the often ill-fitted rules and regulations.

Many other federal agencies played important roles in the Mount St. Helens disaster. Some, like the FAA, became involved early in controlling the dangerous level of air traffic around the mountain. Others, such as the Corps of Engineers and the EPA, came in after the major eruption to perform vital roles in responding to the disaster. The Corps of Engineers cleared the Columbia River to open it to ocean-going traffic once more, and dredged the Toutle and Cowlitz rivers to lower the flood risk. The EPA was involved in assessing the effects of ash on air and water quality.

The reactive mode of many federal agencies made their efforts less effective than they might have been. The military capabilities for search and rescue operations were not fully exploited because most active duty personnel could not go in until the event was declared a national disaster. By then, the search and rescue operations had already passed through their most critical phases. Nor did FEMA's entry come in time for them to play an effective coordinating role in the search and rescue operations. It has been argued that federal disaster policy should adopt a more proactive approach to disaster (Kilijanek 1981, 121). This approach would use the immense capability of FEMA with respect to public information and co-ordination of disaster agencies before the event, when much of the disaster planning must take place if it is to be effective.

Chapter 8

SUMMARY OF AGGREGATE DATA

The previous chapters have presented the events of the Mount St. Helens emergency from the point of view of specific agencies or groups of agencies. It is also useful to summarize and analyze the data from our interviews to provide a general picture. Significant themes to be discussed in this chapter include the changes in expectations of eruption, the perceived magnitude of the May 18 eruption, the effectiveness of the warnings, the role of the warning information in decision making, the problems encountered in the response, the lessons learned, and future expectations and plans. Before turning to these topics we will discuss briefly the sample and questionnaire.

Our sample of 130 was selected to include the individuals most directly involved in the Mount St. Helens hazard warning and response by virtue of their positions in local, state, or federal government agencies, or with private industry or volunteer organizations. Since one of the authors had participated in the aftermath of the May 18 eruption, many of the key actors were known. As individuals were interviewed they in turn were asked to suggest the names of other people deeply involved in the event who might provide other perspectives. We deliberately sought out a broad range of people with different roles, while trying to focus on those most directly involved. In appendix B we list the affiliations of those we interviewed. Many of these individuals were mentioned many times as key actors, by a variety of people so we feel confident that we managed to reach almost all those who played major roles within the USGS, the USFS, the state of Washington Department of Emergency Services, and FEMA.

In only a few cases were some individuals unavailable in the state of Washington during the summer of 1980, when most of the interviewing was done, or in the summer of 1981, when some follow-up interviews were completed.

At the local level, we selected for broad geographic coverage within the communities most directly impacted. For west of the Cascades we often had the names of key individuals when we arrived. East of the Cascades we would start by telephoning such people as the director of the local office of emergency services or the local sheriff to start our list of key local actors. A few telephone calls were sufficient to provide corroboration, as individuals from different agencies would tend to include some of the same individuals. Since time in any one locality was limited, all key actors there would not be interviewed, but, as we gained an appreciation of the range of different roles, we would often select those representing roles not already sampled, e.g. a Red Cross representative who was involved in providing shelter, a city engineer in charge of ash removal, or a social worker dealing with psychological reactions to the ash. Usually these were individuals recommended as having played an important role.

Each of the individuals was interviewed using the questionnaire in appendix D. In some cases, questions obviously inappropriate were excluded, and in a few cases, where time was limited, only the most pertinent questions were asked. For this reason, all tables do not include results for the entire 130 respondents. In most cases, however, the entire set of questions was used and much probing extended the response regarding the individual respondent's special knowledge or interest.

While we feel that the descriptive and qualitative approach adopted is appropriate because of the small numbers within any subgroup of the sample, we present here a few of the results based on the entire sample. These results highlight points where there is substantial agreement in the entire sample, as well as some of the major differences separating groups.

EXPECTATIONS OF ERUPTIONS

The questionnaire response can be used to document changes in expectations about the possibility of an eruption. The use of questions on expectations after the actual event must be interpreted with caution, because of the opportunity for respondents to claim "hindsight" knowledge. The fact that most reported they did not expect much from Mount St. Helens, when they could have looked better if they did, aids in our assessment of the reliability of these data (tables 6 and 7).

The actual experience of the eruption obviously changed expectations about the likelihood of another event. Before the 1980 activity, although nearly three-quarters of the respondents knew Mount St. Helens *could*

Table 6.   Perceived Likelihood of an Eruption (Percent)

	Prior to *Recent Activity (71)*	*Future Activity (125)*
Very Likely	9	81
Somewhat Likely	11	7
Not Likely	76	1
Not Sure	4	10

Table 7.   Perceived Seriousness of an Eruption (Percent)

	Early Activity *(March 20-* *May 18, 1980) (103)*	*Future Activity (101)*
Very Serious	16	20
Somewhat Serious	8	13
Not Serious	56	55
Not Sure	20	13

erupt, most thought it *would not* erupt, and if it did, it would not be a serious hazard. After the first four eruptions most people expected more events to occur, only 2 percent thought there would be no more eruptions. At the beginning of the activity, 24 percent felt an eruption could be at least somewhat serious, but after May 18, 33 percent thought future eruptions could be a serious threat. Many of those who thought future eruptions probably would not be serious qualified their answers. They stressed the low probability of another blast of the magnitude of May 18, as well as the importance of the warning and access restriction system that has been improving through successive trials since May 18. Expectations changed from a denial of the possibility of a hazard to the acceptance of the possibility with the knowledge that they could cope with the effects.

PERCEIVED MAGNITUDE OF EFFECTS

As is quite evident in table 8, the magnitude of the May 18 eruption took almost everyone, including the experts, by surprise. As one FEMA respondent noted, "We were hit by the low end of the probability scale. The mudflows were far greater than expected. We didn't expect extensive ashfall, maybe just Yakima. We didn't envision the disruption caused by ash."

Table 8.   Comparison of Actual versus Expected Effects (116)

	Percent Respondents
Much Greater Than Expected	63
Greater Than Expected	18
About the Same As Expected	8
Less Than Expected	3
Much Less Than Expected	1
Had No Idea What To Expect	8

The extent of the lateral blast was the most unexpected event, even many of the USGS scientists did not feel this was likely. The violence of this blast went beyond the Red and Blue Zone limits and killed people in areas thought relatively safe. The magnitudes of the mudflows, ashfalls, and pyroclastic flows were about the same as those outlined in the Blue Book.

Many people, however, were not well informed and taken by surprise. The best example of this lack of information is the case of local officials on the east side. Over a third of them said they had no idea what to expect from Mount St. Helens, making such comments as "never gave it a thought," "never dawned on me," "totally unprepared personally," "we didn't expect anything," or "truthfully, I didn't know what to expect." The rest of the east side group said the effects were greater or much greater than expected, the majority stated the latter. Their spontaneous comments in response to this question indicates they were thinking of local effects around the mountain, as in the following quotations:

I thought a plume of smoke and some lava, forest fires, and some local effects.

I figured on a short "poof" and a little lava.

I expected to see a little dust. I didn't expect to be smothered in the stuff.

Others with more access to information were shocked by the actual events even though they were expected. For example, "I expected mudslides, but they came further than I expected. The mud was as heavy as the concrete on the bridges and would float them away, the same with houses."

Many of the personal, social, economic, and environmental impacts were unexpected; obviously lack of experience with volcanoes had an effect of its own. As one respondent noted, "One geologist pointed out that volcanoes are popping off all the time, but they are usually in remote or rural areas, not affecting a highly technological society."

That two inches or less of ash could isolate communities for days, ruin machinery, short out transformers, threaten health, and cause other problems was hard to believe until it happened. There were psychological impacts as well from the initial fear and stress plus the uncertainty about the future. In Morton, for example,

> The psychological effect was by far the worst effect on people. People were scared at first, from news reports of high acidity leading to radiation burns. Everyone who's working in it is pretty much aware that there's going to be a long term effect on health.

This stress also affected interpersonal relationships. As one person noted, "People relationships got thin. I had 25 people from Toutle in my house and there were strained interrelations. Even my dog was crazy."

There were also positive effects from the eruption, especially in community feeling. One law enforcement person commented on the "drastic" drop in crime during and shortly after each eruption. Another official felt there were good social and political effects: "A sense of community developed, with altruism operating against 'me-first' thinking. Local government gained credibility, its image improved." Other positive effects cited were the increase in tourism and the flood control works—dams and dikes—on the Cowlitz and Toutle rivers, built in anticipation of future flooding on the mud-clogged rivers.

There were a number of long-term effects mentioned by the local officials. The impact on health and psychological well being was thought to be long lasting, as well as the effect on out-migration, in Castle Rock reported to be 40 percent of the original population. There was a sense of loss for a place important to local identity. As one person thought, "We lost a wilderness area, which will affect natives around Longview. It's like losing a member of the family."

Although there was some talk about the damage to the forest and watershed, most comments on long-term effects centered around the economic impact. Some people felt there would be losses in the lumber industry from timber loss, the restrictions, and the extra cost of harvesting because of ash abrasion on equipment. Others feared loss of investments or new industry because of the volcano hazard, and expected a drop in tax revenue. Still other people think the long-term effect will be positive, citing the "boom" created by federally supported flood control projects, the increase in tourism, and the opening of new areas for logging. Also among local officials is the awareness that Mount St. Helens represents a recurring hazard, one the governments and people of the area will have to live with for a long time. As one said, "In most disasters you recover and then life goes on. In something like this that may go on 25 years, you have to accept that and learn to live with it."

EXPERIENCE AND PREPARATION

Many of the people in our survey (selected from people involved in the planning and response to the volcanic eruptions) were not well experienced with natural hazards. Over 50 percent of the individuals questioned said they had either very little or only a moderate amount of personal experience. However, over 50 percent of the respondents felt their agencies had considerable experience. Our analysis found that although personal hazard experience was not generally significant in pre-eruption planning and activities, agency experience was. Those agencies with considerable hazard experience were more likely to have acted in response to warnings and were more involved in plan development (table 9).

Table 9. Agency Experience and Action Prior to Eruption (49)

Agency Hazard Experience:	Percent Acted in Response to Warnings	
	Yes	No
Considerable	90	10
A Moderate Amount	80	20
Very Little	38	62
Total	80	20

Chi-Square = 10.9
Degrees of Freedom = 2
Significance < .005

Possibly special, more carefully worded warnings have to be sent to inexperienced agencies that may be involved in future emergencies, and special efforts should be taken to include them in a planning process. Experience provides knowledge not only of *when* to do something but *what* to do. Lack of action by inexperienced agencies can be from either deficiency; so, it may be very important to couple the warnings with some sort of advice or planning process. Scientists may not feel qualified to do this, so it may be important for them to join their warnings to that of a hazard response agency such as FEMA or a state DES. The USGS was most effective when joined with the USFS in the contingency planning process.

THE WARNINGS AND THEIR EFFECTIVENESS

Slightly under half (45 percent) the respondents received their first warning through official channels; the rest heard about the impending eruption through the news or other informal contacts. Analysis of the data indicates that the hazard warnings which came through official channels were much more effective in stimulating action than unofficial information. As tables 10 and 11 show, those receiving information through official channels were more likely to be involved in pre–May 18 activity and plan development. Perhaps a better explanation for the data is that those who received no official information targeted directly to them were less likely to do anything.

Table 10. Relationship of Official First Warning Source to Action in the Warning Period (119)

	Channel of Information (Percent)	
Action	Official	Unofficial
Yes	55	45
No	27	73
Total	44	56

Chi-Square = 8.1
Degrees of Freedom = 1
Significance < .005

Table 11. Relationship of Official First Warning Source to Involvement in Plan Development (130)

	Channel of Information (Percent)	
Plan Development	Official	Unofficial
Yes	65	35
No	29	71
Total	44	56

Chi-Square = 13.2
Degrees of Freedom = 1
Significance < .001

The news media was the dominant source of first warnings received by the respondents (table 12), some 42 percent of whom first found out through the news. The news was an especially important source for local government officials; 59 percent first received news reports. Other channels of some importance were the Washington State DES, the USGS, and channels in the respondents' own agencies. Of these sources, only the USGS (table 13) was significantly associated with action before May 18. Nearly three-quarters of the people first notified by the USGS did something, while most of those whose first information came through other channels did nothing.

Table 12.   First Warning Sources (130)

	Percent Respondents
News media	42
Washington DES	15
USGS	12
Own Agency	11
USFS	4
Informal Contacts	3
Sheriff	2
University of Washington Seismic Laboratory	1

Table 13.   Relationship between Action in Warning Period and USGS as First Warning Source (126)*

	Channel of Information (Percent)	
Action	USGS	Other
Yes	73	31
No	27	69
Total	12	88

Chi-Square = 8.7
Degrees of Freedom = 1
Significance < .005
* USGS respondents not included

The USGS sent out five official documents to governmental agencies—the original hazard notification of 1978; the hazard watch in March, 1980; the notice of harmonic tremor in April, 1980; the notice of the bulge on the north flank in late April; and the Blue Book (Crandell and Mullineaux 1978). Of the five documents, accurate counts could only be made for the hazard notification, the hazard watch, and the Blue Book. The activities of April and May, 1980, were so confusing that many respondents could not remember where they heard about the harmonic tremor or bulge. Many who did not receive the official notices heard about them through the news or other individuals, and many who probably did receive the official notices were so overwhelmed by work that they did not read them and relied instead on personal contacts. So, little reliable analysis can be made of the last two notices, aside from a general comment that in a time of confusion and intense activity, as during the seven weeks before the May 18 catastrophe, the transmission of warnings through written notices is not nearly as effective as personal contact.

Analysis of the reaction to the USGS warnings by the survey respondents indicates that although the original notification had no overall effect, both the hazard watch and the Blue Book were significantly associated with pre–May 18 activity and plan development. The hazard watch was significantly associated with action in the warning period and involvement in planning (tables 14 and 15). Nearly two-thirds of the people who saw the report were among the minority who acted before May 18.

Table 14. Relationship between Awareness of Hazard Watch and Action in Warning Period (109)

	Hazard Watch (Percent)	
Action	Yes	No
Yes	65	35
No	30	70
Total	45	55

Chi-Square = 11.8
Degrees of Freedom = 1
Significance < .001

There is a spatial aspect to the distribution of the Blue Book. As illustrated by map 14, the report was not distributed to any of our respondents in eastern Washington, despite the fact that Yakima and Ellensburg were included in the report's map of probable ashfall hazard areas. The Blue Book was seen by about one-third of the respondents before May 18. As in the case of the hazard watch, those people who received the Blue Book tended to be more involved in pre-eruption activity and

Table 15.   Relationship between Awareness of Hazard Watch and Involvement in Plan Development (109)

	Hazard Watch (Percent)	
Plan Development	Yes	No
Yes	61	39
No	28	72
Total	45	55

Chi-Square = 10.6
Degrees of Freedom = 1
Significance < .005

plan development than those who did not (tables 16 and 17).

Apart from the first warnings and the official USGS information, 39 percent of the survey respondents received other warnings. The highest proportion of these other warnings (table 18) came from the Washington DES. Although no single source of these other warnings had a significant effect, table 19 shows a general relationship between receipt of other warnings and activity before May 18.

Table 16.   Relationship between Receipt of Blue Book and Action in Warning Period (109)

	Received Blue Book (Percent)	
Action	Yes	No
Yes	74	26
No	22	78
Total	45	55

Chi-Square = 27.2
Degrees of Freedom = 1
Significance < .001

Table 17. Relationship between Receipt of Blue Book and Involvement in Plan
Development (109)

	Received Blue Book (Percent)	
Plan Development	Yes	No
Yes	68	32
No	25	75
Total	45	55

Chi-Square = 18.1
Degrees of Freedom = 1
Significance < .001

Table 18. Other Warning Sources

	Percent Respondents
State DES	17
Univ. of Wash. Seismic Lab.	7
Federal Agencies	5
County DES	2
County Sheriff	2
Other State Agencies	2
USGS	1
None	63

Table 19. Relationship between Receipt of Other Warnings and Action in
Warning Period

Other Warnings	Action in Warning Period (Percent)	
	Yes	No
Yes	69	31
No	30	70
Total	38	62

Chi-Square = 32.06
Degrees of Freedom = 1
Significance < .001

From the foregoing discussion, obviously the USGS warnings were not the only ones able to stimulate action and planing prior to May 18. The receipt of warnings through official channels and of other warnings in addition to the USGS were also associated with activity in the warning period. Many of these warnings went to the same people, resulting in an accumulation of material. It is important to note, then, that receipt of multiple warnings also is important in motivating action. As shown in tables 20 and 21, the more warnings people received the more likely they were to become involved in predisaster planning and action. In fact, apparently the receipt of three warnings significantly increased the likelihood of response.

Table 20.   Multiple Warnings and Action in the Warning Period (113)

Number of Warnings	Action in Warning Period (Percent)	
	Yes	*No*
0	0	100
1	16	84
2	35	65
3	69	31
4	87	13
5+	79	21
Total	46	54

Table 21.   Multiple Warnings and Involvement in Plan Development (112)

Number of Warnings	Involved in Plan Development (Percent)	
	Yes	*No*
0	0	100
1	24	76
2	35	65
3	75	25
4	73	27
5+	64	32
Total	47	54

INFORMATION AND DECISION MAKING

Two questions were asked about the role of information in decision making. One asked if there were problems making decisions based on the information available, and the other asked what type of information in a hazard warning would be most helpful in decision making. As table 22 illustrates, about one-third of the respondents to the former question reported problems with the information. The majority of problems were at the state level, especially in the Department of Emergency Services. The problems in the DES began with the USGS hazard warning system, starting with, "Confusion of the Survey's mandate and how they classified their information—'Watch,' 'Warning,' 'Notification.' It was hard to know which it was and what it meant."

Table 22.   Problems in Decision Making Based on Available Information (48)

	Percent Respondents	
	Yes	*No*
Local	40	60
State	57	43
Federal	8	92
Private	0	100
Total	31	69

The confusion resulted in an overreaction to the first notification of potential hazards in December, 1978, necessitating a meeting between the USGS and DES, as well as with other concerned agencies, to clarify the situation. With the beginning of activity, DES respondents reported difficulties with the way the information was presented, finding it hard to interpret a "pure scientific approach using only information based on factual data without speculations going beyond the data." The major problem for the DES was the delay in receiving information, especially confirmation, of events on the volcano. On May 18, for example, one respondent noted,

> There was no confirmation of the amateur report [the radio message from a ham operator in the path of the blast—who was killed immediately after sending his report]. We knew there was a major event but there were no details—We did not know what we had. "A major event and we'll get back to you," was the report from Vancouver . . . The news on TV and radio was actually our confirmation, we still didn't have details.

It is hard to avoid the picture of the DES standing in isolation, waiting for confirmation, while all around them information was flowing. Aside from the amateur's report, which they received immediately, and the report given them soon after on the open line to the Vancouver headquarters, there were warnings from the National Weather Service, the FAA was tracking the cloud on their radar scopes, the National Guard was in communication with the USGS, a staff member of the State Division of Geology and Earth Resources had witnessed the event first hand while flying over the volcano, and most people in Cowlitz and Clark counties could see it. One suspects that the confusion in the DES was not from lack of knowledge that the event was occurring, but from lack of knowledge of specific effects that would have to be dealt with. In addition, other respondents suggested that a lack of leadership was a primary factor in the DES failure. Because the information on effects was in the Blue Book (except for the lateral blast), the DES helplessness may have been largely from their own lack of preparation, in understanding the USGS information and understanding their own plan (which was based on the USGS information). One other problem the DES people experienced was the delay of "one-half to two hours" while the USGS analyzed the information. To compensate for this delay, the DES personnel felt they had to rely on "unofficial" information sources, such as the Newport Observatory, the University of Washington seismologists, and the ham radio network.

Other problems faced by state respondents included the "guarded" nature of the scientists' statements—"They weren't willing to make firm statements about the nature of the eruption." Another problem was noted by a member of the governor's staff: "We had to take immediate action based on sketchy information. The governor took precipitous action on April 29, to close the Red Zone." This comment relates to another possible area of communications or leadership breakdown. There was no dearth of information between March 20 and April 29. The Survey geologists had been carrying on intensive studies and Crandell and Mullineaux had been doing all they could to transmit information; Crandell even met with the governor. To call an action taken nearly a month after the USFS and surrounding counties had established restricted areas "immediate," or "precipitous," may be stretching the point.

Most of the problems the local officials had were in obtaining sufficient information. Before May 18, several people reported difficulty with the state information system, for example, " . . . the state DES sent out a teletype asking what actions would be taken and I sent a note saying the action taken would depend on the answers to our questions. They referred us to the bulletin which we already had."

Others said they had no information at all, other than news reports, or that there was a "six to seven hour delay." Another official received most of the USGS information but felt it was speculative and hard to believe at first—

> Before [May 18], there was scientific speculation about what was going to happen. The nature of society is to be less sensitive to speculation. They were geologists who deal about happenings over long periods of time. We had to see it to believe it; to believe it would happen in our lifetime. After the eruption every speculation that the geologists had made was believed.

Some 42 percent of those having no problems with the information cited the quality of the USGS warnings. The most useful USGS warnings were the Blue Book, the hazard map, and (most commonly) personal contacts with the geologists. As one local official noted, "The USGS information was outstanding. Whatever they told us came true. They were pretty well right on from the beginning. Without them we'd have been in really tough shape."

Some felt that although the Survey information was very good, it was difficult for the general public to believe it. One person who attended one of the early meetings with the geologists thought, "If all the people had been sitting at that meeting, they wouldn't have been near the mountain. The breach is in public dissemination of information."

This problem—convincing the public—was seen to affect the ability of the agencies to maintain the Red Zone. As one official put it,

> I felt that Dr. Mullineaux and Dr. Crandell supplied adequate truthful, matter-of-fact information. The difficulty of putting some of it into actual practice was in establishing credibility with the citizenry. For example, the Red Zone was based on scientific information, but people put on great pressure to get into their cabins. On May 17, the Washington State Patrol took a group in, and on May 18 at 10:00 a.m., another group of cabin owners was scheduled to go in. The explosion established credibility.

There was a wide variety of answers to the question about the kind of information most useful in decision making. The largest proportion of answers, about one-third, thought the most important information was about the potential effects and their nature. Several respondents emphasized that the information must be understandable. For example, one official asked for "a lay explanation of possible scenarios, simply stated. I would like to have known that a cataclysm was possible. I need an idea of the range of possibilities."

Some of those concerned with emergency response actions felt they needed a good idea of the nature of the risks but no demands on how to deal with them. One military respondent answered that he wanted to know

> what the problems are, not what they want or what they think they want . . . . The eruption itself was not seen as a real problem. Ash-fall, mudflows and pyroclastic flows are problems we could solve. With the USGS—they told us all the things that could happen and we wrote a plan. Our plan was built on a worse case scenario plus 50%.

Several respondents were also concerned that the scientists were not giving enough information on what could happen in the future, spending more time explaining past events than predicting future possibilities. One official specified that the warning should

> speak to the potential at a given time for a given eruption, and what type of eruption—not give a historical account of what has happened. For example, the bulge report—if you know the growth rate, somebody should be able to predict at least when there would be a slide.

Another felt this hazard potential could be expressed in some sort of rating system, similar to the fire hazard ratings. This type of rating would give some idea of the degree of danger at any given time. An additional point was made about consistency in giving warnings to the public and the government officials:

> The information that was supplied was adequate. If I were to ask them to improve on anything—they were very reluctant to talk about what could actually occur. They soft-pedalled it with the public and the press when they were more matter-of-fact with government people.

There were several other comments about the geologists' lack of consistency. One noted that, at first, "they were aggressive and then backed off." This official felt that attitudinal change caused economic hardship before the eruption. Another respondent thought the geologists' assertions lacked force: "These people who are studying volcanoes are inclined to qualify their remarks to the point where people don't take them seriously. They should have a more positive approach."

This cautiousness in interpreting the risks to the public may have resulted in the increased pressure on the Red Zone. On the other hand, the odds of catastrophe were so low and the risks so incomprehensible, it was hard for many officials to believe anything would happen.

The time of eruption was another major concern. The respondents were aware that eruption prediction is difficult, but those especially concerned with emergency responses such as evacuation or search and rescue need to know when an eruption is imminent:

> The search and rescue business needs real time guesses as to blast hazards; direction, velocity, type of eject, range of blast, and a reasonable guess on time. This should be as close to the volcanic eruption as possible, so we can go to alert. It should be within a few hours.

The search and rescue people also needed to know where they should *not* go because of the danger. This knowledge was especially important to them while operating close to the volcano immediately after the May 18 eruption.

Other people also stressed the importance of charts and maps of potential effects, citing the usefulness of those prepared by the geologists. One need mentioned was good, up-to-date base maps to locate potential hazards or affected areas. According to one respondent, "The best the USGS had was the Gifford Pinchot National Forest map, sometimes they had worse."

There was a variety of other kinds of scientific information thought to be important, including wind and plume trajectories, changes in conditions, health effects, or type of eruption. Some respondents also wanted to know about emergency actions: what type of protective measures would work, possible need for evacuation, where to obtain equipment, and what was being done by others.

About one-fourth the respondents to this question felt what was provided by the USGS was the type of information they needed in a hazard warning. One state official was "impressed" by the "great lengths" the geologists went to, including the early meeting to explain the warning system, the Blue Book, the hazard notification, and even the meeting about Mount Baker. A local respondent in Cowlitz County also praised the USGS information: "The information provided by the USGS could not be improved upon. I felt we had all the information the USGS had and immediate notice when conditions changed."

There were other indications that the information was not well distributed. For example, one Army officer commented on the Blue Book:

> I would like to have seen the Blue Book by Mid-April. I'm not sure Ft. Lewis got copies. Whenever there is an agency in an area that might be faced with disasters, it should be placed on the distribution list. We have seen nothing on volcanoes or floods.

Some question arises about the existence of a distribution list at all. There is no indication that any adequate records were kept on who received copies of the Blue Book or, more importantly, who did not. Several hundred copies of this document were distributed at meetings, but our survey only found fifty people who saw the book. Very importantly, more control must be exercised in the distribution of information, to ensure that those who may need the information receive it.

To summarize the role of the USGS information in decision making, many receiving it thought it was useful. About one-third of the respondents to this question reported problems with the warnings; these included the slow speed in transmitting or confirming information and the tendency of the geologists to qualify their statements. The greatest problems with the information were reported by the Washington Department of Emergency Services. Many felt the USGS did well and provided all the information needed. The information most people wanted was about the nature of risks and possible effects, where the affected areas were likely to be, and something on the potential and timing of eruptions. Others wanted the geologists to be more positive, more consistent, and more understandable. Apparently, the USGS should have planned the distribution of their warning ahead of time to make sure those needing the necessary information received it.

PROBLEMS IN THE MOUNT ST. HELENS RESPONSE

More than half the total number of respondents (53 percent) reported problems in responding to the Mount St. Helens emergency. According to table 23, the most common problem was lack of information, cited by a majority of the officials. Also significant were lack of funds and equipment or facilities. About one-third reported problems with interagency coordination and manpower. Lack of public and news media cooperation were least mentioned; however, both were thought to be problems by at least one-fifth of the sample. As might be expected, different agencies and levels of government experienced all the above problems in different ways, and it is useful to examine each in greater detail.

Lack of information was a significant problem at all levels of government, but most especially for FEMA and the local officials of the east side. The FEMA respondents worked closely with the USGS, but felt they needed more practical information about volcanic impacts on health, machinery, and the environment, as well as how to cope with these effects. They also reported trouble obtaining the necessary information to process state and local requests for assistance and financial reimbursement. For the east side local people, there was no adequate warning before May 18. On May 18, the first warning of ashfall was when the ash fell. After May 18, communications were slow; no one knew the effects of ash, or how to clean it up. Other agencies were strongly affected by the lack of information

Table 23. Problems in the Mount St. Helens Response (130)

Percent Yes

	Total	USFS	FEMA	Other Federal	Wash. DES	Other State	Local Officials West	Local Officials East	Business & Volunteers
Lack of Information	59	56	80	46	54	44	55	79	62
Lack of Equipment or Facilities	49	67	0	22	92	44	72	58	23
Lack of Funds	48	0	20	25	85	61	61	53	23
Lack of Coordination with Other Agencies	41	33	60	50	39	28	55	53	54
Lack of Manpower	37	11	0	8	77	39	50	47	8
Lack of Public Cooperation	25	67	20	15	69	33	22	5	15
Problems with the News Media	20	22	0	31	31	33	33	0	31

as well. Poor communications between agencies, slow information transmission, lack of adequate pre-eruption information for planning, lack of analysis or interpretation of data, inconsistent or contradictory information, and lack of information on eruption impacts (especially ash) and how to deal with them were all important problems related to information.

Lack of equipment or facilities was the second most important problem. The officials of the state DES were most handicapped by this problem. The DES headquarters was not adequate for an emergency operations center, and the communications systems were inferior and subject to failure. Local officials were also hampered by the lack of equipment, especially those on the west side. Mentioned as important were equipment for ash cleanup, personal protection, transportation, communications, and replacements for equipment damaged by ash. Another problem, potentially important for future urban disasters, was water supply equipment, as seen by the trouble obtaining a water purifier for Toutle. In general, the most important equipment needs for other agencies were communication equipment, masks for personal protection, and equipment for remote and aerial surveillance of the volcano and the restricted area.

Closely parallel to lack of equipment were problems with funding. Money was a special problem for state agencies, especially the DES. Many other state agencies also felt financial strain. The state of Washington did not have adequate funds to pay for its own emergency response. Outlays for overtime, equipment, travel, or living expenses affected the regular state operating budget, especially when an alert posture had to be maintained for an extended period of time. A similar problem was faced by the local governments—the sudden emergency depleted their normal operating budgets, leaving basic services operating in the red. The slow speed of federal reimbursement, the cumbersome eligibility rules, and the extra work and expense of preparing and justifying requests all contributed to the problem.

Coordination with other agencies was a big problem, especially for the federal and local respondents. FEMA experienced the greatest trouble with the state agencies after they refused to move from Olympia to Vancouver. FEMA's coordination with the locals was affected by this state bottleneck, as well as by an inadequate field staff borrowed from other federal agencies. Other federal personnel involved in the search and rescue also found coordination difficult between the local sheriffs, the state-directed National Guard and Civil Air Patrol, and the Army, USFS, and FAA. The lack of clear-cut, continuous lines of authority throughout the SAR led to some confusion and took time to iron out. The USFS also had difficulty organizing the state, federal, local, and private agencies in their planning process; but after May 18 these organizations saw the need for cooperation and worked together better.

Coordination problems on the local level involved both state and federal agencies. These criticisms seemed especially directed at the state, citing a lack of warning and later of information. Communications with the governor and other state agencies were poor; many local officials felt they were ignored. Complaints about federal coordination problems were mainly directed at FEMA, citing red tape and the slow speed of processing request for assistance. The business and volunteer organizations experienced problems coordinating with local officials; apparently lack of knowledge about the capabilities of many of these organizations left them ignored or included only as an afterthought.

Manpower was a major problem for the state DES and the local agencies. The DES was understaffed and could not have operated at all without aid from other state agencies as well as from emergency service people from the other Pacific Coast states and provinces. The lack of trained manpower was especially acute; many specialized personnel were forced to stay continuously at work until reduced to exhaustion. Another deficiency at the DES was in people with geologic training to interpret the information from the USGS and seismologists. The DES failed, however, to take advantage of the geological expertise available in the state government and universities. Lack of trained personnel was also a problem cited by local officials. The public response was described in superlative terms on both sides of the Cascades, with large numbers of volunteers offering their help; however the task of coordinating these volunteers taxed the trained staff, taking them away from other duties.

Problems with public cooperation were primarily experienced by the DES and USFS, mainly over enforcing the Red Zone. Violations of the restricted zone around the mountain were common both before and after the May 18 eruption. Arguments over where the boundaries should be and who should be allowed access, in addition to the effort of chasing violators, consumed a lot of time. Perhaps the ultimate example of this difficulty would be the demonstration by Red Zone cabin owners, which resulted in their being escorted on May 17 into what became the blast zone the following day. For most of the other agencies, public cooperation was considered exceptionally good. This was especially the case on the east side, where the isolated communities pulled together and helped neighbors and strangers alike.

There was no question asked specifically about problems with the news media, but it was a recurring theme when the respondents were asked about other problems. Newspeople were especially troublesome to local officials in Cowlitz County as well as to state agencies and federal personnel working in the search and rescue. The main problems mentioned were interference with emergency activities, violations of the Red Zone, distortion of information in news reports, and transmission of rumors without verification. Many respondents differentiated between local and network news agencies, suggesting that the coverage of the local press was good and that excesses were the products of major network personnel. Local news agencies in Cowlitz and Kittitas counties were especially praised. At least part of the reason for news media problems was the lack of experience among many of the officials in dealing with news coverage of national interest. For the most part, the agencies with public information officers had no problems with the press. FEMA was especially careful to maintain a very large, well-manned, and well-financed public information office. They felt they had a very good relationship with the news media.

LESSONS LEARNED

A question on which almost all respondents agreed was, "Did you learn anything from your experience in dealing with this eruption which you think could be helpful in dealing with a future one?" Of the 117 who answered this question, 115 (98 percent) said "yes," a rare instance of agreement in such a diverse group. The "yes" was often followed up with such remarks as "No doubt about it," "absolutely," or "Oh boy! I could give you a whole long list of things." One of those who said "no" may be considered an example of "the exception which proves the rule," for he obviously considered the event a learning experience when he added: "I learned the lesson in previous emergencies—always think in terms of 'what if'—always anticipate system break-up." A question everyone answers the same is not the most useful in a survey, but in this case it does once more underline the extraordinary nature of the event.

More interesting are the responses to the second portion of the question, asking specifically what they had learned. Table 24 indicates our classification of the open-ended replies to this question. The most important single lesson learned by our respondents was the importance of planning. This was mentioned in one form or another by respondents from all major groups interviewed. The answers ranged from very general statements about the need for planning to more specific comments about the type of planning required for particular agencies or people. At the general level were such statements as:

Contingency plans must be kept up-to-date and written on everything.

People who have the responsibility learned they have to get organized more quickly.

Appraise and accept the worst case and provide staff and funds to be ready for it.

Table 24. Lessons Learned from Dealing with the Eruption (Percent of 115 Respondents)

Lessons Learned	Total	USGS[a]	USFS	FEMA	Other Federal Agencies	State DES[b]	Other State Agencies	Business & Volunteers	Local Officials West	Local Officials East
1) Importance of Planning	39	88	67	40	44	57	19	15	36	30
2) Information and Communication Needs	36	37	56	100	38	64	18	8	36	30
3) Experience	22	13	22	20	11	36	10	15	32	35
4) How to Deal with a Volcano	15	38	11	40	6	0	5	8	9	45
5) The Power of a Volcano	12	0	44	20	11	7	19	8	14	0
6) Sense of Pride in Coping	9	13	33	0	16	7	5	0	14	10
7) Other Agency Roles	9	0	22	0	17	0	0	8	9	20

[a] Also includes three other geologists, two from the state government, the other from a university.
[b] Includes a representative from the Oregon Department of Emergency Services.

. . . should be able to breeze through other situations if ready for the worse case.

Prior planning is essential. Without preplanning you're just playing catch up ball and it doesn't work.

Planning was seen as essential at all levels of government. This can be illustrated by comments of respondents dealing with the national level:

Volcanoes that could be potentially hazardous in the near future should be studied; hazard zones should already be mapped out from a geological standpoint;

the regional level:

Don't expect Mount Hood to blow, but it's no harm to have a plan;

the community level:

Mount St. Helens will be there for some time. Communities will have to plan for that—how to design their public facilities, equipment modification and maintenance, will have to budget for emergency response;

and also:

. . . have to set up plans even on an individual level.

More specific suggestions involving planning were the need for:

Memorandums of understanding of fiscal responsibilities in advance.

enough support staff at the beginning

airspace management

SAR missions have to be ready to deploy immediately.

immediate funding at a level adequate to evaluate and deal with the emergency.

A USGS organization ready to respond to a volcanic emergency.

These planning needs emerged even in comments basically positive about various aspects of the response:

> This was the largest search-and-rescue response this nation or any nation has had. The initial response, although it was successful, was so because of the talents of the people involved. There should have been an initial response plan.

In planning for a potential disaster, several stressed the; importance of a clear authority structure and coordination among agencies. Typical comments of these types were:

> Need to have one agency in charge of the total situation, like FEMA.

> More effort has to be given to understanding and developing coordinations among various levels of government. Need to clarify who has the authority, who is going to do what.

A second major category of replies to the question on lessons learned focused on the importance of information and its effective communication. A point emphasized over and over was the need for a centralized information center. This was seen as important at the local level within small communities, as in the remark:

> The primary thing in any incident of any magnitude is the need for a mini-emergency operating center where powers meet and make decisions.

It was also recognized as essential at the broadest level:

> The action of FEMA is gathering technical and public affairs people from all agencies into one place was very effective. This should be done in any natural disaster situation where you are dealing with unknowns (or the unusual).

Why a centralized information center is considered valuable may be illustrated by a series of quotations from our respondents:

> It leads to better exchange.

> face-to-face contact . . . to speed the process.

> separate from normal business routine.

> to speak with one voice.

The idea of "speaking with one voice" was important in public information. Several people discovered that "the public does pay heed to information being provided," and if public information is uncoordinated and inconsistent, it will not be useful: "The public will quickly learn to distrust information sources at the first sign of conflicting information." The Mount St. Helens experience was especially important for learning to handle the news media. Several comments referred to the activities of the media and how to control them:

> Any time you have a disaster there's an overwhelming desire by the media to get the news first before the competition. They cause a distraction to the point where it disrupts operations.

> The media should be restricted to certain areas and certain interviews when commanders are available but spokesmen should provide the information immediately.

The next lesson in order of importance was the general experience and confidence resulting from being "tested under fire." Many people looked at the emergency as a "learning experience—we're better able to deal with future ones." The actual operation provided practice and also allowed people to evaluate their actions: "Like any new experience, the more you deal with it the better you get. We also feel more comfortable with our decisions as it is borne out that they are correct."

The confidence gained from having acted successfully in the emergency was also important, as seen in such statements as "the overall pattern would be the same for responding to other eruptions." Part of the confidence also relates to the feeling that a volcanic eruption is now a known situation instead of fraught with unknowns. This knowledge adds to the power of the simple assertion of one respondents: "We know what to do now."

Also learned was how to deal with a volcano in terms of prediction: "We've very definitely learned about prediction in a geological sense"; emergency management: "We've learned we have to deal with it in terms of an events structure—a flexible structure but still something for a starting point and quick response"; and planning: "You should prepare to have facilities big enough. Don't hesitate to manage it like anything else. You must be prepared for the worst." The actual experience also provided officials with firsthand knowledge of the power of a volcano and the effects an eruption can have on people and their environment. For some it was a lesson in vulnerability: "There's no question—until we forget about it—that government agencies and the public are aware that we are vulnerable to natural hazards."

Some were particularly aware of specific problems to be especially prepared for:

Prepare plans and damage estimates for a 20-30 mile radius.

We have a lot of respect for what a mudflow can do and what a tremendous task it was to clean up.

It was our first experience with mental health which affected such a large portion of the state.

Take precautions for ash fallout in future planning, and damage to equipment.

. . . effects of very slight amounts of ash not recognizable in the geological strata.

Another important gain was a sense of pride in personal and organizational abilities in responding to emergencies:

We learned the tremendous capabilities we have in this district to respond to emergencies.

People responded so nicely and were so disciplined. We were well served by our supervisors in Denver and Reston.

Finally, the multi-agency response provided lessons on how to operate in cooperation with other organizations. Officials on all levels were better aware of other roles and how to coordinate with them: "The areas of responsibility for various organizations are better defined than before."

Especially important was the sense of confidence in other agencies gained from working closely with each other, often for the first time. Illustrations of this can be seen in such statements as:

The USGS—how good they are. FEMA . . . had some super good people.

I'm really impressed by the professionalism of the FEMA public information officers.

FUTURE EXPECTATIONS AND PLANS

As noted previously, most respondents expected the volcano to erupt again in the near future (these expectations, in the summer of 1980, were fully justified). As shown in table 25, half the respondents were unwilling to hazard a guess about the length of time the eruptions would continue. Of those who did, most thought the activity would last more than ten years.

Table 25.   Expected Time of Continued Eruptions

	Percent Respondents
0–1 Year	3
More Than 1–5 Years	5
More Than 5–10 Years	6
More Than 10 Years	37
Don't Know	50

Nearly everyone (96.5 percent) felt they were prepared for future eruptions. Important to this feeling of confidence were a number of factors, including the knowledge and experience gained from the previous eruptions, more personnel and equipment to deal with future emergencies, the presence of the Red Zone, and the existence of tested, workable plans for warning and response. There was still some uncertainty, however, and a feeling that they could be faced with the unexpected.

Some people felt there was little that could be done to prepare for future eruptions. Some felt helpless and others thought it was easiest to react to problems as they appeared, an attitude expressed in the following comment, "Tell me what type of an eruption and how big, and I'll work on it." Most respondents, however, thought there were positive steps that could be taken to prepare for future possibilities, and they were taking them.

Refining and developing contingency plans were the most common types of preparatory activities. Some respondents emphasized "fine-tuning" their response plans based on their actual experience, and adjusting for contingencies that were unexpected before May 18. Several respondents felt continued planning was necessary to maintain a high-level response posture:

Right now we are about as razor-sharp in our system as we can get; to maintain it will not be easy if a long period elapses between activity.

We are trying to ensure help in planning, to institutionalize plans. We must try to keep a state of readiness even if the volcano quiets.

Improving information flow and coordination between agencies and levels of government was also stressed. The working relationships developed during the major eruptions were considered important, especially between agencies with little previous experience with one another. One FEMA respondent pointed out: "We have established working relationships and the confidence of agencies which may have been skeptical of us prior to May 18."

Plans for expanding cooperation between agencies include formalizing working relationships through interagency agreements as well as installing a reliable communications network through dedicated telephone lines and a common interagency radio network. Some people have also set about simplifying the chain of command by dealing directly with field units. One local official stated, for example: "We're beginning to coordinate with state agencies here in the county to see what resources we have available to use and to get agreements locally, since it [the chain of command] doesn't work as it is supposed to."

A significant part of the planning involves mechanisms for disseminating public information. One official emphasized that need by saying,

The people's curiosity has to be satisfied. There is a need for state or local government to step in and give public information. There should be an appropriation either to an existing department, or to create a new agency specifically devoted to information on Mount St. Helens.

Provisions for emergency public information have been added to existing contingency plans, or expanded in some cases. FEMA has established a long-term, standby public information facility at Vancouver, ready to expand operations if necessary. To provide information about the hazard and satisfy curiosity about the volcano, the USFS has established several visitor centers.

Better facilities and equipment were being acquired to support future volcano response actions. The USFS respondents were working on a permanent volcano watch and emergency operations center with a permanent, trained staff assigned specifically to Mount St. Helens. Most agencies were gathering special equipment such as face masks, respirators, radios, water trucks, generators, or emergency supplies, and locating it in strategic places. Others also stressed modifying equipment to cope with ash, for example, redesigning some ash filter systems. One utility with facilities close to Mount St. Helens planned to automate its operations so that risk to personnel is reduced.

Others have insisted that continued maintenance of the Red Zone is essential. Several state officials reported recommendations for stronger land use and access restrictions in hazard areas. Related to these recommendations is the importance of planning for increased tourism, a concern expressed by many state and local officials. Some business respondents emphasized promotion of Mount St. Helens as an attraction; but many others were concerned with protecting sightseers from the hazards, keeping them from interfering with logging and recovery operations, and keeping them under control. The areas close to the volcano will have to expect some social change as tourism increases and lumbering declines (at least temporarily) in economic importance. One law enforcement officer hinted at this change when he noted: "Policing tourists has to be done in a different way. I'm trying to prepare my people for that."

CONCLUSIONS AND RECOMMENDATIONS _____

It is important in coming to any conclusions about what happened at Mount St. Helens in 1980, to bear in mind that an extraordinary event occurred. There is little doubt it will rank as one of the most significant geological events of the century. Beyond that, it was an event of major human significance. All the people in the broad region directly affected by it will remember and hearken back to it for the rest of their lives. For most Americans and many people elsewhere, it will serve as a symbol of the awesome power of nature. As a symbol, it should prove useful for the current crop of natural hazards professionals. The Mount St. Helens example can help make concrete and tangible the meaning of a high-risk, low-probability event. Anyone who reads newspapers or magazines or watches television will be able to recall dramatic examples of the excellent photographic and video coverage of the May 18 eruption and its aftermath; for Mount St. Helens was a fantastic media event, whose climactic eruption lived up to and even went far beyond the promise of the exciting, precursory rumbling, shaking, steaming, and swelling.

The information provided by the warning and response to Mount St. Helens offers a wealth of material for improving emergency service systems and their connections with such scientific agencies as the USGS. After thinking about the successes and failures east and west of the Cascades, we picked for discussion in this chapter a number of issues we consider worthy of further thought and research. The discussion begins at the most broad and general level and proceeds toward specific suggestions for a few individual agencies. At the broadest level, we will consider the psychological impact on our respondents, profound because of the magnitude of the eruption and the perceived efficacy of their actions. We emphasize the element of luck in the Mount St. Helens eruption to illustrate how little control we have over such events and to emphasize the importance of planning, which also stood out as a strong lesson of this emergency. A key issue in planning and response is the need for a clear line of authority in the emergency response system. A more specific look at the emergency services system in the eruption suggests a number of problems on all levels—federal, state, and local. Another set of issues revolves around closure and access to hazard zones. The role of public information and the news media is especially important in hazard situations with many unknowns. Finally, the roles and responsibilities of the USGS require further examination. These issues will be discussed in the following pages.

A PEAK EXPERIENCE

As we interviewed our respondents we could see that this event was indeed a peak experience for them because of their intensity and feelings of awe. This intensity is also seen in the tremendous public response in the disaster areas as people engaged in clean-up activities. Furthermore, a corresponding governmental response was shown by the degree to which huge and powerful governmental agencies set aside their traditional rivalries to cooperate very effectively in attending a task too big for any one of them to manage. Individuals, by virtue of their position at the center of activities at critical periods, unhesitatingly put in the hours and effort necessary to do the best job they could. This was true of sheriffs and citizens at the local level, of DES employees at the state level, and of the Forest Service and the USGS officials at the federal level, as well as of many others.

The magnitude of the eruption and its effects demonstrated the depth and capabilities of many governmental agencies, as well as the resiliency and spirit of the people in the region. The seismologists and USGS officials quickly and competently moved in people and instruments to monitor the volcano and provide hazard information. The Forest Service was very effective in setting up the Emergency Operations Center, taking over the leadership role to coordinate contingency planning, monitoring the mountain, and public information activities. FEMA was impressive in taking over the emergency management activities, in coordinating all agencies, and in enlarging and extending the public information functions. The Weather Service provided almost instantaneous warnings for floods and ash plumes. Many of our respondents paid tribute to the skills of their new colleagues from other agencies in the common task. Both east and west of the Cascades, the public and public officials alike praised each other for the spirit with which they responded to the enormous multidimensional clean-up task.

That the overwhelming majority of respondents felt their actions were effective no doubt contributed to the esprit de corps which developed. The psychological and social effects of a "job well done" under long hours of intense pressure might be worth investigating further. The strong public response to disasters as seen on the east side, could also be investigated and put to use. Strong positive effects were evident in the Mount St. Helens eruption. The involvement was intense enough that virtually all our respondents were convinced they had learned from the experience.

A LITTLE BIT OF LUCK

The consequences of the Mount St. Helens eruption could have been much worse were it not for a little bit of luck. We have started off basically on a positive note because we were very impressed by the effectiveness of the response to the Mount St. Helens eruption by most individuals and agencies we contacted. However, to learn from the experience, it is also necessary to examine in more detail some of the problems, and in an event of that magnitude there are bound to be many. These will be considered below as we provide some general suggestions for dealing with such a low-probability, high-risk event, as well as some specific suggestions for particular agencies. Our main concern was with the USGS and their warning, so we devote more attention to them than the others. But first, we wish to point out a few fortuitous features of the Mount St. Helens eruption which may not be true for the next such event.

It was indeed fortunate that Mount St. Helens was one of the two volcanoes (the other was Mount Baker) in the contiguous forty-eight states for which the USGS had completed a hazard assessment, based on a detailed study of the geologic evidence of past eruptions. This study was not entirely a matter of luck, but a result of careful consideraton by the Survey geologists regarding which volcanoes were of greatest potential danger and deserving of high priority in the allocation of their scarce resources. Hopefully, the rest of the volcanoes in the country will soon be subjected to the same careful research. Without the USGS data, the warning activities would necessarily have been less authoritative, more speculative, and undoubtedly less effective.

A second major element of luck was the timing of the May 18 eruption. If it had been any day but Sunday the death toll would have been higher, for, in spite of all the warnings and the precursory activity, many people were still working in the area on weekdays. An even closer brush with death was encountered by the homeowners and their law enforcement escort, scheduled to go into the blast zone at 10:00 that morning (not to mention the group that went in the day before). The relatively low death toll was due greatly to luck rather than entirely a result of good planning. However, without the amazing "battle of the barricades"—to keep the curious out—an enormous death toll would have been possible, even probable, for crowds of people converged on the area, drawn by the excitement.

That one of the greatest volcanic eruptions in United States history (second only to Mount Katmai, Alaska, in 1912) came from a volcano in the middle of a sparsely populated forest was also lucky. The closest city was Morton, 25 miles north, which suffered under a load of ash—rather insignificant compared to the blast effects a few miles to the south. Both Mounts Rainier and Hood are volcanoes close to more heavily populated areas, with greater potential for catastrophe. The direction of the blast was also lucky, moving to the north rather than west toward Kelso or south into the reservoirs along the Lewis River.

There were other instances of luck as well. The season and the stage of growth of the winter wheat enabled the crop to survive, and even thrive, under the conditions imposed by the ash. The low free crystalline silica content of the ash kept the danger of lung damage and silicosis to a minimum. A different wind direction on May 18 could have dumped tons of ash on Portland, Olympia, or Seattle instead of on areas to the east. It is sobering to consider, for example, the difficulties of communication, evacuation, and search and rescue had the ash gone west instead of east (as it did on May 25 and June 12).

The SAR personnel themselves must have felt quite lucky that there were no crashes with other searchers or sightseers before a centralized control was established for the operation. No doubt other people involved in the emergency could come up with other examples of luck, including the bad luck of the people caught in the eruption. The main point is that the toll of death and damages could have been much higher with minor chance variations beyond human control. Given that such events are largely beyond human control, we should try to make the most of the opportunities we do have to minimize the damage.

THE IMPORTANCE OF PLANNING

Good information, warnings, and contingency planning are essential for effective responses to natural hazards. The idea that nothing can be done to prepare for volcanic disasters or earthquakes or other major hazards is foolish and contrary to the evidence provided by Mount St. Helens. When an eruption like May 18 occurs, it is of such an instant, overwhelming magnitude that no one can simply "react" to it. Those agencies that responded to the Mount St. Helens emergency with some degree of success were those agencies that had planned in advance. True, there were some unforeseen circumstances, but those problems could be attended to without the pressure of other problems that were foreseen.

In a disaster situation where quick reactions are necessary, people and agencies tend to rely on what and who they know; thus, the unknown ash clean-up problem was best handled by analogy with a blizzard or major snowstorm, and local officials contacted people they happened to know elsewhere for needed equipment and supplies. Improvisation, with approaches applied when dealing with snow, enabled those in ashfall areas to eventually surmount the problem. Without proper information and warning the task is more difficult and chances have to be taken which may not always turn out right. Thus, for example, the Washington State Patrol lost a great number of vehicles in their attempt to deal with the emergency situation which could have been avoided by better information and planning before the event.

When relying on habitual patterns, things go well only so long as the new situation remains analogous to the familiar. When unanticipated demands arise, the effectiveness of the habitual patterns diminish. Fortunately, the Forest Service had a good model to follow in responding to the volcanic eruption. Their fire fighting experience stood them in good stead and everyone benefited from the leadership they provided. However, problems began to arise as the magnitude and complexity of the volcanic eruption extended beyond any previous experience, requiring instant improvisation for novel situations. At this limit of previous experience and planning, problems began to show up. Similarly, the USGS did a superlative job in scientific investigation and monitoring geological events. Only when demands were placed on them to extend beyond the point of previous experience, into the social domain, did their scientific excellence provide no guidelines and improvisation was not necessarily always successful.

The need for planning was one of the strongest lessons learned by those who played responsible roles in dealing with the eruption. Planning was seen as important at all levels, from the national to the regional, local, and even individual level. Thousands of people gained experience in the Mount St. Helens eruptions and learned many important lessons which should not be lost. These plans, ideas, and adaptations should be written up into contingency plans for every conceivable type of occupation, agency, or group likely to be involved in another eruption of Mount St. Helens. Of potentially greater significance would be the value of such plans for people in equivalent positions in other areas subject to volcanic eruptions, or in other hazard areas with analogous potential problems (such as earthquakes).

As hazard maps are developed for other Cascade volcanoes (as in the case now for Mounts Rainier, Shasta, and Hood), the warnings would probably be more meaningful if responsible personnel at all levels were exposed to contingency plans developed by counterparts who experienced the Mount St. Helens eruptions. Better yet would be the arrangement of meetings or workshops at which the counterpart describes the experience and reasons why various items were written into the contingency plans. For example, engineers involved in clean-up operations could explain their experience to other engineers who potentially could be affected by a similar event.

There are special problems in planning a multi-organizational response. The questions of jurisdiction and "turf" have to be worked out in advance and in cooperation with all agencies likely to become involved. These issues become especially important where a succession of new actors comes in and has to merge with an already operating response. The search and rescue operation provides an example of what can happen. As successive groups of state and federal, civilian and military support arrived, the original organization set up by the sheriffs and Forest Service was unable to assimilate these groups, and the system verged on chaos. Planners should be aware that large disasters can bring in new actors as new resources become needed. For dealing with such contingencies, an emergency response system has to be flexible, with clear lines of authority and procedures for incorporating more agencies. Thinking about such contingencies is a natural function for emergency services organizations, and they should be involved.

Another point to be made about planning is that the time to think about the worst case is before it occurs. Very few agencies were prepared for the worst possible situation, assuming (correctly) that the odds of its occurrence were low; however, it is not wise to equate low probability with impossibility. The magnitude of the May 18 eruption was of enormous proportions, but other volcanoes have done worse (e.g., the prehistoric Mount Mazama eruption that formed Crater Lake). One common myth we heard in our interviews was that a high magnitude disaster is so overwhelming no one can prepare for it. The success, however, of the agencies that were prepared for Mount St. Helens belies that myth. It takes little more effort to consider the worst case as one of the contingencies in a plan. This planning need not involve massive stockpiling of emergency supplies or funds; but, developing priority lists for operations, plans for expanding operations, or lists of whom to contact for help would create some sense of control if the "worst case" happens again.

Some thought must also be given to the role of FEMA in disaster planning. A high magnitude disaster is usually declared a national disaster, in which case FEMA is placed in charge. Yet many people in that agency believe their mandate is to concentrate on disaster response and recovery, not planning. In the case of Mount St. Helens, the FEMA role in the planning process was primarily as a spectator rather than as a leader. After the disaster declaration, the transition to FEMA control was a source of anxiety to the USFS, of problems with the state DES over how to coordinate, and of anger to the local officials who had little experience in federal regulations. The transition might have been much smoother if FEMA had taken a more active role in preparation, had it been better acquainted with the personnel and roles of other agencies, had the other agencies known what FEMA would do, or had the local officials been better briefed on federal assistance requirements.

THE NEED FOR A CLEAR CHAIN OF AUTHORITY

One important task in planning is to determine how the various agencies will cooperate. The Mount St. Helens emergency provides a good example of what can happen if coordination is not established immediately. The federal and state support activities operated out of two different headquarters, with communications hampered by overloaded phonelines and a certain feeling of animosity. Neither group seemed well linked with the local people east and west of the Cascades; and so, local officials had problems coordinating with others in their own or neighboring counties. The SAR operation around the mountain was in a state of confusion for the first few days before some agreements were ironed out.

The most successful coordinating effort seemed to be in Vancouver, starting with the USFS contingency planning efforts and later supplemented by FEMA. The Forest Service officials were already familiar with many state, local, and lumber company officials in the area, and drawing them together was relatively easy. There was, however, a bias in favor of local officials known by the USFS, for example, the county sheriffs were drawn into the planning while the county DES directors were not (except for one county where the sheriff was also the DES director). After the national disaster declaration of May 21, the federal coordinating officer established his headquarters at Vancouver. Immediately, a Disaster Field Office was established there, with enough facilities to support representatives from the agencies involved in the response. This act—putting all major federal operating agencies "under one roof"—was felt by the respondents there to considerably aid coordination. State agencies were also invited to send representaives, but staffing at Vancouver seemed hampered by state-federal friction.

THE ROLE OF THE EMERGENCY SERVICES AGENCIES

In general, our interviews suggest that evaluation of the various emergency services agencies were variable—FEMA seemed to be good, the Washington DES was not good, and the county DES's ranged from good to bad. As a case study of the emergency services system at work, the Mount St. Helens response enables some observations and fruitful avenues for thought and research.

Despite its "youth," the Federal Emergency Management Agency appears to have in its ranks some highly trained, experienced professionals, whose management of the later part of the volcano response impressed most people coming into contact with them. FEMA was particularly lauded about the way its people took control, establishing a central coordinating position but having the restraint to let other agencies continue in their response activities with little interference. The information coordination effort of FEMA was impressive; the technical information network was innovative, and the public information operation was the largest ever for a disaster. Part of FEMA's success was based upon their use of a general disaster program, in essence a plan that has been tested and refined in disasters of all types around the country. There is also evidence that a great deal of thought about the effect of uncertainty and misinformation in hazard situations took place after Three Mile Island, resulting in the superlative job at Mount St. Helens (Cogan and Lodato 1981).

FEMA's efforts, however, were late. The superb public information office was set up three days after the catastrophe of May 18. Brochures about what to do in case of ashfall were sent out a week late; by then the people in the ashfall areas were more expert in coping with ash than FEMA. The Technical Information Bulletins were even later. Before May 18, the NAWAS warning system was not working well. In addition, there was the lack of involvement in planning discussed previously. Part of this problem is jurisdictional; before a national disaster is declared, hazard planning is the responsibility of the state. But when the state is not able to provide that type of leadership, should FEMA officials at least offer more advice?

The Washington Department of Emergency Services suffered from a combination of neglect and lack of resources. Obviously the DES was not taken seriously as a state agency. It did not have the funding, resources, or expertise to deal with volcanic eruptions, and, apparently, what little leadership capacity remained was undermined by the establishment of the Mount St. Helens Watch Committee under the chairmanship of the chief of the state patrol. So the few trained hazard professionals in the DES had little chance to do the jobs they were trained to do. Preempted from coordinating the state effort by the Watch Committee, and from handling the west side local response by the Forest Service, they did little to oversee the planning efforts in Washington. When the catastrophe came, they were not prepared and very much isolated from the action in the local areas and Vancouver. For the most part, the state DES function appears to have been primarily in public information, a function secondary to the training of most the DES personnel.

The county DES offices were not well integrated with the state office, or with Vancouver headquarters for that matter. Most local emergency service people seemed to be on their own. Their degree of success seemed largely related to their own abilities. In one case, the local DES person was felt to be useless and completely excluded from emergency planning; in others, they were deeply involved in local coordinating activities. Part of the reason for the DES isolation can be traced to the problems of the state DES. The state planning effort mainly coordinated state agencies, including field units in the local areas. The USFS contingency planning group seems mainly to have channelled their coordination efforts through the sheriffs on the west side, a channel already familiar to the Forest Service personnel. In both channels, the county DES offices were bypassed, their involvement with the emergency response more a result of their relationships with the sheriffs' departments than anything else.

In short, the emergency services system in Washington did not work well. Whether from neglect, ignorance, lack of authority, or their own shortcomings. the state and local DES agencies were largely bypassed. Consequently, FEMA was often left to coordinate or respond to the demands of state and local officials ignorant of the limitations of federal support and the procedures for obtaining help; and, the potentially valuable chain of communication from local DES to state DES to FEMA became more of a bottleneck than an aid. Perhaps a rethinking of the DES system would be useful. Emergency services agencies should be planning and coordination agencies for all kinds of disasters; yet, in many cases their association with wartime civil defense has left them virtually ignored when the threat of war is not a major issue. Now, however, our technological society is highly vulnerable to natural and human-made disasters, best illustrated by the effect of less than two inches of ash in bringing the east side of Washington to a standstill. The Washington DES system was inadequate because the state government had done nothing to upgrade it beyond 1950's civil defense. The emergency services system needs better lines of communication, more trained staff (especially field staff), more involvement in overall hazard planning, and, above all, public awareness that hazard planning and mitigation is not just a wartime function but of increasing peacetime importance.

A related issue is the civilian-military interface in disaster management. The military is not allowed to provide disaster assistance except under very strict conditions, and in national disasters they are subordinate to civilian authority, usually FEMA. In a way this restriction is good—avoiding excessive use of military power such as in General Funston's control of San Francisco after the 1906 earthquake. In the Mount St. Helens disaster, however, situations arose that quick military aid could have helped, for example, support for search and rescue operatons or finding a water purifier for Toutle. The military's capabilities for disaster response, in terms of equipment, manpower, and training, are immense, and can be just as easily turned to peacetime use as to wartime purposes. In some cases those resources are unique and unmatched in the private sector. Such unique resources should be immediately available for use in disasters. In the Mount St. Helens response, the resources used by the military, mainly medical, rescue, and support services, were not excessive and probably did little to reduce preparedness for war, but they were enough to help tremendously in a serious natural disaster. There were benefits for the military as well, suggested by our respondents—high troop morale, better relations with civilians, and practice in life-threatening situations. Part of the picture in May 1980, however, was the Ninth Army Division at Fort Lewis, with its plans made and troops on alert, waiting for three critical days before being allowed to help. Procedures for supplying military aid to civilian authorities in disaster situations should be made more flexible. Procedures for determination of civilian aid should be prompt and unambiguous.

Inflexibility of rules for disaster assistance was a common complaint about FEMA that should be further investigated. Mount St. Helens was a unique disaster, with unusual and unexpected situations for which the rules were perhaps not fully prepared. So, also, was Three Mile Island. As an increasingly complex society interfaces with an already complicated environment, other unusual situations will undoubtedly arise. To cope with these unknowns, some provision for flexibility in the rules might be useful. A logical possibility might be to allow the presidentially appointed federal coordinating officer some latitude for change. There was, in addition, some ignorance of federal regulations on the part of local officials, and some briefing or training sessions by FEMA personel would be helpful. Along with both these suggestions comes a need for better information collection by FEMA and state DES officials. Without a good knowledge of the impacts of these unique sorts of hazards, emergency management will be operating somewhat in the dark. This need suggests it is urgent to organize networks of experts and field staff for assessing actual impacts and problems in local areas. The technical information network provides a model for overall information sharing, and perhaps teams of government or academic personnel can be organized for field assessment.

More consideraton is also necessary in determining how much federal aid should be provided for state and local assistance. To attempt to restore disaster areas to predisaster conditions would obviously discourage preparation, caution, and self-reliance on the part of state and local governments, as well as being exceedingly expensive. The federal policy now is to provide necessary assistance after local resources have been commmitted, always demanding strict accountability and evidence that no local resources (public or private) are available. In some cases, however, the definition of just what is a local resource appears to have been distorted. In the case of a water purification unit for Toutle, resources available in California and Oregon (both considered inadequate for the task by county and state authorities) were defined as "local," thereby denying use of the federal equipment at Fort Lewis (which really was local, within easy driving distance of Toutle). The same situation refers to contractors from all over the nation, who offered to sell their services to agencies facing hazard problems. Is it cost-effective to pay the expense of moving, say, a fleet of earthmovers and tanker trucks halfway across the United States when the same equipment is nearby at Fort Lewis? There is also an opposing side—that too quick use of federal resources, or threat of its use, can be unfair competition against private contractors. There are ethical and legal questions here, as well as economic and practical ones to be more carefully considered.

The political authority of FEMA over other federal agencies was established by presidential appointment of a FEMA official as federal coordinating officer. The relationship between the state DES and other state agencies, or between the county DES agencies and other local organizations, was less well defined. Steps should be taken to clarify the chain of command and the role of the state and local DES offices. Something perhaps akin to the Mount St. Helens Watch Committee, but more thoughtfully organized, might be useful on the state level. County DES organizations seem more prone to local experimentation in working relationships, and this experimentation should be encouraged and closely examined. In counties around Mount St. Helens there are some interesting variations: in one the sheriff is also the DES director; in another the DES director is a deputy sheriff; in still another the sheriff is the deputy DES director; and in several others the DES and sheriffs' departments are officially separate. This situation provides a wealth of case study information that might offer valuable insights into emergency services coordination.

All levels of the emergency services system in the state of Washington, at least, need to be in closer contact with one another. The state DES should make sure local DES offices are closely coordinated with overall state level plans and all DES offices must practice these plans. Practice can also be provided by developing a system of exchange with other states in the area. The help sent to the Washington DES from counterparts in Oregon, California, and British Columbia was greatly appreciated, and no doubt also paid benefits to these agencies in experience. By providing aid to other states facing similar disasters, a DES agency can build up a valuable reservoir of experienced personnel and create a system of reciprocal arrangements allowing for help from other states when faced with a high magnitude event. Such an exchange system ought to be developed.

The relationship of FEMA to the emergency services system should be better defined. In the Mount St. Helens disaster, FEMA was little involved in the contingency planning and in the immediate aftermath of May 18. Then, on May 21, the presidential disaster declaration suddenly made it the dominant agency. It might be worthwhile to consider a more flexible arrangement, in which FEMA can gradually become more involved as a disaster widens. At the preliminary stage, some FEMA officials might serve as advisors to the state emergency services. FEMA can then eventually build up to their usual role, if and when a disaster declaration is made.

ACCESS INTO HAZARD AREAS

The most beneficial action taken during the warning period was the establishment of the Red and Blue Zones by the Forest Service, county, and state authorities. This action most certainly saved lives by keeping many people away from the danger areas. Although in hindsight the Red Zone was obviously too small, creating and maintaining it took great fortitude. Its creation also required well-supported, clearly communicated information on the volcano danger from the geologists. As a model for future actions, the restricted area provides some insights into the role of scientific information, economic and social effects of the restriction, and under what conditions access should be allowed.

There is a fascination for hazards on the part of many people, and some dangers, especially if they are not well understood or part of something exotic (such as a smoking volcano), are attractive. This "convergence phenomenon" was especially evident for Mount St. Helens. From the start, the area near the volcano was crowded with curious people, often coming from great distances. Closing the area around the mountain helped keep these people at a distance. This closure was not easy to maintain. The crowds had to be stopped at the limits of the Red Zone, calling for signs, barricades, and personnel to enforce, or explain, the restriction. To satisfy the curiosity of the crowds, it was also necessary to develop areas where people could see the volcano and obtain information in safety. The two Mount St. Helens Information Centers set up by the USFS are good examples of a way to divert people away from danger zones. Planning for future hazard events should include some means of safely dealing with the convergence phenomenon.

The establishment of the restricted area had impacts of its own, apart from protecting people from danger. There were economic effects; people whose livelihoods were tied into forestry and recreation industries suffered.

In some cases there were feelings that the damage caused by the Red Zone was greater than that caused by the volcano. This economic loss appeared to be true in the small tourist town of Cougar, which for a while was in the Red Zone, but had not been subjected to any severe volcanic damage. There were psychological effects as well. People finding themselves in a zone of restricted access would be expected to feel fear. Along with the fear is the isolation from normal social activity. Several residents living in the Red Zone complained of their friends' difficulties in obtaining permission to visit them. So people living or working in the restricted area suffered increased economic and psychological stress because of the governmental action.

The economic, political, and public pressures on the people involved in establishing and maintaining the Red and Blue Zones were tremendous. Some of these pressures were reflected in the initial shape of the Red Zone, whose boundaries excluded state or private land outside Gifford Pinchot National Forest (map 7), land that was later overwhelmed in the eruption of May 18. The decision to create a restricted area, and where to draw the boundaries, requires solid scientific evidence regarding the dimensions of the hazard. In providing that information, the Survey geologists performed an important service. They were greatly aided by the study they had just completed on the past eruptive record and impacted areas of Mount St. Helens. Without the Blue Book and their own research, the geologists probably would not have had the detailed information to support the access restrictions. The Red Zone was set up partly on the basis of expectations of future eruptions, and those expectations were supported by what was known of past events. Governmental authorities need strong evidence to support their decisions, including up-to-date monitoring and predictions based on past behavior. Within the limits of the state-of-the-art volcanic hazards assessment, the Survey geologists provided what they could.

Access to the restricted area is a complicated issue, especially when multiple landowners are involved. Problems appeared with people working in the area, living there, and trying to obtain information inside the hazard zone. The forest industries working in the restricted area were able to work out an "industrial pass" where each corporation was responsible for controlling and warning its employees. This system involved close coordination with the volcano watch at Vancouver, and these companies were very much concerned with communications between working crews and the USGS. The larger issue here regards the question of safety versus economics in hazard situations. For industrial interests to claim and exercise their "rights" to expose workers to hazards, they should also demonstrate some responsibililty. These corporations will need to develop their own contingency plans and be prepared to work with governmental agencies. Within these companies there should be personnel to interface with government planning agencies. Private industrial approaches developed at Mount St. Helens for working safely in hazard zones may be useful for other corporations facing similar problems.

Access to the area to obtain information was an important issue in scientific research. For geologists, ecologists, and other scientists this event was a "once in a lifetime" chance to conduct studies on the effects of an active volcano in the Pacific Northwest; however, their opportunity for research collided with governmental obligations to protect people. Some Survey geologists were not personally affected by these restrictions because of their federal support and their necessary hazard assessment function, although even some USGS people were kept out of some places some times. Academic researchers, however, had varying degrees of difficulty in obtaining access. The difficulty lay not with the USGS, but with the Forest Service, whose personnel feared they would be held liable for death or injury to any nongovernment scientist allowed entry. On the scientists' side was the argument that the USGS could not possibly study everything, and without help much information would be lost. In addition, there was a feeling among geologists that they were better able to assess the risk and weigh the potential benefits of their research than the Forest Service personnel. With many geologists from all over the world clamoring to do research, the Allen Committee was set up and guidelines established to provide a measure of safety. There was much fumbling through all this, and some scientists felt that a great deal of valuable information was lost. For similar situations in the future, some sort of scientific clearing-house and guidelines for research in hazardous zones should be established. Some thought should also go into the legal aspects of liability for hazard zone research, perhaps by establishing conditions under which researchers and governmental agencies can or cannot be held responsible.

Dealing with people with homes inside the Red and Blue Zones was awkward. Before and during the emergency, homeowners were forced either to evacuate or be placed in a position of fear and isolation. The emotional tie to home is often so strong that people will refuse to leave even under great threat, as in the case of Harry Truman. These sorts of problems will always happen when government fiat suddenly imposes a restricted zone. A better alternative is to develop a carefully considered land use policy. Land use restriction is a common means of coping with environmental hazards, although in the case of Mount St. Helens it was complicated by the fact that the American settlement of the area had never been affected by a volcanic eruption. Yet the danger to anyone residing in the area, especially the area between the mountain and Spirit Lake, was potentially great. The best way to deal with property owners in a danger area may be to acquire their land. For a long-term, low-probability hazard, this acquisition can be done with minimal disturbance by a deliberate, long-term policy of buying or trading for land as it becomes available, coupled with forthright and forceful discussions of the dangers with the owners. When people at risk are told that eventually their property (and perhaps their or their children's lives) could be destroyed in an eruption, and that the authorities are taking the risk seriously enough to install special monitoring equipment and institute special plans, many will decide to leave on their own. In contrast, the sudden imposition of a regulatory wall between people and their possession, pets, and livelihoods—as a re-action to potential volcanic activity never before thought possible—is bound to bring disbelief, hard feelings, and political pressure.

HAZARD INFORMATION AND THE PUBLIC

In United States society, public information is very important. The public right to know becomes a need to know in hazard situations. There are many channels of information available to people; personal communication with officials, the news media, official statements, or informal "grapevines" are all examples. Emergency activities may be hampered if these channels carry contradictory information. In the face of the uncertainty of volcanic eruption, a good public information organization is essential. The FEMA response to the Mount St. Helens disaster is perhaps the finest example of a public information operation in a hazard situation. The Vancouver Joint Information Center was set up immediately after FEMA took control. It was budgeted at about two hundred thousand dollars and employed twenty-eight public information officers working around the clock. This operation gathered news from the emergency operations, provided regular press conferences, arranged for newspeople to meet key actors when avail-able, and fielded requests for information from around the world. The facilities were open to all disaster agencies and aided the fledging USGS public information officers with on-the-job training. The major benefit of the FEMA operation was in establishing a central point where public information could be exchanged between all the responding agencies and disseminated in a consistent fashion. The agencies that were involved at the Vancouver Joint Information Center were able to "speak with one voice," enabling the information to be sent to the public quickly and with minimal confusion. This center also provided a central point for the news media to gather, close to the action but enough apart from the more urgent emergency activities so agencies could work without interference. The public information officers interviewed in our survey were very un-derstanding of the needs of the newspeople and did their best to help supply those needs without interfering with other activities; in turn, they all thought the press behaved very well.

The Vancouver Joint Information Center was only able to provide help to those agencies that could, or would, use its services. The state DES tried to run its own public information center from its Olympia office and found itself overwhelmed by calls to the point where it could do little else. Local officials, especially those in Cowlitz and Lewis counties, were not prepared for the "hordes" of newspeople that descended on them. Without their own public information officers to screen the press, the same people responding to the emergency had to respond to requests for interviews. People carrying on emergency activities, major or minor, were at the mercy of those thrusting microphones at them and saying, "You're on national TV." It takes some experience not to freeze up and to field questions about all kinds of things asked by a news professional looking for information or sensation. Some people were not up to this exposure and complained about press excess.

As previously mentioned, problems with the news media were not part of our survey questionnaire, however, enough people volunteered this information that we felt we should include it in our results. We found the most problems in places where public information offices were either inadequate or nonexistent. The press was felt to be out of control in those areas, misusing their mandate to obtain information, interfering with important activities, slanting the news, and actually breaking the law in some cases. Some of the respondents in these areas made a distinction between local and national news agencies, people from national organizations being considered the worst offenders. There were suggestions that competition between national networks led to excess. Perhaps, also, the previously existing relationship between the local news agencies and local officials, and a feeling that the local press had a "stake" in the community, may have given these newspeople a more responsible outlook or led local officials to regard their efforts with more empathy. The Pulitzer Prize–winning effort of the *Longview Daily News* may be seen as an example of this responsible coverage. This relationship between local communities and local and national news agencies in hazard situations deserves more investigation. The role and responsibility of the news media in disaster coverage also requires a more intensive look. In terms of governmental action, the evidence strongly suggests that agencies involved with hazards will require well-staffed, well-equipped public information offices as an integral part of their emergency response organization.

VOLCANIC HAZARD PLANNING AND THE USGS

Considering the relative inexperience of the USGS geologists in hazard assessment and warning, their short-term performance from the time the volcano came to life until the present was excellent. However, dealing with high-risk, low-probability hazards requires more than short-term reactions which are quickly overwhelmed by events. These kinds of hazards require long-term planning, for monitoring, mobilization of emergency services, and reduction of the population at risk to the danger. Regarding this long-term planning process, the USGS effort was successful with other professional geologists, especially the seismologists at the University of Washington, but not successful in terms of public and governmental awareness in most of the Pacific Northwest. The brief stir of activity in December, 1978, was not developed into any constructive activity that helped the situation a year and a half later (aside from plans for lowering the level of Swift and Yale reservoirs—Nichols, personal communication, 1982). There is no evidence that the information provided about Mount St. Helens stimulated any long-range planning in terms of establishment of an effective, permanent geophysical monitoring program, development of a coordinating system for organizing an emergency response, or governmental acquisition of private landholdings in the danger area. All of these programs are evident now, stimulated by the catastrophe of May 18 rather than by the USGS warning.

The Mount St. Helens eruption provided some clear lessons which the USGS should apply in their hazard warning activities.

(1) The USGS should follow through to make sure its information gets to the people who should use it, in an understandable form. The initial distribution of information about Mount St. Helens worked very well with the professional geologists, seismologists, and others who might be expected to understand the message. The warnings worked well on the west side of the Cascades, where special efforts were made to interpret the information in public meetings and through face-to-face communication. The warnings to the ashfall areas in eastern Washington and beyond did not work because they were not properly targeted to the people most likely to be affected. When the transmission of the warnings was left to the DES and the news media, these mediums not only failed to target the information but also lacked the scientific credibility of the USGS. To say that Mount St. Helens might erupt and expect people with limited geological understanding to grasp the significance for themselves is not enough. The information must be taken to those likely to be affected, and presented to specific, selected people in terms of specific possible impacts to be faced. If USGS personnel are not prepared to follow through, they should make sure someone else does, for others are less likely to perceive the full implications of particular geological events.

(2) Communicating this information must occur before a major hazard event takes place. Now is the time to get out the information about other Cascade volcanoes, Mammoth Lake, or the next California earthquake. When the event occurs it is too late to control activities, to decide

whom to warn about what. At Mount St. Helens, when the eruption seemed imminent the USGS, like everyone else, was swept along by the events—reacting to the situations as they occurred.

(3) During the hazard event the USGS should make every effort to evaluate the pertinent data and provide it to other scientists and the public as quickly as possible. This information was useful in reducing rumors at Mount St. Helens and could be helpful to other scientists involved in either scientific research or interpretation for the public.

(4) The USGS should try to enlist the services of other geologists in their research and warning for major geologic hazards. When they used such services during the Mount St. Helens disaster, they and the public derived great benefits. They very effectively enlisted the aid of specialized scholars to study special aspects of the Mount St. Helens event such as landslides, gas chemistry, or seismology. The Allen Committee was also useful in screening and aiding non-USGS research. The local geologists were not as effectively drawn in by the USGS, though they were drafted by the news media. In future events, local geology personnel should become more closely integrated. This integration would aid in the mammoth task of interpretation and would also decrease the chances that the geologists would provide the public with conflicting interpretations.

(5) Hazard monitoring, hazard assessment, and hazard warning are *equivalent* functions. As long as the USGS expects to be in the warning business, more attention must be paid to public information. This requires a stable organization of trained public information officers who can combine geological knowledge with social science and communications. The role of such people would be to obtain information from the research scientists, interpret that information in ways understandable to the general public and public officials, and transmit it to the people who need to know. Such a public information office is needed to protect the scientists from being overwhelmed by demands for public information. Before May 18, the burden of warning was primarily shouldered by two geologists, Crandell and Mullineaux, who already had full-time jobs as leading scientists in the geological research. The strain on these individuals was tremendous. People in such crucial positions should not be subjected to such pressures, which could lead to their exhaustion and possibly impair their ability to function.

Much of our criticism relates to the overwhelming institutionalization of scientific research in the United States Geological Survey, to which all other functions are secondary. There is no subunit in the USGS adequately staffed with professional experts on hazard information and mitigation. It is a function taken over by geologists whose knowledge of hazards as they relate to human systems is limited. Scientists admirably equipped for geologic research were given the additional function of providing information for the organization of public policy and planning, a field about which they knew little. The wonder is that they performed so splendidly in helping to organize the short-term response in the spring of 1980. The individuals assigned to the task did well; it was the supporting agency that failed to provide adequate resources and expertise to ensure the information would reach the necessary people and, once there, would be understood and used properly.

The USGS has gained significantly from the eruptions of Mount St. Helens. It almost goes without saying that they have greater knowledge of vulcanism and volcanic hazards, as indicated by their increasing ability to predict eruptive activity. They also have greater credibility. Our research suggests that the USGS was the most effective warning agency before May 18. On May 18, the predictions made by the Survey geologists were remarkably accurate (aside from the magnitude of the lateral blast) and many people were very impressed. When a hazard watch was instituted for Mount Hood in the summer of 1980, people listened. There is also evidence of an increased awareness in the USGS of its role in providing information to emergency response agencies and the general public (Rowley et al. 1984; Krinsley 1980).

There should also be a greater awareness of their own limitations among Survey geologists. When an overwhelming amount of information must be collected in a short period of time, the USGS needs help. Some sort of coordinating body, perhaps including members of the USGS, FEMA, academic scientists, and the National Science Foundation, needs to operate as a sort of expanded technical information network for gathering scientific data and transmitting it to the necessary people. Awareness of their limitations in dealing with social and political systems is also important. Professional geologists, no matter how highly respected as scientists, are still amateur social scientists. The transmission of information to the public and public officials requires professional social scientists and public information officers.

The Mount St. Helens eruption was a once-in-a-lifetime event. It provided many valuable lessons for those involved in warning and response to volcanic hazards and other major hazard events. For the USGS, it was a baptism-under-fire of a new operation—providing scientific information to the public and public officials in a hazard situation. It is essential that the lessons learned be incorporated into plans before they are forgotten. In this way, responses to future volcanic eruptions and other major hazard events can benefit from the experience gained on Mount St. Helens.

DES WARNING MESSAGES, MAY 18, 1980

FIRST WARNING (10:15 A.M.)

RELAY THE FOLLOWING MESSAGE IMMEDIATELY TO ALL COUNTY AND METROPOLITAN AREA EMERGENCY SERVICES DIRECTORS . . . . ! ! ! ! ! !

AN APPARRENT [sic] MAJOR ERUPTION OF MT. ST. HELENS OCCURRED AT APPROXIMATELY 0833 THIS MORNING.

A WATCH WARNING IS IN EFFECT. AND APPROPRIATE CONTINGENCY PLANS ARE BEING IMPLIMENTED [sic]. ALL LOCATIONS NORTH AND EAST OF MOUNTAIN MAY RECEIVE ASH FALL AS IT HAS ALREADY BEEN REPORTED IN YAKIMA AND PIERCE COUNTIES. PRECAUTIONARY MEASURES ARE ENCOURAGED.

MT. ST. HELENS PLUME TRAJECTORY FORECAST PLUME EJECTION ABOVE MT. TOP . . . . . .

ELEVATION	WIND FROM	SPEED	PLUME GOES TO
12000 FEET	240	15	NORTHEAST
18000 FEET		20	NORTHEAST
24000		35	EAST NORTHEAST
30000		40	EAST NORTHEAST
40000		60	EAST NORTHEAST
50000		20	EAST NORTHEAST

SECOND WARNING (1:38 P.M.)

PLEASE RELAY THE FOLLOWING MESSAGE TO YOUR LOCAL EMERGENCY SERVICES DIRECTOR IMMEDIATELY . . . . . .

THE FOLLOWING BULLETIN IS RETRANSMITTED FOR YOUR INFO AND USE;

WHAT TO DO WHEN A VOLCANO ERUPTS

MOST IMPORTANT—DON'T PANIC, KEEP CALM.

IF VOLCANIC ASH BEGINS TO FALL HEAVILY;

STAY INDOORS

IF YOU ARE OUTSIDE, SEEK SHELTER, SUCH AS A CAR OR BUILDING

IF YOU CANNOT FIND SHELTER, BREATHE THROUGH A CLOTH, SUCH AS A HANDKERCHIEF, PREFERABLY A DAMP CLOTH TO FILTER OUT THE ASH

WHEN AIR IS FULL OF ASH, KEEP YOUR EYES CLOSED AS MUCH AS POSSIBLE

HEAVY FALLS OR ASH SELDOM LAST MORE THAN A FEW HOURS, ONLY RARELY DO THEY LAST A DAY OR MORE.

A HEAVY FALL OF ASH MAY CAUSE DARKNESS DURING DAYLIGHT HOURS, AND MAY TEMPORARILY INTERFERE WITH TELEPHONE, RADIO, AND TELEVISION COMMUNICATION.

DO NOT TRY TO DRIVE A CAR DURING A HEAVY FALL OF ASH. THE CHANCE OF AN ACCIDENT WILL BE INCREASED BY POOR VISIBILITY.

A THICK ACCUMULATION OF ASH COULD INCREASE THE LOAD ON ROOFS, AND SATURATION OF ASH BY RAIN COULD BE AN ADDITIONAL LOAD. ASH SHOULD BE REMOVED FROM FLAT OR LOW-PITCHED ROOFS TO PREVENT A THICK ACCUMULATION.

VALLEYS THAT HEAD A VOLCANO MAY BE THE ROUTES OF MUDFLOWS, WHICH CARRY BOULDERS AND RESEMBLE WET, FLOWING CONCRETE.

MUDFLOWS CAN MOVE FASTER THAN YOU CAN WALK OR RUN, BUT YOU CAN DRIVE A CAR DOWN A VALLEY FASTER THAN A MUDFLOW WILL TRAVEL.

WHEN DRIVING ALONG A VALLEY THAT HEADS ON A VOLCANO, WATCH UP THE RIVER CHANNEL AND PARTS OF THE VALLEY FLOOR FOR THE OCCURRENCE OF MUDFLOWS.

BEFORE CROSSING A HIGHWAY BRIDGE, LOOK UPSTREAM. DO NOT CROSS A BRIDGE WHILE A MUDFLOW IS MOVING BENEATH IT.

THE DANGER FROM A MUDFLOW INCREASES AS YOU APPROACH A RIVER CHANNEL, AND DECREASES AS YOU MOVE TO HIGHER GROUND.

RISK FROM MUDFLOWS ALSO DECREASES WITH INCREASING DISTANCE FROM A VOLCANO.

IF YOU BECOME ISOLATED, DO NOT STAY NEAR THE RIVER CHANNEL—MOVE UPSLOPE.

HAZARDS ARE GREATEST AT THE VOLCANO ITSELF, AND DIMINISH WITH INCREASING DISTANCE. DURING AN ERUPTION, MOVE AWAY FROM A VOLCANO, NOT TOWARD IT.

NOTE TO EDITORS: THE FOLLOWING GENERAAL [sic] INFORMATION WAS PREPARED BY THE U.S. GEOLOGICAL SURVEY AT THE REQUEST OF STATE AND FEDERAL OFFICIALS.

LIST OF AGENCIES REPRESENTED IN THE MOUNT ST. HELENS WARNING AND RESPONSE SURVEY (JUNE–SEPTEMBER, 1980)*

Federal
    Environmental Protection Agency: Seattle
    Federal Aviation Administration: Auburn, Seattle
    Federal Emergency Management Agency: Bothell, Vancouver
    National Oceanic and Atmospheric Administration (Includes National
        Weather Service): Portland (Ore.), Seattle
    United States Air Force: Fort Lewis
    United States Army: Fort Lewis
    United States Army, Corps of Engineers: Portland (Ore.), Vancouver
    United States Forest Service: Packwood, Portland (Ore.), Randall,
        St. Helens, Vancouver
    United States Geological Survey, Vancouver

Washington State
    Attorney General's Office: Olympia
    Department of Emergency Services: Olympia, Vancouver
    Department of Fisheries: Olympia
    Department of Game: Olympia
    Department of Licensing: Olympia, Vancouver
    Department of Natural Resources: Castle Rock, Olympia
    Department of Transportation: Ritzville, Olympia, Vancouver, Yakima
    Department of Planning and Community Affairs: Olympia
    Department of Social and Health Services: Olympia
    Division of Geology and Earth Resources: Olympia
    National Guard: Camp Murray
    Office of the Governor: Olympia

*Locations cited are in Washington unless otherwise noted.

State Patrol: Olympia, Vancouver, Yakima
University of Washington (Geophysics): Seattle

Oregon
Department of Emergency Services: Salem
Department of Geology and Mineral Industries: Portland
Portland State University (Geology): Portland

Local Government
Department of Emergency Services: Chehalis, Kelso, Portland (Ore.),
Spokane, Tillamook (Ore.), Yakima
Police or Sheriff's Department: Castle Rock, Chehalis, Ellensburg,
Ephrata, Kelso, Moses Lake, Ritzville, Spokane, Stevenson,
Vancouver, Yakima
Fire Department: Moses Lake, Yakima
Health Department: Spokane
Hospital: Ritzville
Mayor or City Manager: Morton, Moses Lake, Woodland
County Commissioner: Chehalis, Kelso, Spokane, Vancouver
Department of Public Works or Engineering: Ellensburg, Kelso,
Moses Lake, Portland (Ore.), Ritzville, Spokane, Woodland, Yakima
Air Pollution Agency: Spokane
Parks and Recreation: Chehalis

Private Industry
Pacific Power and Light: Portland (Ore.)
Portland General Electric: Portland (Ore.)
Washington Water and Power: Spokane
Burlington Northern: Longview
International Paper: Longview
Weyerhauser: Longview
Chamber of Commerce: Longview, Spokane, Vancouver, Woodland

Volunteer Organizations
Amateur Radio Relay Service: Longview
Red Cross: Longview, Vancouver, Yakima
Search and Rescue: Longview

Appendix C

LIST OF TECHNICAL INFORMATION NETWORK BULLETINS

1.   The Nature of Mount St. Helens Ash
2b.   Driving and Vehicle Maintenance in Heavy Ash Areas
3.   Precautions in Handling Volcanic Ash
4.   Current Volcanic Hazards at Mount St. Helens, Washington
5.   Volcanic Ash Could Reduce Insect Population . . . Permanently
6.   Advice for Farmers from Washington State University—Tractors and Water Pumps
7.   Ash Particles and Home Clean-Up Problems—Advice from the University of Idaho
8.   Physical and Chemical Characteristics of Mount St. Helens Deposits of May 18, 1980
9.   Volcanic Ash Advice to Berry Growers
10.   Center for Disease Control (CDC) Community Based Health Surveillance Program (Update)
11.   Poultry—Bees—Livestock
12.   Foodstuffs and Volcanic Ashfall
13.   Research into the Free Crystalline Silica Content of Mount St. Helens Ash
14.   Protecting Children from Volcanic Ash-Related Health Hazards
15.   Volcanic Ash and Your Water Supply
16.   Health and Medical Update
17.   Insurance Concerns
18.   Health and Medical Update
19.   Controlling Blowing Dust from Volcanic Ash
20.   Health and Medical Update
21.   Aviation Considerations
22.   Electric/Electronic Protection—Commercial and Major Systems

MOUNT ST. HELENS WARNING AND RESPONSE QUESTIONNAIRE _____

Hello, I'm _____ from the University of Arizona. We are conducting a study of the warnings for the Mt. St. Helens volcanic eruption. I would appreciate it if you would help us by answering a few questions.

First, I would like to ask you a few background questions about your-self and your job.

1. What is your current position?

Government Level	Function	Private Enterprise
1. City ___	1. Police or Sheriff ___	1. Power Company ___
2. County ___	2. Forest Service ___	2. Lumber Co. ___
3. State ___	3. Transportation ___	3. Paper Co. ___
4. Federal ___	4. Natural Resources ___	4. Railroad ___
5. Other ___	5. Emergency Services ___	5. Other ___
	6. National Guard ___	
	7. Water ___	
	8. Health Dept. ___	
	9. Wildlife ___	
	10. Agriculture ___	
	11. Other ___	

2. (If area of jurisdiction not obvious) How far does your area of responsibility extend (geographic and functional)?

3. How long have you been in your current position?

    1. less than 1 year _____
    2. 1–2 years _____
    3. 2–5 years _____
    4. 5–10 years _____
    5. more than 10 years _____

    If less than 5 years: What sort of work did you do before?

4. During the time you have worked here has your job ever been involved with natural hazards such as earthquakes, landslides, floods, volcanoes or tidal waves?

    1. Yes _____   go to 5
    2. No _____   skip to 6

5. With respect to dealing with such natural hazards would you say you have had considerable experience, a moderate amount of experience or very little experience?

    1. considerable _____
    2. a moderate amount _____
    3. very little _____

6. With respect to dealing with such natural hazards would you say your agency has had considerable experience, a moderate amount of experience, or very little experience?

    1. considerable _____
    2. a moderate amount _____
    3. very little _____

Now I'd like to ask you about Mt. St. Helens.

7. Can you tell me approximately how many miles your place of work is from Mt. St. Helens?

    _____ miles   _____ do not know

8. Prior to its recent activity, did you know that Mt. St. Helens might erupt?

    1. yes _____   go to 9
    2. no _____   go to 12

    How and when did you first find out about the possibility of an eruption on Mt. St. Helens?
    (Probe)

    1. always known _____
    2. learned in school _____
    3. learned from local residents _____
    4. learned from displays in national parks _____
    5. common community knowledge _____

10. Prior to its recent activity, how likely did you think it was that Mt. St. Helens would erupt? Did you think it was . . .

    1. very likely _____
    2. somewhat likely _____
    3. not likely _____   go to 12
    4. not sure _____

11. How serious a threat to public safety did you think such an eruption might be?

    1. very serious _____
    2. somewhat serious _____
    3. not serious _____
    4. not sure _____

Now I'd like to talk to you about the recent eruption and events leading up to it.

12. Do you remember when you first received information about the imminent possibility of a volcanic eruption on Mt. St. Helens?

    1. yes _____   go to 13
    2. no _____   go to 20

13. When was it? What was it?

14. Did this information first reach you in your official capacity or from some other source?

    1. official capacity _____
    2. other source _____

15. What was the source of your warning information?

    1. USGS _____
    2. State Dept. of Emergency Services _____
    3. Own Agency _____
    4. TV _____
    5. radio _____
    6. newspaper _____
    7. other _____

16. What was your first reaction on hearing about this? (Probe—actions taken, belief in source)

17. At that point, how serious a threat to public safety did you think such an eruption might be?

    1. very serious _____
    2. somewhat serious _____
    3. not serious _____
    4. not sure _____

18. Did you contact other people or agencies about this?

    1. yes _____   go to 19
    2. no _____   skip to 20

19. Who? Why? (Probe) What did you tell them?

20. The USGS has issued several warnings. Could you tell me which of these you have received and what action, if any, you took as a result?

Warning	Received		Reaction	
	yes	no	yes	no
1. Original Hazard Notification (12/20/79)				
2. Hazard Watch (3/27/80)				
3. Blue Book Distribution (after hazard watch)				
4. Notice of Harmonic Tremor (4/3/80)				
5. Notice of Bulge—N. Flank (4/30/80)				
6.				
7.				

Reactions

21. Did you receive official warnings from any other sources?

    1. yes _____   go to 22
    2. no _____   go to 25

22. Where did they come from?

    State Dept. of Emergency Services _____
    Other State Agencies _____
    Federal Agencies _____
    Other _____

23. Did you take any action as a result of these?

    1. yes _____   go to 24
    2. no _____   go to 25

24. What actions did you take?

25. Did you have problems making a decision based on the information that was available?

26. What type of data or information would you like to see in a hazard warning that would help you in your decision making?

27. At which point, if any, did you begin to take those warnings seriously?

28. What information in that warning led to this?

29. Were you involved in the development of the Mt. St. Helens Contingency Plan?

    1. yes _____   go to 30
    2. no _____   go to 31

30. What was your role in the development of the plan?

31. Was your company or agency assigned a role in the Mt. St. Helens Contingency Plan?

    1. yes _____
    2. no _____
    3. don't know _____

32. If yes, what was your assigned role?

If no, why not?

33. Did you take action to deal with the effects of any of the volcanic eruptions?

1. yes _____
2. no _____

34. What did you do? (Specify which eruption what action)

35. How well do you think you performed your role?

1. excellently _____
2. very well _____
3. adequately _____
4. not very well _____
5. poorly _____

36. Do you think your actions led to any positive results? (such as prevention of damage, deaths, or injuries)

1. yes _____
2. no _____

If yes, What?

37. Did you have any problems in performing your role?

1. yes _____
2. no _____

If yes, What?

38. I want to read to you a list of possible problems which could have negatively affected your role in responding to the volcanic eruption. I would like you to tell me whether any of these posed problems and if so how important they were.

	Posed Problems		If Yes: Would you say this was		
	Yes	*No*	*Very Important*	*Important*	*Unimportant*
lack of manpower	_____	_____	_____	_____	_____
lack of equipment or facilities	_____	_____	_____	_____	_____
lack of funds	_____	_____	_____	_____	_____
lack of information	_____	_____	_____	_____	_____
lack of coordination with other agencies	_____	_____	_____	_____	_____
lack of public cooperation	_____	_____	_____	_____	_____
Others	_____	_____	_____	_____	_____
	_____	_____	_____	_____	_____
	_____	_____	_____	_____	_____

For all problems rated very important ask:

> You said that _____ was a very important problem. Could you tell me a little more about this? (repeat for all problems rated very important)

39. Did you learn anything from your experience in dealing with this eruption which you think could be helpful in dealing with a future one?

    1. yes _____
    2. no _____

    If yes: Specify

40. What were the major effects, if any, of this eruption in the area under your jurisdiction?

41. Were there any (other) positive or negative effects?

42. Were the effects of the volcanic eruption about what you expected they might be, greater than expected, less than expected, much greater than expected, much less than expected?

    1. much greater than expected _____
    2. greater than expected _____
    3. about the same _____
    4. less than expected _____
    5. much less than expected _____

43. How did the effects differ from what you had expected?

44. Do you expect any of these to have long term effects?

45. Are you prepared to deal with any future eruptions?

    1. yes _____
    2. no _____

46. Why not?

47. How likely do you think it is that Mt. St. Helens will erupt again in the near future?

    1. very likely _____   (go to 48)
    2. somewhat likely _____   _____
    3. not likely _____   (End Interview)
    4. not sure _____

48. How serious a threat to public safety do you think such an eruption might be?

1. very serious _____
2. somewhat serious _____
3. not serious _____
4. not sure _____

49. How long do you expect the volcano will continue to erupt?

50. What are you doing to help overcome problems related to future eruptions?

Thank you for your cooperation—(End Interview)

INTERVIEWER NOTES:

Date _____

Agency _____

Location _____

Miles from Mt. St. Helens _____

Comments:

REFERENCES

Allen, J. E. 1980. *Final Report on the Operations of the Mount St. Helens Research and Educational Coordinating Committee*. Earth Sciences Department, Portland State University, Portland, Oregon.

Anderson, D. R. 1980. "Volcano Debris—A New Maintenance Problem." Paper Presented to WASTO Conference, Sun Valley, Idaho, Aug. 3–6.

Anderson, J. 1983. "Mount St. Helens May 18 Ashfall: The Human Ecology of an Unanticipated Natural Hazard." In S. A. C. Keller, ed., *Mount St. Helens: One Year Later*. Cheney, Washington: Eastern Washington University, pp. 181–189.

Austin, D. 1980. "Mount St. Helens." Memorandum, Seattle Air Route Traffic Control Center, Federal Aviation Administration, Auburn, Washington. April 8, 1980.

Banks, N. G., and R. P. Hoblitt. 1981. "Summary of Temperature Studies of 1980 Deposits." In P. W. Lipman and D. R. Mullineaux, eds., *The 1980 Eruptions of Mount St. Helens, Washington*. U.S. Geological Survey Professional Paper 1250. Washington, D.C.: Government Printing Office, pp. 295–313.

Baxter, P. J. 1980. "Scope of Current Center for Disease Control (CDC) Efforts." In J. W. Kerr, ed., *Mount St. Helens Scientific Workshop, November 13–14, Proceedings*. Washington, D.C.: Federal Emergency Management Agency, pp. 15–17.

Brugman, M. M. and M. F. Meier. 1981. "Response of Glaciers to the Eruptions of Mount St. Helens." In P. W. Lipman and D. R. Mullineaux, eds., *The 1980 Eruptions of Mount St. Helens, Washington*. U.S. Geological Survey Professional Paper 1250. Washington, D.C.: Government Printing Office, pp. 743–746.

Christiansen, R. L. 1980. "Eruption of Mount St. Helens: Volcanology." *Nature* 285:531–533.

Christiansen, R. L. and D. W. Peterson. 1981. "Chronology of the 1980 Eruptive Activity." In P. W. Lipman and D. R. Mullineaux, eds., *The 1980 Eruptions of Mount St. Helens, Washington*. U.S. Geological

Survey Professional Paper 1250. Washington, D.C.: U.S. Government Printing Office, pp. 17–30.

Chuan, R. L., D. C. Woods, and M. P. McCormick. 1981. "Characterization of Aerosols from Eruptions of Mount St. Helens." *Science* 211:830–832.

Cogan, P. and P. Lodato. 1981. "She's Blowing Again! Return to Headquarters! Disaster Information Center at Work." *PR Casebook* (1): 11–18.

Cook, R. J., J. C. Barron, R. I. Papandick, G. J. Williams, III. 1981. "Impact on Agriculture of the Mount St. Helens Eruptions." *Science* 211:16–22.

Corps of Engineers, U.S. Army. 1980. *Mount Saint Helens Recovery Operations: Draft Environmental Impact Statement*. Portland District, U.S. Army Corps of Engineers, Portland, Oregon.

Crandell, D. R. and D. R. Mullineaux. 1975. "Technique and Rationale of Volcanic-Hazards Appraisals in the Cascade Range, Northwestern United States." *Environmental Geology* 1:23–32.

Crandell, D. R. and D. R. Mullineaux. 1978. *Potential Hazards from Future Eruptions of Mount St. Helens Volcano, Washington*. U.S. Geological Survey Bulletin 1383-C. Washington, D.C.: U.S. Government Printing Office.

Crandell, D. R., D. R. Mullineaux, and M. Rubin. 1975. "Mount St. Helens Volcano: Recent and Future Behavior. *Science* 187:438–451.

Decker, R. W. 1981. "The 1980 Activity—A Case Study in Forecasting Volcanic Eruptions." In P. W. Lipman and D. R. Mullineaux, eds., *The 1980 Eruptions of Mount St. Helens, Washington*, U.S. Geological Survey Professional Paper 1250. Washington, D.C.: U.S. Government Printing Office, pp. 815–820.

Decker, R. W. and B. Decker. 1981. "The Eruptions of Mount St. Helens." *Scientific American* 244(3):68–80.

DeMott, John S. 1980. "Decoding the Volcano's Message." *Time*, Sept. 22:48–49.

Dillman, D. A. 1980. "After Mount St. Helens: Seven Grey Days in May." Department of Sociology, Washington State University, Pullman, Washington.

Dillman, D. A. 1981. "Communication Behavior and Social Impacts Following the May 18, 1980, Eruption of Mount St. Helens." Paper presented at Conference on Mount St.Helens, One Year Later, Cheney, Washington.

Dueker, K. J., P. Pendleton, L. Robinson, T. Gihring, B. Rabiega. 1980. *Impacts of Volcanic Ashfall on Travel Behavior*. Center for Urban Studies, School of Urban Affairs, Portland State University, Portland, Oregon.

Endo, E. T., S. D. Malone, L. L. Noson, and C. S. Weaver. 1981. "Locations, Magnitudes, and Statistics of the March 20-May 18 Earthquake Sequence." In P. W. Lipman and D. R. Mullineaux, eds., *The 1980 Eruptions of Mount St. Helens, Washington.* U.S. Geological Survey Professional Paper 1250. Washington, D.C.: U.S. Government Printing Office, pp. 93–107.

Federal Emergency Management Agency (FEMA). 1980. *Disaster Response and Recovery: Program Guide.* Washington, D.C.: Federal Emergency Management Agency.

Findley, R. 1981a. "Eruption of Mount St. Helens." *National Geographic* 159:3–65.

Findley, R. 1981b. "Mount St. Helens Aftermath." *National Geographic* 160:710–734.

Fruchten, J. S., D. E. Robertson, J. C. Evans, K. B. Olsen, E. A. Lepel, J. C. Laul, K. H. Abel, R. W. Sonders, P. O. Jackson, N. S. Wogman, R. W. Perkins, H. H. Van Tuhl, R. H. Beauchamp, J. W. Shade, J. L. Daniel, R. L. Erikson, G. A. Sehmel, R. N. Lee, A. V. Robinson, O. R. Moss, J. K. Briant, W. C. Cannon. 1980. "Mount St. Helens Ash from the 18 May 1980 Eruption: Chemical, Physical, Mineralogical, and Biological Properties." *Science* 209:1116–1125.

Gandrud, B.W. and A. L. Lazrus. 1981. "Filter Measurements of Stratospheric Sulfate and Chloride in the Eruption Plume of Mount St. Helens." *Science* 211:836–837.

Geophysics Program, University of Washington. 1980. "Eruption of Mount St. Helens: Seismology." *Nature* 285:529–531.

Greene, M. R., R. W. Perry, and M. K. Lindell. 1980. *The March 1980 Eruptions of Mount St. Helens: Citizen Perceptions of Volcano Hazard.* Battelle Human Affairs Research Centers, Seattle, Washington.

Hammond, P. 1973. "If Mount Hood Erupts." *The Ore Bin* 35(6):93–102.

Hammond, P. E. 1980–81. "Mount Saint Helens Box Score." Unpublished manuscript, Department of Earth Sciences, Portland State University, Portland, Oregon.

Harris, S. L. 1980. *Fire and Ice: The Cascade Volcanoes.* Seattle: The Mountaineers.

Hoblitt, R. P., D. R. Crandell, and D. R. Mullineaux. 1980. "Mount St. Helens Eruptive Behavior During the Past 1,500 Years." *Geology* 8:555–559.

Hooper, P. R., I. W. Herrick, E. R. Laskowski, C. R. Knowles. 1980. "Composition of the Mount St. Helens Ashfall in the Moscow-Pullman Area on 18 May 1980." *Science* 209:1125–1126.

Hunt, C. E., and J. S. MacCready. 1980. *The Short Term Economic Consequences of the Mount St. Helens Volcanic Eruptions in May and June, 1980*. Washington State Department of Commerce and Economic Development, Olympia, Washington.

Inn, E. C. Y., J. F. Vedder, E. P. Condon, and D. O'Hara. 1981. "Gaseous Constituents in the Plume from Eruptions of Mount St. Helens." *Science* 211:821–823.

Janda, R. J., K. M. Scott, K. M. Nolan, and H. A. Martinson. 1981. "Lahar Movement, Effects and Deposits." In P. W. Lipman and D. R. Mullineaux, eds., *The 1980 Eruptions of Mount St. Helens, Washington*. U.S. Geological Survey Professional Paper 1250. Washington, D.C.: Government Printing Office, pp. 461–478.

Johnson, S. 1980. "Volcano: Lots of Paper, No Money." *The Seattle Times*, Aug. 22: A1.

Kartez, J. D. and W. J. Kelley. 1980. *Emergency Planning and the Adaptive Local Response to the Mount St. Helens Eruption. Summary Report*. Environmental Research Center, Washington State University, Pullman, Washington.

Keiffer, S. W. 1981. "Fluid Dynamics of the May 18 Blast at Mount St. Helens." In P. W. Lipman and D. R. Mullineaux, eds., *The 1980 Eruptions of Mount St. Helens, Washington*. U.S. Geological Survey Professional Paper 1250. Washington, D.C.: U.S. Government Printing Office, pp. 379–400.

Kerr, J. W. 1980. "Mount St. Helens: Learning the Hard Way." *Emergency Management* 1(1):16–21.

Kerr, J. W. 1981. *Mount St. Helens Scientific Workshop, November 13–14, 1980, Proceedings*. Washington, D.C.: Federal Emergency Management Agency.

Kerr, R. A. 1981. "Mount St. Helens and a Climate Quandry." *Science* 211:371–374.

Kilijanek, T. S. 1981. *There She Blows: The Search and Rescue Response to the Mount St. Helens Volcano*. SAR Research Project Report 11, Department of Sociology, University of Denver, Denver, Colorado.

Korosec, M. A. 1980. "Mount St. Helens, May 18, 1980—A Scenario." In M. A. Korosec, J. G. Rigby, and K. L. Stoffel, eds., *The 1980 Eruption of Mount St. Helens, Washington, Part I: March 20–May 19, 1980*. Information Circular No. 71, Division of Geology and Earth Resources, Washington State Department of Natural Resources, Olympia, Washington, pp. 12–17.

Krinsley, D. B. 1980. *U.S. Geological Survey Interim Emergency Response Plan for Volcanic Hazards in the United States*. U.S. Geological Survey, Reston, Virginia. December 3, 1980.

Leik, R. D., T. M. Carter, and J. P. Clark. 1981. *Summary Final Report: Community Response to Natural Hazard Warnings.* NTIS.

Lipman, P. W. and D. R. Mullineaux, eds. 1981. *The 1980 Eruptions of Mount St. Helens, Washington.* U.S. Geological Survey Professional Paper 1250. Washington, D.C.: U.S. Government Printing Office.

Lipman, P. W., and D. R. Norton, J. E. Taggart, Jr., E. L. Brandt, and E. E. Engleman, 1981. "Compositional Variations in 1980 Magmatic Deposits." In P. W. Lipman and D. R. Mullineaux, eds., *The 1980 Eruptions of Mount St. Helens, Washington.* U.S. Geological Survey Professional Paper 1250. Washington, D.C.: U.S. Government Printing Office, pp. 631–640.

May, P. J. 1982. "Formulating Disaster Relief when Needs are Unknown." *Journal of Policy Analysis and Management* 2:39–54.

McLucas, G. B. 1980a. "Petrology of Current Mount St. Helens Tephra." *Washington Geologic Newsletter* 8(3):7–13.

McLucas, G. B. 1980b. "Cleanup and Disposal of Mount St. Helens Ash in Eastern Washington." *Washington Geologic Newsletter* 8(4):1–7.

Miller, C. D., D. R. Mullineaux, and D. R. Crandell. 1981. "Hazard Assessments at Mount St. Helens." In P. W. Lipman and D. R. Mullineaux, eds., *The 1980 Eruptions of Mount St. Helens, Washington.* U.S. Geological Survey Professional Paper 1250. Washington: U.S. Government Printing Office, pp. 789–802.

Moore, J. G. and W. C. Albee. 1981. "Topographic and Structural Changes, March-July 1980—Photogrammetric Data." In P. W. Lipman and D. R. Mullineaux, eds., *The 1980 Eruptions of Mount St. Helens, Washington.* U.S. Geological Survey Professional Paper 1250. Washington, D.C.: U.S. Government Printing Office, pp. 123–134.

Murcray, D. G., F. J. Murcray, D. B. Barker, and H. J. Mastenbrook. 1981. "Changes in Stratospheric Water Vapor Associated with the Mount St. Helens Eruption." *Science* 211:823–824.

National Weather Service. 1980. "Mount St. Helens Plume Trajectory Forecast." Bulletin issued May 18, 1980.

Nelson, D. 1981. "Monitoring Nature's Big Blow-Up." 1981. *Dartmouth Alumni Magazine* 74, 48–49.

Newhall, C. 1981. "Volcanic Hazards at Mount St. Helens." Bimonthly Update #8, August 5, 1981, U.S. Geological Survey, Mount St. Helens Project.

Office of the Governor. 1980. Executive Order E080–05. State of Washington, Olympia, Washington. April 30, 1980.

Osmond, E. 1980. *Mount St. Helens Contingency Plan.* U.S. Forest Service, Gifford Pinchot National Forest, Vancouver, Washington.

Ota, A. K., J. Snell, and L. L. Zaitz. 1980. "A Terrible Beauty." *The Oregonian*, Portland, October 27.

Perry, R. W., M. R. Greene, and M. K. Lindell. 1980. *Human Response to Volcanic Eruption: Mount St. Helens, May 18, 1980*. Battelle Human Affairs Research Center, Seattle, Washington.

Pollack, J. B. 1981. "Measurement of the Volcanic Plumes of Mount St. Helens in the Stratosphere and Troposphere: Introduction." *Science* 211:815–816.

President's Commission on the Accident at Three Mile Island. 1979. *The Need for Change: The Legacy of Three Mile Island*. Washington, D.C. U.S. Government Printing Office.

Rainier National Bank, Economics Department. 1980. *The Economic Implications of the Eruption of Mount St. Helens*.

Ressler, J. Q. (n.d.) *Mount St. Helens Ashfall in the Ellensburg, Washington Area: Impacts and Response*. Department of Geography, Central Washington University.

Robock, A. 1981. "The Mount St. Helens Volcanic Eruption of 18 May, 1980: Minimal Climatic Effect." *Science* 212:1383–1384.

Rowley, P. D., M. H. Hait, Jr., D. R. Finley, D. B. Kelly, S. L. Russell-Robinson, J. M. Buchanan-Banks, K. V. Cashman, and E. G. King. 1984. "Between Mount St. Helens and the World," *USGS Circular 921*.

Saarinen, T. F. and H. J. McPherson. 1981. "Notices, Watches, and Warnings: An Appraisal of the USGS's Warning System With a Case Study from Kodiak, Alaska." *Natural Hazard Research Working Paper 42*. Boulder, Colorado, Institute of Behavioral Sciences.

Sarna-Wojcicki, A. M., S. Shipley, R. B. Waitt, D. Dzurisin, and S. H. Woods. 1981. "Areal Distribution, Thickness, Mass, Volume and Grain Size of Air-Fall Ash from the Six Major Eruptions of 1980." *The 1980 Eruptions of Mount St. Helens, Washington*. U.S. Geological Survey Professional Paper 1250. Washington, D.C.: U.S. Government Printing Office, pp. 577–600.

Schiffer, R. 1980. "National Aeronautics and Space Administration (NASA) Programs." In J. W. Kerr, ed., *Mount St. Helens Scientific Workshop, November 13–14, Proceedings*. Washington, D.C.: Federal Emergency Management Agency, pp. 31–53.

Schuster, R. L. 1981. "Effects of the Eruptions on Civil Works and Operations in the Pacific Northwest." In P. W. Lipman and D. R. Mullineaux, eds., *The 1980 Eruptions of Mount St. Helens, Washington*. U.S. Geological Survey Professional Paper 1250. Washington, D.C.: U.S. Government Printing Office, pp. 701–718.

Sear, C. B. and P. M. Kelly. 1980. "Eruption of Mount St. Helens: Effects on Climate." *Nature* 285:533–535.

Shadel, D. 1980. "Activities of Disaster Relief Center in Kelso (May 23–27)." Office of the Attorney General, State of Washington, Olympia, Washington.

Shake, K. 1980. "A Mountain Erupts." *Northwest Intercom: Mount St. Helens Special Edition*. Federal Aviation Administration, Seattle, Washington.

Shearer, C. 1981. "United States Geological Survey (USGS) Programs." In James W. Kerr, ed., *Mount St. Helens Scientific Workshop, November 13–14, 1980 Proceedings*. Washington, D.C.: Federal Emergency Management Agency, pp. 11–14.

Shearer, C. F. 1981. "Hazard Warning Procedures and Problems." Unpublished Manuscript, U.S. Geological Survey.

Sheets, P. and D. Grayson. 1979. *Volcanic Activity and Human Ecology*. New York: Academic Press.

Smith, R. 1981. "Tight Screening for EPA Data," *Science* 213:1345–1346.

Smith, W. K. 1980. "A Plotting Program for Producing Ashfall Prediction Maps from Output of the NOAA Forecast Trajectory Program: Application to and Examples from the 1980 Mount St. Helens Eruptions." U.S. Geological Survey, Open File Report 80–2005.

Sorensen, J. H. 1981. "Emergency Response to Mount St. Helens Eruption: March 20, 1980 to April 10, 1980." *Natural Hazard Research Working Paper 43*. Boulder, Colorado, Institute of Behavioral Science.

State of Washington, Division of Mental Health. 1981. Unpublished proposal to National Institute of Mental Health.

Stoffel, K. L. 1980. "The May 18, 1980 Eruption of Mount St. Helens: A View from the Top." In M. A. Korosec, J. G. Rigby, and K. L. Stoffel, eds., *The 1980 Eruption of Mount St. Helens, Washington, Part I: March 20–May 19, 1980*. Information Circular No. 71, Division of Geology and Earth Resources, Washington State Department of Natural Resources, Olympia, Washington, pp. 9–11.

"Toutle River Receives Extensive Damage." 1980. *Washington Geologic Newsletter* 8(3):17–18.

"Towns Have a Blast a Year After The Big One." 1981. *Arizona Daily Star*, Tucson, May 18.

U.S. Department of the Interior, U.S. Geological Survey. 1977. "Warning and Preparedness for Geologic-Related Hazards: Proposed Procedures." *Federal Register* 42 (April 12):19292–19296.

Voight, B. 1980. "Slope Stability Hazards, Mount St. Helens Volcano, Washington." Unpublished Manuscript, U.S. Geological Survey Investigation for Mount St. Helens Volcano, Vancouver, Washington.

Voight, B., H. Glicken, R. J. Janda, and P. M. Douglass. 1981. "Catastrophic Rockslide Avalanche of May 18." In P. W. Lipman and D. R. Mullineaux, eds., *The 1980 Eruptions of Mount St. Helens, Washington*. U.S. Geological Survey Professional Paper 1250.

Washington, D.C.: U.S. Government Printing Office, pp. 347–377.

Warrick, R. A., J. Anderson, T. Downing, J. Lyons, J. Ressler, M. Warrick, T. Warrick. 1981. *Four Communities Under Ash*. Monograph 34; Program on Technology, Environment and Man, University of Colorado, Boulder, Colorado.

Washington National Guard, Executive Summary. 1980. Operation Mount St. Helens II, Camp Murray, Washington.

Washington State Area Command. 1980. *Oplan Mount St. Helens*. Washington National Guard, Camp Murray, Washington.

West, Susan. 1980. "The Right to Research." *Science News*, July 26, pp. 61–62.

Wichels, J. 1980. "Chronicle of a Cataclysm." *World* 10(7):5–11.

SUBJECT INDEX _____

NAME AND
AUTHOR INDEX

GEOGRAPHIC NAME INDEX